SCREENING DISABILITY

Essays on Cinema and Disability

Edited by
**Christopher R. Smit
Anthony Enns**

University Press of America,® Inc.
Lanham · New York · Oxford

Copyright © 2001 by
University Press of America,® Inc.
4720 Boston Way
Lanham, Maryland 20706

12 Hid's Copse Rd.
Cumnor Hill, Oxford OX2 9JJ

All rights reserved
Printed in the United States of America
British Library Cataloging in Publication Information Available

Library of Congress Cataloging-in-Publication Data

Screening disability : essays on cinema and disability /
edited by Christopher R. Smit, Anthony Enns.
p. cm
Includes bibliographical references and index.
1. Handicapped in motion pictures.
I. Smit, Christopher R. II. Enns, Anthony.
PN1995.9.H34 S39 2001   791.43'6520816—dc21   2001027398 CIP

ISBN 0-7618-2016-7 (cloth : alk. paper)
ISBN 0-7618-2017-5 (pbk. : alk. paper)

◯™ The paper used in this publication meets the minimum
requirements of American National Standard for Information
Sciences—Permanence of Paper for Printed Library Materials,
ANSI Z39.48—1984

Contents

Acknowledgments	vii
Introduction: The State of Cinema and Disability Studies Christopher R. Smit and Anthony Enns	ix

Theorizing Cinema and Disability

Screening Stereotypes: Images of Disabled People Paul K. Longmore	1
The Hollywood Discourse on Disability: Some Personal Reflections Martin F. Norden	19
The Fusion of Film Studies and Disability Studies Thomas B. Hoeksema and Christopher R. Smit	33

Disability as Monstrosity in Classical Hollywood Cinema: Tod Browning and *The Hunchback of Notre Dame*

None of Us: Ambiguity as Moral Discourse in Tod Browning's *Freaks* Méira Cook	47

The Horror of Becoming "One of Us": Tod Browning's   57
Freaks and Disability
Sally Chivers

Disabling the Viewer: Perceptions of Disability in Tod   65
Browning's *Freaks*
Nicole Markotic

Tod Browning and the Monstrosity of Hollywood Style   73
Oliver Gaycken

Lost and Found in Translation: The Changing Faces   87
of Disability in the Film Adaptations of Hugo's *Notre
Dame de Paris: 1842*
Laurie E. Harnick

Disability as Trauma, Mental Illness, and Dysfunction in Post-Vietnam Cinema

Trapped in the Affection-Image: American Cinema's   99
Post-Traumatic Cycle (1970-1976)
Christian Keathley

The Inner Life of *Ordinary People*   117
Patrick E. Horrigan

Disability and the Dysfunctional Family in Wayne Wang's   127
Smoke
Lou Ann Thompson

Disability as Spectacle in Contemporary Cinema

The Noble Ruined Body: Blindness and Visual Prosthetics   135
in Three Science Fiction Films
Susan Crutchfield

The Spectacle of Disabled Masculinity in John Woo's   151
"Heroic Bloodshed" Films
Anthony Enns

**Sexy Cyborgs: Disability and Erotic Politics
in Cronenberg's *Crash*** 165
James L. Cherney

Index 181

About the Contributors 189

Acknowledgments

The editors would like to thank those people and institutions without whom this book could not have been realized. Our special thanks to James Prakash Younger for his belief in the project, his reading of the manuscript, and his help with the introduction. Thanks, too, to Dudley Andrew and the staff of the Institute for Cinema and Culture at the University of Iowa, in particular Alison Latendresse and Caitlin Horsman. The editors would also like to thank Martin F. Norden, Rick Altman, Douglas Trank, Kathleen Buckwalter, Carol Schrage, Cindy Stevens, Kris Bevelacqua, Elizabeth Van Arragon, and Abe Geil for their help and support, as well as the members of the Cinema and Disability Group, including Tom Walz, Douglas Baynton, Martti Lahti, Lisa Schmidt, and Emily Cervantes. And special thanks to our fellow contributors for their excellent work and their longstanding commitment to the study of cinema and disability.

Excerpts from Paul Auster's book *Smoke and Blue in the Face* (Hyperion Miramax Books, 1995) have been used with the permission of Hyperion.

Excerpts from David Cronenberg's film *Crash* (FineLine Features, 1996) have been used with the permission of Alliance Atlantis Communications, Inc.

The editors would also like to express their thanks to the following sources for permission to reprint articles:

Paul K. Longmore's "Screening Stereotypes: Images of Disabled People" first appeared in *Social Policy* 16.1 (Summer 1985).

Anthony Enns' "The Spectacle of Disabled Masculinity in John Woo's 'Heroic Bloodshed' Films" originally appeared in *Quarterly Review of Film and Video* 17.2 (2000).

Introduction:
The State of Cinema and Disability Studies

Christopher R. Smit and Anthony Enns

Depictions and portrayals of persons who live with disability in motion pictures have changed over time, sometimes reflecting, at other times influencing, societal attitudes and beliefs. Yet disability itself has no easily recognizable form. When isolated from the mainstream of human existence by artistic representations, the disabled individual is effectively transformed into an object of cultural fascination, a fragment of humanity, the Other. The disabled experience, defined only in relation to a perceived lack of human potential, becomes significant as a distorted mirror image of what we take to be "human" and thereby reveals our culture's preconceived notions of normalcy. By analyzing films involving disability we are thus able to expose, critique, and reconsider social and political relations between normative and minority groups. Recent scholarship in Film Studies has further complicated the relationship between cinema and culture by analyzing the ways in which films are not merely carriers of ideology but rather present us with ambiguous or conflicting ideologies. These theories thereby challenge the passive model of the film spectator and force us to reconsider film spectatorship itself. This movement in Film

Studies has added a new urgency to the study of cinema's portrayal of disability.

Historically, the scholarship on cinema and disability has followed the assumption that negative images of people with disabilities on the screen create negative situations for people living with disabilities in society. Early criticism on cinema and disability frequently attacked films for presenting derogatory and discriminating images of people with disabilities. This work was primarily done under the umbrella of Disability Studies, which gained status in the academy in the mid-eighties as part of a growing awareness of disability rights in the broader culture. The tendency towards political correctness during the late eighties and the passage of the Americans with Disabilities Act in 1990 were among the catalysts for the advancement of Disability Studies in the academy. The close relationship between political movements and the emergence of Disability Studies focused early disability scholarship on ways of critiquing society's prejudice towards people with disabilities and ways of effecting positive change. For the most part, Disability Studies remains committed to this agenda today, and many disability scholars continue to use it as their theoretical lens. As Lennard Davis states, "The exciting thing about disability studies is that it is both an academic field of inquiry and an area of political inquiry" (1).

The scholar who pioneered this approach in the study of cinema and disability was Paul K. Longmore, whose influential essay "Screening Stereotypes: Images of Disability," published in 1985, offered a comprehensive overview of the negative stereotypes seen in Hollywood films that deal with disability. This essay set the theoretical tone of cinema and disability studies, which remained primarily focused on exposing and reversing the discriminatory ideology underlying most portrayals of disability in film. This impulse could still be seen in 1994 when Martin F. Norden published his groundbreaking study *The Cinema of Isolation: A History of Physical Disability in the Movies*. Norden's book offered the first complete documentation of negative images of physical disability in American cinema, and even its title shows the continuing influence of Longmore's methodology.

Longmore and Norden's work mirrored early feminist film criticism, which made possible the study of representations of minorities in cinema based on gender, race, class, and sexuality. Laura Mulvey's seminal essay in this field, "Visual Pleasure and Narrative

Cinema," published in 1975, identified the essentially patriarchal structure of classic Hollywood cinema, and her work became a catalyst for feminist film criticism in the mid-seventies. Longmore's essay established a similar model for cinema and disability, claiming that Hollywood films were essentially ableist in their depiction of people with disabilities. Both approaches shared a common top-down view of ideological interpellation, derived from theorists such as Theodor Adorno and Louis Althusser, in which the spectator is figured as a passive receptacle for the film's ideological content. This underlying assumption in Mulvey's work was questioned more than a decade ago by feminist scholars like Jacqueline Rose and Constance Penley, who challenged Mulvey's claims about the stereotypes of women and female spectatorship. These critics resisted Mulvey's totalizing theory by looking at sites of contradiction in the text and acts of resistance in the audience. These developments in feminist film criticism suggest that the study of cinema and disability must reexamine its basic assumptions.

Such a reexamination began in March of 1999, when scholars in both Film Studies and Disability Studies gathered at the University of Iowa for the first conference on cinema and disability. These scholars attempted to visualize where the study of cinema and disability had come from and where it needed to go. This book was conceived to continue that effort by both providing an overview of the traditional methods of analyzing portrayals of disability in cinema as well as suggesting new directions for cinema and disability scholars to take. The essays collected here not only show where the study of cinema and disability began, but it also marks a potentially new phase in the study of cinema and disability by incorporating elements of Film Studies that reemphasize the priority of reception and the complexity of texts.

The first section of the book, "Theorizing Cinema and Disability," presents three different theoretical models one could use to study the portrayal of disability in cinema, beginning with Paul K. Longmore's "Screening Stereotypes: Images of Disability." Seen as the foundational article in the study of cinema and disability, Longmore's work is reprinted here because it was the catalyst for the study of disabled images and it illustrates what could be called the first wave of scholarship in this field. Longmore was the first to ask the important question, "Why do television and film so frequently screen disabled characters for us to see, and why do we usually screen them out of our consciousness even as we absorb those images?" For Longmore, this question opens onto the different ways in which cinema and television have affected the societal condition of disability, and thus it forwards a political critique of the medium which has remained instrumental in the further development of the study of cinema and disability.

In the second essay, "The Hollywood Discourse on Disability: Some Personal Reflections," film historian Martin F. Norden provides a second theoretical model for the study of cinema and disability. In this essay, he reexamines the argument he originally made in his book *The Cinema of Isolation*. This now canonical text ushered in a new moment for cinema and disability studies by basing its argument firmly in the specificities of film history. Norden's book followed the approach outlined in Longmore's work, yet added a much needed historical element, citing examples from early silent cinema to contemporary film. In the essay included in this collection, Norden reflects on this project and articulates three phases in the development of disability in cinema, critiquing what he sees to be a historical discourse of unjust representation of people with disabilities in American films and offering some solutions on how such systems of representation might be changed.

"The Fusion of Film Studies and Disability Studies," by Thomas B. Hoeksema and Christopher R. Smit, offers yet a third theoretical model for the study of cinema and disability. Hoeksema and Smit have taught cinema and disability since 1995, and through that work have come to the conclusion that the activist agenda of earlier film and disability scholarship must be challenged in order for the discipline to productively engage with contemporary scholarship in the humanities. Hoeksema and Smit want to refocus critical attention back to the idea of film as art by applying an aesthetic methodology to the study of these films, thus offering a potentially new wave of film and disability scholarship.

The second section of the book, "Disability as Monstrosity in Classical Hollywood Cinema: Tod Browning and *The Hunchback of Notre Dame*," offers various perspectives on classical Hollywood's representation of people with disabilities as monstrous and grotesque, particularly in the films of Tod Browning. Méira Cook's essay "None of Us: Ambiguity as Moral Discourse in Tod Browning's *Freaks*" looks at the ways in which Browning's 1932 landmark film creates a complex and at times seemingly contradictory relationship between the spectator and images of disabled bodies. Cook argues that while the first half of the film appears to be highly progressive in its deployment of audience identification with the freaks, the second half returns to a more traditional horror film structure by presenting the freak performers as horrifying spectacles which threaten the viewers' own humanity. Cook uses the freaks' recurring phrase "one of us" as emblematic of this contradiction: "[W]hile it entrenches identification within the community of freaks, it holds up the presumably 'normal' or able-bodied viewer as a subject at once cut off from this unified group at the same time that s/he is guiltily implicated in the construction of just such a group identity." In other words, while the phrase "one of us" would seem to "hail" the viewers, asking them to identify with the freaks, it actually serves as a reminder of the strong division between the able-bodied viewers and the freaks, thus revealing the freaks' segregation from society.

Sally Chivers' essay "The Horror of Becoming 'One of Us': Tod Browning's *Freaks* and Disability" addresses a similar tension in Browning's film by analyzing the ways in which it complicates the horror genre's use of disabled bodies as a threat to the spectator's notion of normalcy and "health." Chivers points out that although *Freaks* continues to be marketed as a horror film, the only element it actually shares with this genre is that "it forces an uncomfortable audience identification," and this uncomfortable identification, unlike most horror films, is not the result of the horrifying appearance of the Monster but rather the disjuncture between the Monster's appearance and its behavior. Chivers thus argues that the representations of people with disabilities in Browning's film become horrific only insofar as they challenge "pervasive understandings of what comprises a healthy body, and how a body signifies moral fortitude."

Nicole Markotic's essay "Disabling the Viewer: Perceptions of Disability in Tod Browning's *Freaks*" addresses the difficulties of constructing an "authentic" representation of people with disabilities. Markotic begins by addressing Longmore's claim that in horror films "the deformity of the body symbolizes a deformity of the soul." Markotic points out that Browning's film both fulfills and contradicts this common metaphor by depicting people with disabilities as "vengeful and murderous" while at the same time defining disability itself as a medical problem rather than the manifestation of a moral disorder. However, Markotic also examines the ways in which this medical understanding of disability mobilizes another set of assumptions by reinforcing the able-bodied audience's belief in "the universal power of the human spirit to overcome adversity." In the end, Markotic concludes that Browning's film "reinscribes the essentialism it purports to challenge."

In his essay "Tod Browning and the Monstrosity of Hollywood Style," Oliver Gaycken employs film history to challenge the assumption that Browning was primarily a horror filmmaker. Rather than minimizing Browning's impact on cinema by categorizing him as a "cult director," Gaycken points out that "Browning was a mainstream artist, a director whose classical pedigree began with his assistant directorship under D. W. Griffith on *Intolerance* (1916) and that spanned the rest of the silent period and well into the early era of sound, periods during which he worked for major studios." By exploring different facets of Browning's career as a filmmaker, such as his use of melodrama, his ongoing relationship with star Lon Chaney, and his keen narrative sense, Gaycken puts forth an articulate understanding of this seemingly enigmatic director. In the end, Browning is shown as the paradoxical figure of classical Hollywood; while fitting succinctly into what David Bordwell calls the "classical Hollywood style," Gaycken's essay argues that he also served to stretch, challenge, and at times invert that very genre. Unlike the authors of the other essays regarding Browning's film *Freaks*, Gaycken approaches this important filmmaker holistically and offers an intriguing view of his contributions to the portrayal of disability in American cinema.

Laurie E. Harnick's essay "Lost and Found in Translation: The Changing Faces of Disability in the Film Adaptations of Hugo's *Notre Dame de Paris: 1842*" looks at how the representation of disabled bodies as monstrous and grotesque has changed since the age of classical Hollywood cinema. Building off of Norden's historical model, Harnick's essay provides a comprehensive guide to the film adaptations of Hugo's novel since 1923 and offers a detailed analysis of the ways in which their portrayals of disability have changed over time. While the earliest adaptations depicted Quasimodo as a horrific monster, Harnick claims that over time further versions gradually transformed him into a saint and martyr. Harnick argues that these adaptations thus provide a "barometer" for society's changing attitudes towards people with disabilities over the past century.

The third section, "Disability as Trauma, Mental Illness, and Dysfunction in Post-Vietnam Cinema," addresses the unique critical and theoretical issues raised by representations of non-physical disability since the 1970s. Following the Vietnam War, disabled veterans introduced a new political dimension to disability and new advocacy groups such as ADAPT worked to broaden the ways in which society defined disability itself. Christian Keathley's "Trapped in the Affection-Image: American Cinema's Post-Traumatic Cycle (1970-76)" serves to identify a persistent pattern of climactic dysfunction as characteristic of American films of the 1970s. Extending Gilles Deleuze's theory of the crisis of the action image, Keathley argues for the links between the closing images of traumatized and disabled protagonists in the films of Robert Altman, Francis Ford Coppola, and Alan J. Pakula and the larger political events of the period, such as Vietnam and Watergate. He argues that this crisis of confidence at the national level is symbolically embodied in the individual. By carefully placing this cycle of films in the context of the confident action-oriented films that preceded and followed it, Keathley vividly demonstrates that American cinema compulsively figures human possibility by the measure of physical ability.

Patrick Horrigan's "The Inner Life of *Ordinary People*" applies this notion of dysfunction and trauma to his own personal reading of Robert Redford's 1980 film. In an effort to understand the suicide of his close friend Gary Lucek, Horrigan reads his life and image in tandem with that of the suicidal character Conrad Jarrett (Timothy Hutton) from *Ordinary People*, a film his friend loved, revealing in the process the extent to which narrative and character patterns derived from fiction can play a role in producing disabling narratives in real life. Through several close readings of scenes from the film, he demonstrates the intricate mechanisms of transference that are figured through the relationship between Conrad Jarrett and his mother Beth (Mary Tyler Moore). Challenging received notions of suicide as a product of isolation, the essay illustrates the intimate relation between family history and dysfunction and provides a model for how personal memoir can be used to serve the purposes of critical analysis.

Lou Ann Thompson's "Disability and the Dysfunctional Family in Wayne Wang's *Smoke*" identifies the emotional disabilities that paralyze the 1995 film's ensemble of characters and demonstrates how their dysfunctions serve as the expression of personal traumas. The emotional paralysis that seems to govern all the characters in this film is sustained until they recognize the value and importance of the informal family structure into which they have been interpellated, a structure which allows them to work out their traumas and hence their dysfunctionality. Echoing this social dynamic, the physical disabilities of some characters are used by them and others as symbols that mediate relations with the past; like the emotional dysfunctions, they are seen as having a "history" and their disabling function is shown to depend on the degree to which the characters understand and accept this history. Because it figures disability as the product of a social response to circumstances, Thompson primarily sees the film as progressive.

The final section of the book, "Disability as Spectacle in Contemporary Cinema," addresses the ways in which disabled bodies see and are seen in contemporary cinema. Susan Crutchfield's essay "The Noble Ruined Body: Blindness and Visual Prosthetics in Three Science Fiction Films" applies Donna Haraway's cyborg theory and Michel Foucault's notion of bodily discipline to understand the complex ideologies at work in the use of visual prosthetics in science fiction films. While the characters in these films frequently employ visual prosthetics to enhance or regain their vision, these devices inevitably cause damage and even blindness to their users. Crutchfield sees this relationship between user and prosthetic as a Foucaultian "discipline of the body" which shows "that ability is gained through disciplines which amount to physical restrictions in themselves." According to Crutchfield, these representations of "dis/enabling" prosthetics critique the notion that vision is technologically mediated by revealing "the repressed and undervalued content of humanity that technology attempts to control, and even efface." These films thus evoke "a postmodern fantasy of the return to the noble ruined body, which is every-body, once stripped of modern technology's prosthetics." However, Crutchfield also points out that these films simultaneously "suggest that no vision can escape the influence and inflection of visual technology." Vision in these films is never "natural or so-called normal," but rather it is depicted as either "prosthetically enhanced, *media-ted* vision or its alternative, *blindness*." Disability then becomes "a rhetorical figure for the postmodern *norm* of human/technology interfaces," and Crutchfield concludes that film itself serves as one such human/technology interface which interpellates the spectator into the ideology of the prosthetic.

Anthony Enns' essay "The Spectacle of Disabled Masculinity in John Woo's 'Heroic Bloodshed' Films" examines the ways in which masculinity is empowered through disability in the films of John Woo. Enns points out that critics have read Woo's "heroic bloodshed" films as a response to the anxiety of Hong Kong's citizens in the wake of the Tiananmen Square protests in 1989; by evoking a nostalgia for chivalry within a climate of impending doom, these critics argue, Woo's films offer a potentially radical image of masculinity which incorporates both physical prowess and emotional intimacy. Enns analyzes the connection between this new image of masculinity and the frequent presence of disabled men in Woo's films. While these men are sometimes depicted as weak characters who need to be protected or avenged, they are more often empowered by their suffering. Disability also enables a new kind of masculinity by predicating difference on the figure of disability rather than gender. Enns' analysis not only reveals the complex role of disabled masculinity in these narratives but also how this role is related to a specific cultural and historical moment.

In "Sexy Cyborgs: Disability and Erotic Politics in Cronenberg's *Crash*," James L. Cherney attempts to challenge the predominantly asexual treatment of people with disabilities in film. Working from within a critique of cultural ableism, Cherney uses the concepts of the eroticized other, the sexual oppression of disabled individuals, and contemporary cyborg theory to articulate the ways in which film treats the issue of sex and disability. He also examines how current ideologies of the body and technology are ushering in new models for cinematic depictions of disabled sexuality. Cherney employs Norden's term "the cinema of isolation" to discuss cinema's failure to represent disability and sexuality, and he presents David Cronenberg's film *Crash* (1996) as an innovative way of portraying disability in film. As Cherney points out, by forcing its viewer "to question and confront repulsion of the disabled body and to accept the sexuality of even the sterile cyborg, Cronenberg's film works to undermine the political power of the ableist repression of sexual desire for the other."

The primary goal of this collection is to give attention to the variety of representations of people with disabilities in film and the ways in which these images can be read. Developing and enriching our knowledge of the complex historical traditions that go into cinematic representations, the essays collected here apply sophisticated theoretical and critical methodologies to enable a deeper understanding of the role of disability in cinema. Our hope is that this book will become the catalyst for further work in this field, and that it will suggest new avenues of inquiry into cinema, disability, and their points of intersection.

Works Cited

Adorno, Theodor, and Max Horkheimer. *Dialectic of Enlightenment*. Trans. John Cumming. New York: Continuum, 1999.

Althusser, Louis. *Lenin and Philosophy.* Trans. Ben Brewster. London: Monthly Review Press, 1971.
Davis, Lennard J. "Introduction: The Need for Disability Studies." *The Disability Studies Reader.* Ed. Davis. New York: Routledge, 1997. 1-6.
Longmore, Paul K. "Screening Stereotypes: Images of Disabled People." *Social Policy* 16.1 (Summer 1985): 31-37.
Mulvey, Laura. "Visual Pleasure and Narrative Cinema." *Screen* 16.3 (1975): 6-18.
Norden, Martin F. *The Cinema of Isolation: A History of Physical Disability in the Movies.* New Brunswick: Rutgers UP, 1994.
Rose, Jacqueline. "Paranoia and the Film System." *Feminism and Film Theory.* Ed. Constance Penley. New York: Routledge, 1988. 141-158.
Penley, Constance. *The Future of an Illusion: Film, Feminism, and Psychoanalysis.* Minneapolis: U of Minnesota P, 1989.

Theorizing Cinema and Disability

Screening Stereotypes: Images of Disabled People

Paul K. Longmore

When one examines images of people with disabilities in television and film, one encounters two striking facts. First, one discovers hundreds of characters with all sorts of disabilities: handicapped horror "monsters"; "crippled" criminals; disabled war veterans, from *The Big Parade* (1925) to *The Best Years of Our Lives* (1946) to *Coming Home* (1978); central characters of television series temporarily disabled for one episode; blind detectives; disabled victims of villains; animated characters like stuttering Porky Pig, speech-impaired Elmer Fudd, near-sighted Mr. McGoo, and mentally retarded Dopey.

The second striking fact is how much we overlook the prevalence of disability and the frequent presence of disabled characters. Why are there so many disabled characters, and why do we overlook them so much of the time? Why do television and film so frequently screen disabled characters for us to see, and why do we usually screen them out of our consciousness even as we absorb those images?

The critic Michael Wood has some useful observations that apply here. "All movies mirror reality in some way or other," he writes:

> There are no escapes, even in the most escapist pictures . . . . Movies bring out [our] worries without letting them loose and without forcing us to look at them too closely . . . . [I]t doesn't appear to be

> necessary for a movie to solve anything, however fictitiously. It seems to be enough for us if a movie simply dramatizes our semi-secret concerns and contradictions in a story, allows them their brief, thinly disguised parade . . . . [E]ntertainment is not, as we often think, a full-scale flight from our problems, not a means of forgetting them completely, but rather a rearrangement of our problems into shapes which tame them, which disperse them to the margins of our attention. (16-18)

Often, as Wood says, film and television programs do touch upon our areas of concern without explicitly acknowledging or exploring them. At other times, for instance in the "social problem" dramas seen during the 1970s and '80s, the subjects of our worries were addressed, but without a deep examination. In such cases, television and film supply quick and simple solutions. They tell us that the problem is not as painful or as overwhelming as we fear, that it is manageable, or that it is not really our problem at all, but someone else's.

Disability happens around us more often than we generally recognize or care to notice, and we harbor unspoken anxieties about the possibility of disablement, to us or to someone close to us. What we fear, we often stigmatize and shun and sometimes seek to destroy. Popular entertainments depicting disabled characters allude to these fears and prejudices, or address them obliquely or fragmentarily, seeking to reassure us about ourselves.

What follows is a brief consideration of the most common screen images of people with physical, sensory, and developmental disabilities and some thoughts about their underlying social and psychological meaning. This article by no means exhausts the range of images or their significance; although it concentrates on live-action fictional depictions, it also compares them to nonfictional images in order to illuminate further the social and cultural attitudes and concerns they reflect and express. Further, it is important to show the connections between recent changes in those characterizations and the emergence of a new socio-political consciousness about disability, particularly among disabled people themselves.

Disability and Criminality

Disability has often been used as a melodramatic device not only in popular entertainments, but in literature as well. Among the most persistent is the association of disability with malevolence. Deformity of body symbolizes deformity of soul. Physical handicaps are made the emblems of evil.

Richard the Third's hunchback and Captain Ahab's peg leg immediately come to mind, but "bad guys" still frequently have handicaps. Doctor No and Doctor Strangelove both have forearms and hands encased in black leather. The overpowering evil embodied in Strangelove's leather-wrapped hand nearly makes him strangle himself. He is also "confined to a wheelchair." The disabilities of both doctors apparently resulted from foul-ups in their nefarious experiments. They are "crippled" as a consequence of their evil.

One of the most popular adversaries of the TV adventure series *The Wild Wild West* (1965-1970) was the criminal genius, yet another doctor, Miguelito P. Loveless, a hunch-backed "dwarf." Michael Dunn, a marvelous and talented actor, spent much of his career relegated to such horrific roles. In one episode, Dr. Loveless says to the story's hero, "I grow weary of you, Mr. West. I weary of the sight of your strong, straight body." This brilliant villain repeatedly hatches grandiose schemes to wreak havoc and overthrow the U.S. government, with an obvious motive: he wants revenge on the world, presumably the able-bodied world. Disabled villains, raging against their "fate" and hating those who have escaped such "affliction," often seek to retaliate against "normals."

Other criminal characters may operate on a less magnificent scale, but act from the same animus. In the "Hookman" (1973) episode of *Hawaii Five-O*, a double-amputee sniper who had lost both hands in a foiled bank robbery blamed the series' hero and pledged to avenge his "maiming" by killing the police detective. Or consider the "one-armed man," the real murderer in one of the most popular series in television history, *The Fugitive* (1963-1967). (Bill Raisch was another handicapped actor confined to criminal roles because of his disability.)

The connection between criminality and disability continues. In 1984 the short-lived series *Hot Pursuit* unsuccessfully tried a variation on the "fugitive" formula. This time an innocent woman accused of murder was chased by the real killer, a one-eyed hit man. Another recent series, modern-day western, *The Yellow Rose* (1983-1984), featured Chuck Connors as Hollister, a greedy and vengeful oilman who walks with a limp, supporting himself with a cane. The scene introducing this character made clear the connection between his nastiness and his handicap. An establishing long shot showed him "hobbling" toward the camera, with a cut to a close-up of the "bad" leg and the cane.

Another recent disabled villain—not a criminal, but a "bad guy" just the same—appeared in the popular British miniseries, *The Jewel in the Crown* (broadcast on American public television in 1984-1985). This dramatization of the last years of British colonial rule in India revolved around one Ronald Merrick, a police investigator and army intelligence officer who is arrogant, deceitful, and viciously racist. Because of a battle injury, the left side of his face is disfigured and he loses his left arm. Like Doctor No, Doctor Strangelove, and a number of other maimed or amputee bad guys, he acquires a black leather-covered prosthetic limb. This dramatic device recurs frequently enough that one begins to wonder about the psychosexual significance of the connection between blackness, badness, amputation, and artificial arms.

Giving disabilities to villainous characters reflects and reinforces, albeit in exaggerated fashion, three common prejudices against handicapped people: disability is a punishment for evil; disabled people are embittered by their "fate"; disabled people resent the nondisabled and would, if they could, destroy them. In historic and contemporary social fact, it is, of course, non-disabled people who have at times endeavored to destroy people with disabilities. As with popular portrayals of other minorities, the unacknowledged hostile fantasies of the stigmatizers are transferred to the stigmatized. The non-disabled audience is allowed to disown its fears and biases by "blaming the victims," making them responsible for their own ostracism and destruction.

Closely related to the criminal characterization, but distinct from it, is the depiction in horror stories of the disabled person as "monster." The subtext of many horror films is fear and loathing of people with disabilities. As with the equation of disability and criminality, the horrific characterization long antedates television and persists most frequently in horror films made for theatrical release. Still, television perpetuates the "monster" image not only by broadcasting these theatrical films, but also by producing new versions of horror classics. The most prominent recent examples are the TV movie remakes of those perennial favorites, *The Hunchback of Notre Dame* (1981) and *The Phantom of the Opera* (1983).

The most obvious feature of "monster" characterizations is their extremism. The physical disabilities typically involve disfigurement of the face and head and gross deformity of the body. As with the criminal characterization, these visible traits express disfigurement of personality and deformity of soul. Once again, disability may be represented as the cause of evil-doing, punishment for it, or both.

Further, the depiction of the disabled person as "monster" and the criminal characterization both express to varying degrees the notion that disability involves the loss of an essential part of one's humanity. Depending on the extent of disability, the individual is perceived as more or less sub-human. These images reflect what Erving Goffman describes as the fundamental nature of stigma: the stigmatized person is regarded as "somehow less than human." Such depictions also exemplify the "spread effect" of prejudice. The stigmatized trait assumedly taints every aspect of the person, pervasively spoiling social identity (Goffman 3; Wright 8).

That "spread effect" is evident in an extension of the notion of loss of humanity, the idea that disability results in loss of self-control. The disabled character thus endangers the rest of society. The dangerous disabled person is not necessarily a criminal or a malevolent monster, but may be a tragic victim of fate, as in the non-horror story *Of Mice and Men* (TV versions 1969, 1981). Whatever the specific nature of the disability, it unleashes violent propensities that "normally" would be kept in check by internal mechanisms of self-control.

Violent loss of self-control results in the exclusion of the disabled person from human community. Often in horror stories, and virtually always in criminal characterizations, it is the disability itself and the resultant dangerous behavior that separates and isolates the disabled character from the rest of society. But in some "monster" stories, for instance *The Hunchback of Notre Dame*, the disabled person is excluded because of the fear and contempt of the nondisabled majority. Still, even when the handicapped character is presented sympathetically as a victim of bigotry, it remains clear that severe disability makes social integration impossible. While viewers are urged to pity Quasimodo or Lennie, we are let off the hook by being shown that disability or bias or both must forever ostracize severely disabled persons from society.

For both monstrous and criminal disabled characters, the final and only possible solution is often death. In most cases, it is fitting and just punishment. For sympathetic "monsters," death is the tragic but inevitable, necessary, and merciful outcome. Again we can "sympathize" with the mentally retarded Lennie, while avoiding our fears and biases about him, and escape the dilemma of his social accommodation and integration.

During the 1970s and 1980s another depiction of persons with severe disabilities emerged: the severely physically disabled character who seeks suicide as a release from the living death of catastrophic disablement. This was the theme of the play and motion picture *Whose Life Is It, Anyway?* (1981), the TV movie *An Act of Love* (1981), and the theatrical drama *Nevis Mountain Dew*. In the first two stories, recently spinal cord-injured quadriplegics request assisted suicide, and in the last, a post-polio respiratory quadriplegic asks his family to unplug his iron lung. The ostensible subject of the first and second dramas is the arrogance and oppressive power of a medical establishment gone wild, which at exorbitant expense keeps alive suffering people who would be better off dead. But just beneath the surface of all of these tales runs a second unacknowledged theme, the horror of a presumed "vegetable-like" existence following severe disablement.

These stories present distinct parallels with the "monster" characterization. Disability again means loss of one's humanity. The witty, combative central character in *Whose Life Is It, Anyway?* refers to himself as a "vegetable" and says that he is "not a man" anymore. The disabled persons in the other two dramas make similar statements of themselves. Severe disability also means loss of control. Unlike the criminal and "monster" characterizations, it does not mean loss of moral self-control, since the disabled would-be suicides clearly have a moral sensibility superior to those who would force them to live. Rather, disability means a total physical dependency that deprives the individual of autonomy and self-determination.

Disability again results in separation from the community. This exclusion is not presented as necessary to protect society from danger, as with the monstrous disabled character. Nor is it the result of discrimination or inaccessibility. It is portrayed as the inevitable consequence of a serious physical impairment that prevents normal functioning, normal relationships, and normal productivity. All of these dramas distort or ignore the possibilities of rehabilitation and modern assistive technology. They also totally avoid considering what effects the enforcement of antidiscrimination and accessibility laws would have on the activities, identities, and sense of self-worth of disabled individuals.

Finally, as with the "monster" and criminal characterizations, these dramas present death as the only logical and humane solution. But instead of eliminating the disabled person who is a violent threat, it relieves both the individual viewer and society of the impossible emotional, moral, and financial burden of severe disability. The disabled characters choose death themselves, beg for it as release from their insupportable existence. The non-disabled characters resist this decision, but then reluctantly bow to it as necessary and merciful. Once again, the nondisabled audience is allowed to avoid confronting its own fears and prejudices. It is urged to compliment itself for its compassion in supporting death as the only sensible solution to the problems of people with severe disabilities.

Even when bigotry is presented as a fundamental problem confronting severely disabled persons, as in *The Elephant Man* (1980), the final solution, the choice of the disabled character himself, is suicide. Whether because of prejudice or paralysis, disability makes membership in the community and meaningful life itself impossible, and death is preferable. Better dead than disabled.

Portrayals of Adjustment

The most prevalent image in film and especially in television during the past several decades has been the maladjusted disabled person. These stories involve characters with physical or sensory, rather than mental, handicaps. The plots follow a consistent pattern: the disabled central characters are bitter and self-pitying because, however long they have been disabled, they have never adjusted to their handicaps, and have never accepted themselves as they are. Consequently, they treat nondisabled family and friends angrily and manipulatively. At first, the nondisabled characters, feeling sorry for them, coddle them, but eventually they realize that in order to help the disabled individuals adjust and cope they must "get tough." The stories climax in a confrontation scene in which a nondisabled character gives the disabled individual an emotional "slap in the face" and tells him or her to stop feeling sorry for themselves. Accepting the rebuke, the disabled characters quit complaining and become well-adjusted adults.

These portrayals suggest that disability is a problem of psychological self-acceptance, of emotional adjustment. Social prejudice rarely intrudes. In fact, the nondisabled main characters have no trouble accepting the individuals with disabilities. Moreover, they understand better than the handicapped characters the true nature of the problem. Typically, disabled characters lack insight about themselves and other people, and require emotional education, usually by a nondisabled character. In the end, nondisabled persons supply the solution: they compel the disabled individuals to confront themselves.

The drama of adjustment seems to have developed in the aftermath of World War II, probably in response to the large numbers of disabled veterans returning from that conflict. Note, for instance, that two of the most powerful examples appeared in the films *The Best Years of Our Lives* (1946) and *The Men* (1950). This genre became a staple of television in the 1960s, '70s, and '80s.

Paradoxically, this depiction represents progress in the portrayal of disabled persons. The criminal and "monster" characterizations show that disability deprives its victims of an essential part of their humanity, separates them from the community, and ultimately requires that they be put to death. In contrast, the dramas of adjustment say that disability does not inherently prevent deaf, blind, or physically handicapped people from living meaningfully and productively and from having normal friendships and romantic relationships. But these stories put the responsibility for any problems squarely and almost exclusively on the disabled individual. If they are socially isolated, it is not because the disability inevitably has cut them off from the community or because society has rejected them. Refusing to accept themselves with their handicaps, they have chosen isolation.

A recurring explicit or implicit secondary theme of many stories of adjustment is the idea of compensation. God or nature or life compensates handicapped people for their loss, and the compensation is spiritual, moral, mental, and emotional. In an episode of *Little House on the Prairie*, "Town Party, Country Party" (1974) about a "lame" schoolgirl, Charles the father says that many "cripples" seem to have "special gifts." Laura, his daughter, asks if those gifts include "gumption." Yes, he answers, and goodness of heart too. Other stories represent blind people with special insights into human nature (for instance, the blind old Black man in *Boone*, a short-lived 1983 TV series) or paraplegic detectives with superior skills (*Ironside*). Far from contradicting the image of the maladjusted disabled person, the notion of compensation reiterates it in yet another way. Compensation comes to those who cope. It is a "gift" to handicapped individuals who responsibly deal with their "afflictions."

Nonfictional television programs, particularly magazine shows such as *That's Incredible*, *Real People*, and *Ripley's Believe It Or Not*, frequently present handicapped individuals who are the opposite of the fictional "maladjusted" disabled person. Repeatedly they recount stories of achievement and success, of heroic overcoming. Over and over they display inspiring blind carpenters, paraplegic physicians, and "handicapable" athletes. These "real-life" stories of striving and courage seem the antithesis of the bitter and self-pitying "cripples" in dramas of adjustment, but both stem from the same perception of the nature of disability: disability is primarily a problem of emotional coping, of personal acceptance. It is not a problem of social stigma and discrimination. It is a matter of individuals overcoming not only the physical impairments of their own bodies but, more importantly, the emotional consequences of such impairments. Both fictional and nonfictional stories convey the message that success or failure in living with a disability results almost solely from the emotional choices, courage, and character of the individual.

The Social Function of Disability Images

Both the dramas of adjustment and the nonfictional presentation of people with disabilities stem from the common notion that with the proper attitude one can cope with and conquer any situation or condition, turning it into a positive growth experience. Nothing can defeat us; only we can defeat ourselves. This belief in the power of a positive mental outlook, so widely and successfully marketed in therapies, psychologies, and sects, not only currently but throughout American history, suggests a primary reason for the popularity of stories about disabled people adjusting and overcoming. It points to one of the social and cultural functions of that image and to one of the primary social roles expected of people with disabilities: in a culture that attributes success or failure primarily to individual character, "successful" handicapped people serve as models of personal adjustment, striving, and achievement. In the end, accomplishment or defeat depends only on one's attitude toward oneself and toward life. If someone so tragically "crippled" can overcome the obstacles confronting them, think what you, without such a "handicap," can do.

Another obvious social function of the psychologized image of physical and sensory disability is to make it an individual rather than a social problem. Prejudice and discrimination rarely enter into either fictional or nonfictional stories, and then only as a secondary issue. In fictional productions, nondisabled persons usually treat disabled people badly, not because of bias, but out of insensitivity and lack of understanding. It becomes the responsibility of the disabled individual to "educate" them, to allay their anxieties and make them feel comfortable. For instance, in an episode of *Little House on the Prairie*, "No Beast So Fierce" (1982), a boy who stutters is told that he must patiently help the other children to accept him and then they will stop ridiculing him.

Nonfictional programs also generally avoid or obscure the issue of prejudice. In an interview on *Hour Magazine*, a paraplegic teenage fashion model briefly mentioned repeated professional rejection and discrimination because of her disability. Diverting from that subject, the interviewer concentrated his questions on her strenuous efforts to learn to walk. (By then she was up to twelve steps.) Presumably, walking would make her a more acceptable and attractive model than using a wheelchair.

Segments about disabled people on magazine shows and news broadcasts frequently focus on medical and technological advances. They also often present "human interest" stories about individuals with disabilities performing some physical feat to demonstrate that they are not "handicapped," only "physically challenged." One could argue that these features demonstrate that medical and technological innovations are increasingly neutralizing physical impairments and that they and the "human interest" stories show that attitudes rather than disabilities limit people. But simultaneously they reinforce the notion that disability is fundamentally a physical problem requiring a medical or mechanical fix. They also suggest that disabled people can best prove their social acceptability, their worthiness of social integration, by displaying some physical capability. Finally, these features also reiterate, with the active complicity of the disabled participants themselves, the view that disability is a problem of individual emotional coping and physical overcoming, rather than an issue of social discrimination against a stigmatized minority.

The reactions of disabled people themselves to "human interest" stories are particularly illuminating. Some praise these features for showing that "physically inconvenienced" folks are as able as so-called "normals." Others criticize such "super crip" segments for continuing to portray handicapped people as "incredible," extraordinary, or freakish. Both responses, it would seem, stem from the same concern and aim: increasingly and in various ways, for instance in the debate over the language of disability,[1] people with disabilities are rejecting the stigmatized social identity imposed upon them. They are struggling to fashion for themselves a positive personal and public identity. Whether or not "human interest" stories in fact promote an alternative image, handicapped people themselves clearly intend to oppose stigma and discrimination.

Stigma and discrimination are still especially powerful regarding sexuality and romance. In a sexually supercharged culture that places almost obsessive emphasis on attractiveness, people with various disabilities are often perceived as sexually deviant and even dangerous, asexual, or sexually incapacitated either physically or emotionally. Film and television stereotypes reflect and reinforce these common biases.

Criminal disabled characters convey a kinky, leering lust for sex with gorgeous "normal" women. Dr. Loveless, the hunch-backed "dwarf" super-criminal in *The Wild Wild West*, surrounds himself with luscious women. The Nazi "dwarf" in the film comedy *The Black Bird* (1974) displays a voracious appetite for sex with statuesque beauties. Dr. Strangelove salivates over the prospect of having his share of nubile young women to perpetuate the human race in underground caverns following a nuclear holocaust. "Monster" disabled characters menace beautiful women who would ordinarily reject them. The disfigured "Phantom of the Opera" kidnaps a woman who reminds him of his dead wife. Quasimodo, the hunchback of Notre Dame, rescues and tenderly cares for a woman with whom he has obviously fallen in love. But there is always an undertone of sexual tension, of sexual danger. We are never quite sure what he might do to her.

Mentally retarded adult men also at times appear as sexually menacing figures, partly because of their supposed inability to control their emotions, to gauge their own strength, and to restrain a propensity toward violence. Thus, George mercifully kills his friend Lennie (*Of Mice and Men*) after Lennie accidentally breaks the neck of a beautiful young woman. Sexual menace, deviancy, and danger stem from the loss of control often represented as inherent in the experience of disability.

In other stories, physical paralysis results in asexuality or sexual incapacitation. The quadriplegic characters in *Whose Life Is It, Anyway?*, *An Act of Love*, and *Nevis Mountain Dew* opt for suicide partly because they believe they have lost the ability to function sexually. Neither of the first two films examines the reality of sexual physiology among people with spinal cord injuries, nor the possibilities of sexual rehabilitation. *Nevis Mountain Dew* inaccurately represents sensory deprivation and sexual dysfunction as consequences of polio. But these individuals, and characters with less severe physical disabilities in other stories, have lost something more important than the physical capacity to function sexually. Disability has deprived them of an essential part of their humanness: their identities as sexual beings. More than one male character with a disability refers to himself as "only half a man."

Even when a disability does not limit sexual functioning, it may impair the person emotionally. Disabled characters may be quite capable of physical love-making, but spurn opportunities for romance because of a lack of self-acceptance, a disbelief that anyone could love him or her with their "imperfections." Nondisabled characters of the opposite sex have no trouble finding the disabled persons attractive or falling in love with them, and have no difficulty in accepting them with their disabilities. From the double amputee veteran in *The Best Years of Our Lives* to a quadriplegic accountant in *Highway to Heaven*, "A Marriage Made in Heaven" (1985), disabled characters require convincing that they are loveable and that a romantic relationship is workable despite their disabilities. These depictions fly in the face of the real life experiences of many handicapped men and women who find that even the most minor impairments result in romantic rejection. Once again, popular entertainments invert social reality and allow the non-disabled audience to disown its anxieties and prejudices about disabled people. The source of the "problem" is shifted to the stigmatized person himself or herself, in another version of blaming the victim.

In the past, most stories presenting a positive image of disabled people and romance have involved blind characters. Recently, a few productions have presented people with physical disabilities as attractive and sexual. Most prominent among these are Jon Voight's paraplegic Vietnam veteran in *Coming Home* and an episode of the TV situation comedy *Facts of Life* starring Geri Jewell, an actress with cerebral palsy. What distinguishes these and a handful of other portrayals is the self-assurance of the disabled characters regarding their own sexuality and romantic value. They enter relationships out of the strength of their own identities as persons with disabilities.

Changing Views of the Disabled

These romantic portrayals and other new characterizations have slowly begun to appear, partly as a result of the increasing impact on casting and characterization of the Media Access Office of the California Foundation on Employment and Disability and other disability activist groups within the entertainment industry. Creation of these groups in turn reflects the emergence of the disability civil rights movement and the growing media awareness of the disability community. Even while previous stereotypes have persisted, a few productions have struggled to "read" these evolving events and to respond to a developing sociopolitical consciousness about disabled people. The resulting images are fascinatingly contradictory. Elements of a minority-group view of disabled people jostle uncomfortably with the themes of the drama of adjustment.

This complicated trend first appeared in *The Other Side of the Mountain* (1977) and *The Other Side of the Mountain, Part II* (1979). This film biography of Jill Kinmont turned her story into a traditional account of overcoming severe disability, while almost completely ignoring her struggle to combat discrimination in education and employment. However, one important scene showed her confronting prejudice when a professor praises her as an "inspiration" while declaring that she will never get a teaching job. Subsequently, the TV movie, *The Ordeal of Bill Carney* (1981), dramatized the "real-life" landmark legal battle of a quadriplegic father to gain custody of his two sons. The characterization of Carney, according to Carney himself, distorted his personal life by fitting it into the stereotype of coping, showing him as frequently bitter and depressed, and particularly maladjusted in a sexual and romantic relationship. In contrast, his paraplegic lawyer was portrayed as having an emotionally and sexually healthy relationship with his wife. More importantly, the film showed the attorney militantly defending Carney's legal right to raise his children and the lawyer's own right of physical access to public places.

Contradictions of characterization and theme have also appeared in episodic television. *T. J. Hooker* segment, "Blind Justice" (1983), presented a blind woman in physical danger because she had witnessed a murder. Here is a recurring stereotype: a blind person, usually a woman, in jeopardy who tells of the terror of "living in darkness." But in this instance, the stereotype was mitigated and complicated because the woman was also presented as an advocate of the rights of handicapped people and Hooker was given a speech about the need to end bias against people with disabilities. Similarly, an episode of *Quincy*, "Give Me Your Weak" (1983), showed hundreds of politically active disabled people demonstrating in favor of the "Orphan Drugs Bill" pending in Congress. But the story also followed the descent into self-pity of a woman who succumbed to her disability, until her husband rebuked her and demanded that she act responsibly again. An installment of *Alice* (1984) focused on accessibility for wheelchair users, clearly a response to that pressing social and policy question. But it treated accessibility as an act of generosity that the nondisabled should perform to make things easier for "the handicapped," rather than an issue of the civil and legal rights of disabled people.

A few recent productions have directly dealt with the issue of prejudice. *The Elephant Man* showed the dehumanizing exploitation and bigotry inflicted on a severely disabled man; "Little Lou," an episode of *Little House on the Prairie* (1983), told of a short-statured man denied employment because of discrimination. Unfortunately, instead of showing such bias as widespread, this story had only one prejudiced character, the cartoonishly obnoxious and snobbish Mrs. Oleson. The weakness of both dramas was their indulgence in melodramatic sentimentality.

More realistic was the powerful "For Love of Joshua" on *Quincy* (1983), which examined the denial of medical treatment and nutrition to developmentally disabled new-borns and showed the possibilities of independent living for intellectually handicapped people. The story climaxed with an eloquent courtroom speech by a teenager with Down's Syndrome protesting prejudice against mentally retarded people. In the theatrical film *Mask* (1985), a teenager with a rare facially disfiguring disease confronts discrimination in education, social ostracism, and romantic rejection. He and his mother militantly resist prejudice. Unfortunately, as in *The Elephant Man*, the movie lets the audience off the hook when the youth dies. It is easier to regret prejudice if its victims won't be around (Longmore, "'Mask'").

If stereotyping of handicapped persons has prevailed in both fictional and nonfictional television programming, the problem in TV commercials has been the total exclusion, until recently, of people with disabilities. Sponsors have feared that the presence of individuals with visible handicaps would alienate consumers from their products. They also have failed to recognize the substantial population of disabled Americans as potential customers. Additionally, they have asserted, not without reason, that by casting performers with disabilities in their commercials they would incur the charge of exploitation. As a result, past efforts to integrate commercials have met with massive resistance.

In 1983, '84, and early '85, commercials using handicapped performers began to appear. Departing significantly from past practices, these spots may signal a trend. In mid-1983, CBS broadcast a series of promos for its fall schedule. One showed a paraplegic wheelchair racer. Another had a deaf couple signing, "I love you." "I love you too." Significantly, these commercials not only garnered praise from the disability community, but also criticism from at least one nondisabled TV critic who implied that CBS was exploiting handicapped people.

More important breakthroughs came in 1984. Levi's Jeans, a major sponsor of ABC's coverage of the 1984 Summer Olympics, presented jazzy spots showing hip young adults, including one with a beautiful woman walking next to a young man in a sports wheelchair who pops a wheelie and spins his chair around. Late in 1984, McDonald's "Handwarmin'" commercial featured patrons of the restaurant chain clapping rhythmically and enjoying its food, warmth, and conviviality. One of them is a young woman seated in a wheelchair. In May 1985, network commercials for Kodak and *People* magazine included wheelchair users, and, most importantly, a spot for the Plymouth Voyager prominently featured a middle-aged man on crutches praising the car.

These commercials represent a major departure in several ways. Most obviously and importantly, all include disabled persons in efforts to promote products, whether hamburgers, blue jeans, TV shows, magazines, cameras, or cars. They seek out handicapped Americans as a market and audience; they reject the fear that nondisabled consumers will be distressed or offended. Further, in order to sell their products, these commercials present a new image of disabled persons. They are not portrayed as helpless and dependent, but rather as attractive, active, and "with it," involved and competitive, experiencing "normal" relationships, and in the auto commercial, smart about what they buy. Ironically, these commercials offer perhaps the most positive media images of people with disabilities to date.

Conclusion

Positive images in commercials and other programs reflect the growing socio-political perception of disabled people as a minority group and the increasing impact of the disability civil rights movement. Whether these new depictions will become an important trend depends partly on the response from the disability community itself. Advertisers and broadcasters pay close attention to the reactions of various audiences. They are more likely to expand inclusion of disabled performers in commercials and other programming if they receive positive reinforcement from the disability community. By the same token, they will avoid stereotyping and discrimination only if they know that such practices will evoke a negative reaction from handicapped viewers. It is organized constituencies, of whatever size, that have brought about changes in broadcasting and advertising. Although the disability community and civil rights movement have slowly been becoming more media conscious, concerted efforts to alter media images have thus far remained on a comparatively small scale.

Meanwhile, the study of images of people with disabilities in television, film, literature, and the arts needs more detailed investigation. It seems probable that an analysis of not only the "monster," criminal, and maladjusted characterizations, but other types as well, would reveal a hierarchy of disability, involving a complex interaction among such factors as visibility, severity, mode of functioning, and proximity to the face and head. Such studies should draw upon psychological and social-psychological explorations of the dynamics of prejudice against disabled people. That linkage would deepen our understanding of both the images themselves and the social and cultural attitudes they express. Students of those images should also examine their historical evolution. How did they change over time? These historical developments should also be connected with the historical experience of disabled people in various societies and cultures. What was their social and economic condition? How did their societies regard and treat them? In short, we need a social and cultural history of disabled people.

The scholarly task is to uncover the hidden history of disabled people and to raise to awareness the unconscious attitudes and values embedded in media images. The political task is to liberate disabled people from the paternalistic prejudice expressed in those images and to forge a new social identity. The two are inseparable.

Notes

[1] For more information on the debate over the language of disability, see Longmore's essay "A Note on Language and the Social Identity of Disabled People."

Works Cited

Goffman, Erving. *Stigma: Notes on the Management of Spoiled Identity.* Englewood Cliffs: Prentice Hall, 1963.

Longmore, Paul K. "'Mask': A Revealing Portrayal of the Disabled." *The Los Angeles Times Sunday Calendar* 5 May 1985: 22-23.
---. "A Note on Language and the Social Identity of Disabled People." *American Behavioral Scientist* 28.3 (January/February 1985): 419-423.
Wood, Michael. *America In the Movies.* New York: Basic Books, 1975.
Wright, Beatrice. *Physical Disability: A Psychological Approach.* New York: Harper and Row, 1960.

The Hollywood Discourse on Disability: Some Personal Reflections

Martin F. Norden

Shortly before the University of Iowa's "Screening Disability" conference, the *Chronicle of Higher Education* published an essay by Leonard Cassuto titled "Whose Field Is It, Anyway?: Disability Studies in the Academy." In this essay, Cassuto, an English professor at Fordham, examined the emergent field of Disability Studies and raised some provocative questions about the relevance of teachers' and researchers' own "disability status" to the work that they do. This essay, which elicited dozens of often spirited responses,[1] prompted me to take stock of my own situation and how it led to the writing of *The Cinema of Isolation: A History of Physical Disability in the Movies* and many related articles. What follows, then, is an assessment of my own involvement in the intersecting concerns of Film Studies and Disability Studies, some of the things I learned, and suggestions for future work.

My interest in the Hollywood representation of disability emerged from a confluence of personal and professional concerns. I regard myself as a temporarily able-bodied person—a TAB—but I have known disabled people all my life: in my family, in my place of worship, in my classrooms, at the office, and elsewhere. As a professor long interested in the movie representation of disadvantaged social subgroups, I could not help but notice that the people with disabilities (PWDs) I knew exhibited little resemblance to the disabled characters I saw on theater screens.

A turning point occurred in 1981 when, in the midst of a conference on fantasy and the arts, I attended a screening of the 1932 film *Freaks*. (I had seen this controversial movie before, but my memory of it was quite hazy as the presentation had been on a late-night, commercial-choked television broadcast years before the age of VCRs.) I came out of the auditorium greatly conflicted, and I wanted to know more about this film and others that had disabled characters at their centers. Back at my home campus, I did a library search but discovered nothing, at least in book form, on disability-related films. This gap in the media-stereotyping literature was puzzling, since a tradition of books that examined the movie portrayals of social subgroups such as women, African Americans, Native Americans, and gay men and lesbians was well underway by the early 1980s.

I remember thinking that this lack of scholarly attention could probably be attributed to the long-standing belief among able-bodied society members that disability is primarily an individualistic, medically defined problem, not a socially constructed one. In other words, they believed (and, no doubt, some still do) that society bears little if any responsibility for a disabled person's struggles; it all rests squarely on the shoulders of that person. It was a matter of having the proper "strength of character," abetted usually by sympathetic family and friends. In short, PWDs were not regarded as an oppressed minority group but simply as hard-luck individuals who were forever bitter about their misfortune until some good-hearted able-bodied types "showed them the way."

Such perspectives changed dramatically during the 1980s and '90s with the development of Disability Studies as a discipline and its emphasis on the social construction of disability. We have finally moved away from (or, at least, have *begun* to move away from) the medical model of disability and its seemingly apolitical privileging of health-care professionals to the social model and the role of society and culture in the creation of disability. It was within this new paradigm that I framed the research that eventually led to *The Cinema of Isolation*.

One of the prime questions that prompted my professional interest in the newly conjoined fields of Disability Studies and Film Studies is simple: Where does mainstream, able-bodied society get its ideas from about disability? Not usually from PWDs themselves; social scientists have long known that TABs tend to avoid interacting with PWDs, in part because they are uncertain how to behave in their presence (Thompson 108; Yamamoto 180-189). Also, TABs don't like to be reminded of their own fragility and mortality, as Nancy Mairs has noted: "Most non-disabled people I know are so driven by their own fears of damage and death that they dread contact, let alone interaction, with anyone touched by affliction of any kind" (qtd. in Berubé B4).

Where do the attitudes come from, then, if not typically from direct social interaction with PWDs? Such social institutions as the family, schools, religious organizations, and the various levels of government certainly provide frameworks for imparting perspectives on disability, but I would argue that the ideas are derived to a large extent from movies and the other forms of popular culture that surround us. And that's a scary thought. From a postmodern perspective, it is not simply a matter of movies reflecting reality; for some people, movies *are* reality. Such people perceive the world in terms of the mass-produced, profit-minded imagery that bombards them daily. As film historian Steven Ross has noted, "movies play an important role in shaping the ways in which Americans think about their world—and, especially, aspects of life about which they have little first-hand knowledge" (1).

Armed with the basic assumption that many members of society have drawn on the "reality" of the movies for their ideas about disability, I began examining hundreds upon hundreds of films that represented (or, perhaps more accurately, misrepresented) the disabled experience. Two of my goals were to expose Hollywood's strategies for depicting PWDs and to make people more media-literate—to empower them, in effect—and thus be in a better position to read the images "against the grain" for themselves. Most Hollywood films do not encourage their audiences to think critically; instead they lull them into a seamless, dreamlike world or overwhelm them with the latest special effects technology. They are powerful and seductive—all the more reason to lay bare their techniques so that audiences can resist them when necessary.

For example, I found the issue of audience positioning within films to be a critical issue, for more often than not moviemakers have photographed and edited their works to reflect an able-bodied point of view. This strategy of encouraging audience members to perceive the world depicted in the movies from this perspective and thus associate themselves with able-bodied characters reduces disabled characters to objects of spectacle for the able-bodied majority, among other invidious effects.

In terms of the three spectatorial positions suggested by cultural theorist Stuart Hall—dominant-hegemonic, negotiated, oppositional[2]— I readily admit to having gravitated toward the last of the three while "reading" these texts; in other words, I recognized the "preferred" readings that the filmmakers were trying to convey about disability but often rejected them or, to quote Hall, evaluated them "within some alternative framework of reference" (138). Though I was interested in conducting what in social science circles might be called a trend analysis to see if any general patterns of portrayals emerged during the 100+ years of disability movie depictions, I also recontextualized the films as forms of political discourse designed to keep PWDs "in their place."

Here in very general terms is what I discovered. As I suggested in *The Cinema of Isolation*, the history of disability movie depictions can be divided into three periods: the late 1890s to the late 1930s, the World War II years into the 1970s, and the 1970s through today. Films from the first period tended to feature highly *exploitative* portrayals, with women and children coded primarily as "Sweet Innocents"—pure, godly, docile things eventually rewarded with a miracle cure—and men as "Obsessive Avengers": wronged Captain Ahab types who relentlessly seek revenge. (During the earliest years of the silent-film era, men were also frequently constructed as "Comic Misadventurers"—fellows who cause "funny" problems for themselves or others because of their disabilities.) Seldom rising above a comic-book level of complexity, these movie constructions dominated hundreds of films and defined the disability-movie scene during this time. Prominent films of the time that featured the Sweet Innocent include D. W. Griffith's *Orphans of the Storm* (1921), Charles Chaplin's *City Lights* (1931), and several versions of *A Christmas Carol*, while Tod Browning and Lon Chaney, separately and in collaboration, gave form to the Obsessive Avenger in many films, including *The Penalty* (1920), *The Hunchback of Notre Dame* (1923), *The Unknown* (1927), *West of Zanzibar* (1928), *Freaks* (1932), and *The Devil-Doll* (1936).

After about four decades' worth of such problematic imagery, moviemakers began offering more sensitive and enlightened portrayals. During the World War II era, images of disabled veterans and "Civilian

Superstars"—famous people "struck down" by disabling circumstances only to make an awe-inspiring comeback—began displacing the older stereotypes as the movies took on more of an *exploratory* quality. Disability, which during the first period had been used mainly to telegraph a character's inner qualities to the audience or simply propel the plot, was now treated as a major issue to explore and overcome. Such constructions were not without problems (the movies often presented the disabled characters as larger than life and placed the burden of "overcoming" solely on their shoulders while ignoring problems of prejudice and access), but they represented a major step forward. *Pride of the Marines* (1945), *The Best Years of Our Lives* (1946), *Til the End of Time* (1946), and *The Men* (1951) were conspicuous among the disabled-vet films, while such works as *The Stratton Story* (1949), *With a Song in My Heart* (1952), *Interrupted Melody* (1955), and *Sunrise at Campobello* (1960) promoted the Civilian Superstar. The latter image continued well into the 1970s with such films as *The Other Side of the Mountain* (1975), *The Other Side of the Mountain, Part 2* (1978), and *Ice Castles* (1979).

The third period, which began approximately during the 1970s, began featuring movies that treated disability in more of an *incidental* fashion. Rehabilitative struggles, which took center stage during the second period, began giving way to other concerns: pursuing a career, fighting for social justice, sexually expressing oneself, simply getting on with everyday life. In other words, filmmakers were now framing the characters as people who happened to be disabled and who have a wide range of concerns like anyone else. Though the period has been littered with rather flat character types, characterizations of a more three-dimensional nature began developing during this time. Films such as *Inside Moves* (1981), *The Waterdance* (1992), *Passion Fish* (1992), and particularly those that examined the lives of disabled Vietnam veterans, including *Coming Home* (1978), *Cutter's Way* (1981), and *Born on the Fourth of July* (1989), were among the best of the disability-related films of the time.

Though the general movement from exploitative to exploratory to incidental treatment might suggest a slowly developing enlightenment on disability issues, it is important to note that this general history has been marked by frequent slippage back to the older stereotypes. For example, such movies of the 1990s as *Hook* (1991), *Speed* (1994), and *Wild Wild West* (1999) feature variations on that hoariest and most hateful of images, the Obsessive Avenger. Indeed, the screen continues to be haunted by negative imagery of PWDs. As Arthur Campbell Jr., a disability-rights activist with severe cerebral palsy (and subject of Walter Brock's PBS documentary *If I Can't Do It*), commented in 1998: "Most filmmakers want to make us either some sympathetic, poor little character that no one could have mature and normal relations with, or some kind of a monster who has to be kept away and watched for the safety of society or themselves" (qtd. in Johnson AR23).

Campbell's observations lead us to several broader questions: Why have moviemakers insisted on constructing these images of disability and not more progressive ones? The mainstream movie industry has produced hundreds, perhaps even thousands, of films with disabled characters, yet the vast majority of them follow the historical pattern sketched above. What are the filmmakers' motivations for constructing PWDs the way(s) that they have?

First and foremost, it is important to note that movies are not simply reflections of mainstream attitudes. We live in a consumer culture, and we might well argue that disability, like many other imaged subjects, is a commodity. Hollywood filmmakers are trying to "sell" audiences certain images with the assumption that, if the audiences accept it (or, at least, don't protest it too loudly), they will keep buying tickets for more of the same.

From the filmmakers' perspective, then, we might say that disability is often an issue of commodification—a commodification that, as many social commentators (e.g., Bogdan, Fiedler, Thomson) have pointed out, has had a long and inglorious history well before the age of movies. George Henderson and Willie Bryan suggested that "throughout history, people without disabilities have had a paradoxical repulsion-attraction for those with disabilities" (3), and entrepreneurs have always been around to exploit that repulsion-attraction, most notoriously in the freak shows that helped define the cultural scene during the nineteenth and early twentieth centuries. In many respects, filmmakers—particularly ones before World War II—picked up where the freak show proprietors left off. As Leslie Fiedler has suggested, "human curiosities [have], for most Americans, passed inevitably from the platform and the pit to the screen, flesh becoming shadow" (16).

Disability imagery is not just a simple commodity subject to marketplace demands, however. It's also a *politically charged* product designed to send (and "sell") certain perspectives, and it might prove useful at this point to examine the general topic of political issues and their linkage with movies.

Generally speaking, a mainstream society will do whatever it can to maintain itself in power, and its strategy of keeping minorities such as PWDs dependent by defining the issues represents a significant part of its self-continuance. Specialists in the rehabilitation field, an area dominated by able-bodied people, have certainly exhibited this perspective, as Joseph Stubbins has argued: "[Rehabilitation] professionals define the problems, the agenda, and the social reality of disabled persons in ways that serve their own interests more closely than those of their clients" (23).

The movie industry, so interwoven with other institutions of the dominant culture, has likewise demonstrated this point of view. Its products constitute an important mode of discourse by which the culture perpetuates itself and its perspectives, and they operate on several levels in service to it. Not only do they frequently deal explicitly, if often misguidedly, with contemporaneous social concerns (such as the post-WWII films noted above that examined the lives of extraordinary people with disabilities), but, more significantly, they also contain submerged ideological perspectives, or what Gerald Mast and Bruce Kawin have called "the unspoken, assumed cultural values of films—values that seem so obviously true for that culture that they are accepted as inevitable, normal, and natural rather than as constructs of the culture itself" (5). These values, which typically go undetected and unquestioned by mainstream audiences, often assume the form of stereotyped images that, though sheer repetition, eventually take on a ring of truth in that society.

In attempting to understand the relationship of mainstream society and its disabled minority in life and in the movies, I have found the commentary of the philosopher Roland Barthes to be helpful. In his landmark book *Mythologies*, Barthes suggested that a mainstream society is profoundly uneasy with "Others" and usually tries to neutralize them in one of two ways: cure them or get rid of them. "Any otherness is reduced to sameness," he wrote, "because the Other is a scandal which threatens [mainstream] existence" (151). Though Barthes was not writing specifically about people with disabilities, his dichotomy has found frequent expression in disability-related movies. Disabled characters coded as "good" are often rewarded with a miracle cure and thus reabsorbed into the mainstream (and, intriguingly, are hardly ever affected by their experiences as PWDs). "Bad" disabled characters, on the other hand, are usually dead by the end of the film (via suicide, homicide, or a "convenient" accident) or have been removed from the narrative in some other way. To a certain extent, this second option parallels our society's treatment of PWDs in general; if society can't render them safe through a cure, it rejects them in ways ranging from simply ignoring them to institutionalizing them (and thus moving them out of the public sphere) to outright murdering them.

What purposes do PWDs serve before their disposal through either of the options established by Barthes? Kaoru Yamamoto has suggested that a mainstream society needs to demonize Others, or, in his words, ascribe "evil, intangible dangers" to people regarded as different, to help maintain its cohesion (186). As he observed, "deviance is not inherent in any particular pattern of behavior or physical attribute. Society determines whether some individuals should be regarded as different by selecting certain facets of their being and then attaching to these facets degrading labels and interpretations.... The singled-out individuals personify the kinds of experience that fall beyond the boundary of the accepted group norm. In this sense, they preserve stability in society by embodying otherwise formless dangers" (182). We might add that a mainstream society also has a need to create and then service a charitable underclass. In a study of disability references in Western civilization's major defining text, the Bible, Nancy Weinberg and Carol Sebian underscored "the biblical tradition of giving alms to the disabled but not accepting disabled persons as equals" (281). This centuries-old tradition, which enables mainstream members to "feel good" about themselves, has the insidious effect of allowing them to maintain a sense of superiority and control over PWDs.

There is little question that Hollywood filmmakers have taken their cue from the dominant culture and frequently used fear and pity (and, to a lesser extent, awe and humor) to separate people with disabilities from the rest of society. In so doing, they of course help perpetuate the culture. This situation seems an endless loop, but it need not remain so if certain changes continue to occur. As Nancy Weinberg has suggested, continued intermingling of disabled and able-bodied people has the general effect of minimizing differences as perceived by the latter group: "As contact between able bodied and disabled is intensified, the stereotype of the disabled as different diminishes.... There is a positive relationship between contact and perceived similarity: as contact increases, perceived similarity increases" (123). Though Weinberg was commenting on members of society in general, her observations suggest what undoubtedly will be the key to the improvement of movie depictions of people with disabilities: disabled people working with able-bodied peers within and outside of Hollywood.

Collaborations within the industry, which began during the silent film era with such films as *Deliverance* (1919) and *The Big Parade* (1925),[3] are admittedly few and far between but continue to have impact. Ron Kovic, the disabled Vietnam veteran who wrote the screenplay for *Born on the Fourth of July* with Oliver Stone, proclaimed himself "extremely proud" of the movie based on his like-titled autobiography. "I was able to see my story come out the way I wanted to see it and the way I felt it should come out," he said, adding that his able-bodied colleagues on the film "treated me with a great deal of respect" (qtd. in Seidenberg 56). Another PWD who has enjoyed success in Hollywood is Neal Jimenez, who wrote and co-directed a film based partially on his own experiences called *The Waterdance*. An insightful look at the range of issues facing newly disabled males, *The Waterdance* won critical praise—Vincent Canby of the New York Times gave it a very favorable review, for example, noting that "though small in scale, it is big in feelings expressed with genuine passion and a lot of gutsy humor" (C13)—as well as several awards at the Sundance Film Festival that year.

Activists outside the movie industry have also worked to improve the image of PWDs. Disability-related associations ranging from local to international have been concerned about raising public awareness of the imagery and calling for improvements. For example, participants at the 1997 International Leadership Forum for Women with Disabilities held in Bethesda, MD, issued a statement demanding a greater use of disabled people in mass media productions and that "these portrayals must be positive, sensitive and life enhancing" ("International Leadership" np).

Other activists have gone a step further by directly attempting to influence the production and exhibition of Hollywood films. For instance, Deaf activists tried to convince the producers of *Calendar Girl* (1993), a comedy set in the 1950s about three Nevada boys who journey to Hollywood to meet Marilyn Monroe, to reconsider their decision to hire a hearing actor to play a minor character who is deaf. Though the activists lost that round, they refused to give up the battle and staged a series of protests during the film's premiere (Levitan 21-26).

In similar fashion, Paul Spudich, a man with kyphoscoliosis, organized a letter-writing campaign in 1995 to protest the Walt Disney company's plans to produce an animated version of *The Hunchback of Notre Dame* ("Disney Says No" 4). In addition, the 3,000 delegates who attended the 1997 convention of the National Federation of the Blind unanimously passed a resolution asking Disney to abandon production of *Mr. Magoo*, a film about a hapless, nearsighted man (Bannon A1). Though the Disney juggernaut rolled on in both instances (*Hunchback* debuted in 1996, *Magoo* in 1997), the protests helped raised people's awareness of disability issues and may well have contributed to the relatively poor performances of the two films at the box office.

The creation of films and videos that pose alternative perspectives to those promoted by Hollywood represents yet another strategy. Billy Golfus, who sustained brain damage as a result of a traffic accident during the 1980s, wrote and directed an independently produced film titled *When Billy Broke His Head . . . and Other Tales of Wonder* (1994) that details his experiences as a disabled person in American society. It also explores the lives of many other PWDs and, in the process, reveals a world far different from that constructed in most Hollywood films. Golfus announced at the "Screening Disability" conference that he plans to enter the narrative filmmaking field; if he follows through with his intentions, a powerful voice for PWDs will have been added to the moviemaking establishment.

Those interested in helping improve the movie image of disabled people might use the above examples as guides for developing their own courses of action. Here are several suggestions:

1. Join national or local associations in their campaigns against unfair movie portrayals.

2. Use the internet to find associations, activist groups, and like-minded people interested in discussing disability topics. Two internet mailing lists devoted to disability issues are well worth signing on to:

Disability Research
<disability-research@mailbase.ac.uk>
Disability Studies in the Humanities
<dshum@listserv.georgetown.edu>[4]

Disability concerns are also addressed occasionally on two mailing lists dedicated to the scholarly study of film:

H-Film
<h-film@h-net.msu.edu>
Screen-L
<screen-l@bama.ua.edu>

3. If you have reason to believe that a movie with questionable disability perspectives is about to go into production (or already has), use the *Hollywood Creative Directory* or similar sources to find the name and address of the company in charge and make your views known. Directors and screenwriters can also be reached through their respective unions: the Directors Guild of America <www.dga.org> and the Writers Guild of America <www.wga.org>.

4. Produce your own movie or video that features people with disabilities. Interview several film/video production companies to find a creative team that will work with your conception and within your budget. You might premiere the film at a nearby college or on local access cable TV.

It has been an uphill struggle to make people aware of, and improve, the movie image of people with disabilities. With the continuing domination of Hollywood and the decline in independent filmmaking at home and national cinemas abroad, the challenges are greater than ever before. Through the combined efforts of activists within and outside Hollywood, however, the refinement of that image cannot help but occur. Activists and scholars (most certainly not mutually exclusive categories) in the intertwined fields of Disability Studies and Film Studies need to keep making progress in this area. Only by all of us working together—PWDs as well as their TAB allies—will we start to see some real progress.

Notes

[1] The *Chronicle of Higher Education* invited scholars to respond online to the following questions related to Cassuto's essay: "Should the validity of research on disability and the disabled depend on whether the researcher is disabled?" and "Should scholars in disability studies reveal their 'disability status'?" The responses may be found at the following web address: <www.chronicle.com/colloquy/99/disability/re.htm>.

[2] According to Hall, dominant-hegemonic is the position in which viewers essentially go along with the filmmakers' messages and thereby give the film a "preferred" reading—preferred, that is, from the filmmakers' perspective. Negotiated refers to the position in which the viewers accept some, but not all, of the filmmakers' messages. In other words, they negotiate their way through the movie by accepting some messages while rejecting others. In the

oppositional position, viewers may recognize the "preferred" messages implicit in the film's formal properties but nevertheless reject and/or recontextualize them (136-138). Extending Hall's views, we might argue that a continuum of reading positions exists, with dominant-hegemonic and oppositional serving as the extremes and negotiated as the midway point.

[3] *Deliverance*, which reconstructed the first four decades of Helen Keller's life, featured Keller playing herself in its final act, while *The Big Parade*, a bittersweet tale of a young man who returns from World War I disabled and disillusioned, was developed by Laurence Stallings, himself a disabled WWI veteran.

[4] Links to these mailing lists and many other websites and e-zines devoted to disability research and activism may be found at the following website: <www-unix.oit.umass.edu/~norden/dra.html>.

Works Cited

Bannon, Lisa. "The Vision Thing." *Wall Street Journal* 31 July 1997: A1.
Barthes, Roland. *Mythologies*. Trans. Annette Lavers. New York: Hill and Wang, 1972.
Berubé, Michael. "The Cultural Representation of People with Disabilities Affects Us All." *Chronicle of Higher Education* 30 May 1997: B4-B5.
Bogdan, Robert. *Freak Show: Presenting Human Oddities for Amusement and Profit*. Chicago: U Chicago P, 1988.
Canby, Vincent. "Heroism and Humor as Paraplegics Learn." *New York Times* 13 May 1992: C13.
Cassuto, Leonard. "Whose Field Is It, Anyway?: Disability Studies in the Academy." *Chronicle of Higher Education* 19 March 1999: A60.
"Disney Says No to Disability Consultants." *One Step Ahead* 2.1 (16 January 1995): 4.
Fiedler, Leslie A. *Freaks: Myths and Images of the Secret Self*. New York: Simon and Schuster, 1978.
Hall, Stuart. "Encoding/Decoding." *Culture, Media, Language*. Ed. Stuart Hall, Dorothy Hobson, Andrew Lowe, and Paul Willis. London: Hutchinson, 1980. 128-138.
Henderson, George, and Willie V. Bryan. *Psychosocial Aspects of Disability*. Springfield: Thomas, 1984.
International Leadership Forum for Women with Disabilities. "Final Statement." Unpublished manuscript. June 1997.
Johnson, Mary. "Just One Man's Story, but It Speaks for Many." *New York Times* 5 July 1998: AR23.
Levitan, Linda. "Faking It!" *Deaf Life* August 1992: 21-26.
Mast, Gerald, and Bruce F. Kawin. *A Short History of the Movies*. 5th ed. New York: Macmillan, 1992.
Norden, Martin F. *The Cinema of Isolation: A History of Physical Disability in the Movies*. New Brunswick: Rutgers UP, 1994.

Ross, Steven J. <sjross@almaak.usc.edu>. "Re: On the Waterfront." In H-Film <H-Film@h-net.msu.edu>. 25 March 1999. Archived at: <http://www2.h-net.msu.edu/~film>.

Seidenberg, Robert. "To Hell and Back." *American Film* January 1990: 28-31, 56.

Stubbins, Joseph. "The Politics of Disability." *Attitudes Toward Persons with Disabilities*. Ed. Harold Yuker. New York: Springer, 1988. 22-32.

Thompson, Teresa L. "'You Can't Play Marbles—You Have a Wooden Hand': Communication With the Handicapped." *Communication Quarterly* 30.2 (Spring 1982): 108-115.

Thomson, Rosemarie Garland. *Freakery: Cultural Spectacles of the Extraordinary Body*. New York: New York UP, 1996.

Weinberg, Nancy. "Modifying Social Stereotypes of the Physically Disabled." *Rehabilitation Counseling Bulletin* 22.2 (December 1978): 114-123.

Weinberg, Nancy, and Carol Sebian. "The Bible and Disability." *Rehabilitation Counseling Bulletin* 23.4 (June 1980): 273-281.

Yamamoto, Kaoru. "To Be Different." *Rehabilitation Counseling Bulletin* 14.3 (March 1971): 180-189.

The Fusion of Film Studies and Disability Studies

Thomas B. Hoeksema and Christopher R. Smit

We were intrigued by what the students in our course on the representations of disability in cinema were saying about the current study of disability and film. As a class, they had been reading assorted critics and academics that deal with film's treatment of disabled people: Paul Longmore, Martin F. Norden, David Mitchell and Sharon Snyder, and others who have helped develop this topic. The students noted that something was missing in the works they were reading, that something wasn't right.

Along with the texts and articles that addressed the topic of disability and film, the class also read *Anatomy of Film* by Bernard F. Dick (1997), a classical treatment of film style and technique. Before being told the reasons for reading Dick's book, many students realized its purpose. They observed that the current study of disability and cinema has its historical, cultural, and its critical components. But one student summed up the class' feelings on what was missing in one wonderful phrase, "You can't study film and disability . . . without *film*."

Our concern with the study of film and disability has been growing for some time. The fact of the matter is simple; over the past decade there has been a surge of interesting writing, research, and scholarship surrounding the topic of disability and media, yet the main emphasis in many of these analyses has been the political and social effects of disability portrayals. The questions being asked, and theories being written, reflect a posture of disability activism. While this has helped Disability Studies gain status similar to that of Women's and African-American Studies in the humanities, it has not encouraged a stylistic, analytical or structural study of these films as cinematic expressions.

The literature on film and disability is dominated by those who write from what is being called a Disability Studies perspective. This somewhat amorphous field consists of scholars from a variety of disciplines who are challenging established ways of studying disability in the cognitive, biological and social sciences. Following the model of literary criticism, Disability Studies scholars deconstruct portrayals of disability in places as disparate as novels, public policy, and popular media, in order to expose underlying attitudes and antagonisms. Many of its spokespersons appear to embrace Disability Studies as a form of civil rights activism.

Authors such as Longmore, Norden, and Mitchell and Snyder assume a disability activist posture in their critique of popular culture and its depictions and assumptions about disability. Norden, in his book *The Cinema of Isolation: A History of Physical Disability in the Movies,* for example, asserts that Hollywood is to blame for negative images of disability in film:

> The strategy of isolating disabled people reflects a political agenda of sizable proportions. Mainstream society has long followed a divide-and-quarantine approach to controlling minorities, and . . . movies have always played a conspicuous role in this agenda . . . . The movie industry has perpetuated or initiated a number of stereotypes over the years as part of a general practice of isolation, stereotypes so durable and pervasive that they have become mainstream society's perception of disabled people, and have obscured if not outright supplanted disabled people's perception of themselves. (2-3)

Mitchell and Snyder are also critical of Hollywood. Speaking about their own film, and other documentaries like Billy Golfus' award-winning film *When Billy Broke His Head . . . and Other Tales of Wonder* (1994), Mitchell and Snyder point to their "refusal to capitulate to the trite and sentimental productions of Hollywood films and mass produced TV" (328).

While these claims have some merit and certainly hold an inherent appeal to all of us who resist the many types of injustices that have been perpetuated against people with disabilities, they do not tell the whole story. In our classes, we assert that cinematic depictions of people who live with disability have been enormously diverse. Sometimes they contain negative and erroneous images; at other times their portrayals of disability are accurate and positive. Sometimes they respond to or reflect societal attitudes and beliefs; at other times they influence society's perceptions. We believe that it is inaccurate and insufficient to characterize cinematic depictions of disability as primarily negative and stereotypic. We also think that taking an activist, advocacy perspective when critiquing disability cinema risks missing insights that may be obtained by reviewing films using additional tools from the field of Film Studies. Nonetheless, a major goal for our course is to dissect cinematic depictions of disability in order to understand the cultural beliefs that may have shaped the depictions or been perpetuated by them, for good or for ill. We believe that an understanding of film as art, and the fusion of Film Studies and Disability Studies perspectives, enables a comprehensive analysis of disability cinema that is not possible from only one or the other perspective.

Without the aesthetic contributions of film studies, the study of disability and film ignores an entire corpus of critical understanding. Students of disability films, when denied the appropriate film language, cannot communicate or articulate their ideas coherently. For example, without an understanding of high and low angle shots, panning, close-ups, tracking, the use of sound in film, etc., images in films are interpreted in a bland and one-dimensional fashion, thus causing the image to lose that which defines it as an artistic expression.

When students describe their fondest experiences of films, they respond with descriptions of scenes: the biting conclusion to *The Graduate* (1967), the "I love America" sequence from Coppola's *The Godfather* (1972), the boat ride in *One Flew Over the Cuckoo's Nest* (1975), and so on. While they experienced these films as an audio/visual experience, it is the tangible images that remain lodged in their memories. It is the palpable image that has made them feel things they hadn't before.

Much more than its storyline, character development, and themes, it is the images in Lynch's *The Elephant Man* (1980) that affect the viewer. Since this is the case, we can interpret the film more richly by analyzing the ways in which Lynch's camera presents disability. Going further, why not try to find similar camera work in other films that portray disability? At the end of such a search, we may know much more about disability cinema than if we had looked simply at whether people with disabilities had been portrayed positively or negatively, or at whether persons with disabilities had been treated appropriately in 19th century England.

What do we lose when we fail to use the tools of film theory and criticism? We lose a means for understanding a particular effect that has been produced. We lose a means for understanding a particular purpose a filmmaker is trying to accomplish. We neglect a rich tapestry of communication studies, which includes a history of technique and tradition that points us to how and why images affect us. We forget the power of images, and the cultural influence that film has always held. We neglect the meanings that a film may be communicating, and instead assign only our own agendas to our interpretations. We forget that behind the images of these films are the decisions of the directors. If we lose sight of the intentions of the creators of these films, we lose vital insight.

It is easy to fall into the trap of blaming Hollywood, as if it was its own entity, for the social ramifications of disability portrayals in cinema. Challenging such a top-down ideology, we encourage our students to consider the fact that all filmmakers make films for specific reasons. Tod Browning made the film *Freaks* (1932) to comment on a particular aspect of Weimar Germany. He may or may not have set out to mock disabled circus performers, or to show that all disabled people want to destroy their able-bodied peers. If you come to that conclusion after considering what the film provides cinematically, fine. However, if you skip a cinematic analysis of the film, which includes attempting to identify the aims of the director, then you are missing the boat.

By using a cinematic lens in the study of disability depictions in film, we add a new way in which to understand these films' vernacular. Much of the criticism available on disability films suffers from an incomplete practice of film criticism. Rather than focusing single-mindedly on the social ramifications of images, students of the portrayal of disability in cinema must begin to view the images of these films in a different way. What follows are brief examples of how Film Studies and Disability Studies can be fused in order to do the work of critiquing portrayals of disability in film.

Film and Disability: An Integrated Model

When we first began to think about teaching a course on the portrayals of people with disabilities in film, we postulated some important questions about disability cinema in general, like: what can be learned about disabilities in Hollywood films, if anything? how do people learn about disability, and what part might popular culture play in that process? and most importantly, how might film's portrayal of disability help teach the important lessons of acceptance, awareness, and understanding of not only disability, but of the inherent weakness and need that we all share as human beings? We also began asking questions about film consumption in general: how do we get students to engage films as more than entertainment? how can postsecondary students be taught the rudiments of film theory and criticism? and, can films about disability be used to teach people how to be better consumers of film?

In sum, we were motivated to construct our course in part because we were dissatisfied with the perspective of some critics of disability cinema who, in our view, were failing to look at film holistically. In addition, we were bothered by a sense that most film viewers today do not think critically or analytically about what they have seen. Hollywood depends on passive audience members. Early scholarship in film and disability, ironically, also depended on a somewhat passive viewer. The notion that derogatory representations of disability in film negatively affect societal beliefs relies on the presence of a non-thinking film consumer. Our model of studying filmic portrayals of disability demands a rupture in the idea of passive spectatorship, and demands a reconsideration of the ways in which film is culturally consumed.

A concept of active film viewing has been articulated by Christian Metz as a twofold participation in which the viewer "watches and helps" the film in question; the screen seduces the viewer and demands her attention, while at the same time she is, consciously or unconsciously, translating the visual narrative into a meaningful discourse (90-92). Taken further, we have asked students, when discussing their roles as film viewers, to make certain considerations. First, we ask that they consider the "baggage" which they bring to every screening. Viewers are often affected by particular images or narrative themes because of the way these elements relate to their unique life experiences. Using those experiences as a tool of inquiry, rather than discarding them as emotional barriers, adds vitality to the criticism they perform. Second, this consideration must be followed by a desire to validate film as a significant contributor to the process of creating cultural meaning. This validation includes having an appreciation of film as art, seeing the cinematic experience as a meaningful cultural discourse wherein both the screen and viewer take an active role in creating meaning, and recognizing film as a cultural force—it affects the way we think about our world (i.e., disability). Thus, we ask the student to consider the cultural significance of film as a medium, a concept understood through a consideration of "realism."

As John Ellis has suggested, "The question of realism is indeed a complex one, but it is complex because the word itself is being used to describe a whole series of principles of artistic construction and of audience expectations alike" (6). Such expectations are based on a film's surface accuracy, conformity to audience speculations of psychology and narrative structure, and character motivation. Questioning the realism of a film has definite connections to the interrogation of representations often done when critiquing disability films. However, the manner in which the critic conceptualizes the question of realism depends on the critical frame wherein her analysis is situated. We have asserted that the dominant analysis of disability representations is based in the rhetoric of advocacy, hence questions of realism tend to attack the validity of the disabled experience being forwarded by a particular film. Yet, as Ellis points out, the effects of a film "have more to do with the creation and sustaining of meanings (in the realm of ideology) than they do with any direct action upon individuals" (14).

This concern about realism relates to the issue of how much cultural influence cinema has, when one considers the social distinctions society offers itself to understand the relationship between the "typical" and the Other. Such definitions of difference, "appear as common sense, as the taken-for-granted, a kind of natural horizon of life, beyond which anything is unthinkable" (14). Films not only present these stereotyped depictions of reality, but they also challenge them. An understanding of this relationship between film and cultural activity demands critics to expand their inquiry beyond, for example, a disabled community, and instead focus on the broader cultural manifestations and conditions of cinematic expression.

When one considers Ellis' remarks, questions of realism become less poignant in the critique of portrayals of disability in cinema. Furthermore, inaccurate portrayals of disability can raise useful questions if they are dissected in the classroom. What a film says is not as important as what a film makes the viewer think about. To dismiss some films because of alleged inaccuracies denies the possibilities of varied receptions. When freed of the question of authenticity, the analysis of disability cinema is able to focus on the cinematic expressions, narrative motifs, and image construction. Disability knowledge and attention remains a part of the unpacking of a film, yet is present independently from the visual construction of the movie being studied. This process is illustrated below using the films *Mask* (1985), *My Left Foot* (1989), and *The Elephant Man*.

Most critics writing from the Disability Studies perspective castigate depictions of disability that use sentimentality and melodrama, claiming that such portrayals foster and uphold the pity approach to society's disabled members. On the contrary, we would argue that beyond this one-sided perspective lie forgotten cinematic and cultural lessons. Peter Bogdonavich's film *Mask* depicts the life of Rocky Dennis, a teenager who lived with craniodiaphyseal dyaplasia, a congenital condition which caused the progressive disfigurement of the skeletal structure of his face. A somewhat sachrine film, which climaxes with Rocky's death, *Mask* could be dismissed as a sentimental treatment of a boy's triumphant, yet tragic, struggle with physical disability. Criticism from the Disability Studies perspective would chastise the film's use of sentimentality to foster pity, the director's playing God by increasing the physical effects of Rocky's disease when the narrative needed drama, and the film's portrayal of disability as weakness. Criticism from an integrated perspective of both Film and Disability Studies, however, would argue that the sentimentality in the film is an element of *all* melodramas. Sentimentality in melodrama fosters a real feeling of loss to the viewer, disability-related or not; if we understand the film as a genre (i.e., melodrama), sentimentality has an expected role to play. Furthermore, it could be argued that the film attempts to portray a lived reality. Rocky Dennis did die at a very early age, and in a film that depicts his life, such an ending should not be identified as a negative attribute of the film. The underlying power of film is its ability to move an audience's emotions surrounding the issues of human experience. That notion must be respected and understood as a dynamic cinematic technique. To deny any emotional reaction to portrayals of disability, as do negative reviews of sentimentality, is to deny the power of film, which is to deny the medium being studied in the first place.[1]

The above critique of *Mask* adheres to the perspective of Film Studies, specifically with regards to genre convention. Our integrated model of film and disability scholarship also calls for an attempt to increase the viewers' disability knowledge via other sources besides cinematic expression. By pulling from other resources like secondary texts, teaching guides, and interviews with persons who live with disabilities, we attempt to provide students with real-life exemplars of the disabled experience. Thus, an integrated methodology of studying film and disability relies upon the combination/juxtaposition of cinematic consideration and disability consideration, which is crucial to assuring a well balanced analysis of these films.

The film *Elephant Man* can also be used to illustrate the fusion of Disability Studies and Film Studies perspectives. Thematically, this film offers fertile ground for an exploration of several themes important to disability activists and advocates. The film sheds light on the historical treatment of people who live with disability in western society and provides a revealing look at the freak show phenomenon. The viewer is made aware of many ways in which people with disabilities are abused, even by those who think themselves benevolent. The isolation, staring, and hatred that is so often part of the experience of living with disability are brutally, yet empathically, revealed in this film.

Melding a Film Studies perspective to the above analysis adds layers to the viewer's understanding of the film. The director's choice to film in black and white adds a visual sense of history and provides a textured feel to the figures and scenes captured by the camera. Perhaps more importantly, Lynch's use of a stationary camera and close-ups provides a gratuitous gaze; the viewer is unannounced spectator, as much a ticketholder to the freak show as those in attendance on the screen. Fusing Disability and Film Studies perspectives enables a more comprehensive and complementary analysis.

The widely appreciated *My Left Foot* provides a third example. Disability Studies scholars find much to examine in this film. From the use of a non-disabled actor to portray a man with cerebral palsy, to the glorious rage of disabled protagonist Christy Brown, this film stimulates discussion of numerous issues pertinent to improving societal perceptions of disability. When a cinematic perspective is added, however, additional meanings emerge. The slow pan of the camera as the film opens follows the action and, unlike Lynch's camera, welcomes and invites our participation. We become a member of Christy Brown's family, an identification that enables us to understand better the bonds within families that live with disability. At times, the camera enables the viewer to see from the perspective of one who has a disability. In a memorable scene of a neighborhood street soccer game, the camera shows us what happens from Christy's eye level. As he prepares to kick a penalty shot, the camera pans up from the ball, to Christy's twisted legs, to the brothers holding him up. This cinematic expression of Christy's dependence is juxtaposed with the next event: Christy successfully executes the penalty kick with his very able left foot, revealing the team's dependence on his skill. Through efficient cinematic, rather than verbal, narrative, the viewer is convincingly exposed to the reality of interdependence that exists between all people, disabled or not. Cinematically, we understand that people who have disabilities can participate meaningfully in life. Thus, a film analysis of *My Left Foot* complements a Disability Studies critique.

Conclusion

To conclude, we return to the theoretical considerations of our work, especially in regards to what is possibly at risk of being lost when these films are not considered through the medium they represent. Looking at the study of film and disability as a discipline becomes very important to consider.

Questioning the methodology of disability and cinema criticism is fundamental to establishing it as an academic discipline. If, as it develops, the study of disability and film continues primarily to promote the precepts of political activism, as it has in recent years, it will remain merely an adjunct to Disability Studies. While this may be acceptable to academics in that field, the overall scholarly impact will result in a diminished understanding of these films. Without a multifaceted interpretation, disability films will eventually be seen simply as political commentary, never receiving their proper critique.

So what would be the harm of the study of portrayals of disability in cinema remaining solely a branch of Disability Studies? First, by remaining inextricably attached to the study of disability, the analysis of disability cinema would remain centered around the question of political agency. While such analyses have been instrumental in the development of film and disability scholarship, they have also directed critical attention away from the cinematic aspect of disability depictions. Second, by remaining attached to Disability Studies, the questions being asked of these films will remain centered on disability topics. It is mistakenly forgotten that along with being disability narratives, many portrayals of disability deal with larger societal themes, like cultural interdependence. This element, among others, are overlooked within the framework of minority advocacy. Studying films exclusively from a disabled perspective denies an able-bodied critique of these films. For much of society, disability is something which they only encounter from a distance. If disability is not present in one's family situation, it is possible that one's only extended exposure to disabled individuals occurs through film and television. Knowing this, the able-bodied perceptions of such exposure is vital to understanding the cultural power of these films.

What we are essentially curious about is the nature of film not only as cultural product, but also as art. As does any form of art, film places much responsibility on the viewer. Ask an artist what her painting is about, and she will most likely say, what do you see? In some ways, we must approach disability films the same way. Our intention is to disentangle the study of disability representations from a predominantly political system of analysis, and offer a new balcony from which to view these films. We must move beyond the myopic agenda of an activist critique, and begin to understand that portrayals of disability in film are more than simply one dimensional stereotypes.

Students of disability and film need to be concerned with portrayals of disability, not solely because of their inadequacies, but because they are emotional, relational, and artistic offerings as well. Perhaps what a film says isn't as important as what it makes you think about. For example, in our teaching, often times the so-called negative portrayal offers an avenue of meaningful interactions revolving around the nature of real life disability. We are challenged by the needs and desires of any disabled protagonist. Dismissing films because of alleged inaccuracies denies their teaching and learning value.

The study of disability and film is at a crucial moment. The field of Disability Studies has provided a platform within liberal arts education for the study of the disabled cultural experience, yet if its methods regarding the study of disability films continue there will be no opportunity for alternative approaches that will offer more complete analyses of portrayals of disability in film. Our intention is not to negate the efforts, findings, or accomplishments of contemporary Disability Studies. Rather, we seek dialogue between Film Studies and Disability Studies wherein questions of inquiry and methodology can be debated. The fusion of these two fields remains to be organized, understood, and respected. Until that day, representations of disability in film will remain where they are, on the screen. Lacking the proper tools, Disability Studies alone cannot bring them down.

Notes

[1] This is a radical departure from the tools being used by Disability Studies. Equipped with the tools of identity politics and terms of objectification, such criticism often ignores or chastises the emotional responses to these films. For example, Martin F. Norden concludes that sentimentality only belittles the disabled character's plight and manipulates the viewer's reaction into one of pity rather than respect (118-119).

Works Cited

Dick, Bernard F. *The Anatomy of Film.* 3rd ed. New York: St. Martin's Press, 1998.
Ellis, John. *Visible Fictions: Cinema, Television, Video.* London, Boston, Melbourne, Henley: Routledge and Kegan Paul Publishing, 1982.
Longmore, Paul K. "Screening Stereotypes: Images of Disabled People." *Social Policy* 16.1 (Summer 1985): 31-37.
Metz, Christian. *Psychoanalysis and the Cinema: The Imaginary Signifier.* London: Macmillan Publishing, 1982.
Mitchell, David T., and Sharon L. Snyder, eds. "Talking about Talking Back: Afterthoughts on the Making of the Disability Documentary *Vital Signs: Crip Culture Talks Back.*" *Michigan Quarterly Review* 37.2 (Spring 1998): 316-336.
Norden, Martin F. *The Cinema of Isolation: A History of Physical Disability in the Movies.* New Brunswick: Rutgers UP, 1994.

Disability as Monstrosity in Classical Hollywood Cinema: Tod Browning and *The Hunchback of Notre Dame*

None of Us: Ambiguity as Moral Discourse in Tod Browning's *Freaks*

Méira Cook

In her introduction to an anthology of essays published in 1996 entitled *Freakery*, Rosemary Garland Thomson characterizes the genealogy of the freak discourse as the movement from a narrative of the marvelous to a narrative of the deviant (3). The monstrous body, once celebrated upon the freak show stage as a cue to entertainment and the somewhat voyeuristic emotions of horror, wonder, and awe, is deployed within the cultural narrative of modernity as a pathological body whose proper place is the medical theatre and the proper response to which is shame or pity. At the same time, the movement from the "monstrous" or "freakish" body to what we would today call the "abnormal" or "anomalous" body carries with it a semantic cargo that hovers on what Arnold Davidson calls an "especially vicious normative violation" (51). At once transgressive and flamboyant, the exceptional body, what Garland Thomson calls "the extravagantly marked, pliant figure of the freak" (12), is always an interpretive occasion, a means of sustaining narrative, of encouraging readability, of inciting revelation.

It is within this context that I intend to read Tod Browning's movie, *Freaks*, as a narrative that positions itself ambiguously at the bifurcation of the exceptional body viewed alternately as monstrous pathology and unfortunate error. First produced in 1932, Browning's movie was almost immediately removed from distribution by Metro-Goldwyn-Mayer shortly after its release, and banned outright in Britain. Leslie Fiedler reports that the film was eventually re-released under the apologetic title "Nature's Mistakes" together with an explanatory foreword of some two or three minutes (296). This written blurb is couched in the inflammatory language of the side show, promising the audience a "HIGHLY UNUSUAL ATTRACTION" comprising "amazing subject matter." Conditioned, by such staples of the ringmaster's spiel as "BELIEVE IT OR NOT" and "STRANGE AS IT SEEMS," the blurb suddenly modifies its sensationalist rhetoric to offer instead, "tales of misshapen misfits," "unfortunates," "the abnormal, the malformed and the mutilated." "Never again will such a story be filmed," the foreword promises us, "as modern science and teratology is rapidly eliminating such blunders of nature from the world." This last sentence acts both as a device of reassurance and as a far from subtle incitement to catch this last spectacle before it too vanishes from a dismayingly normalized world.

Browning's movie which, despite its history of censorship and bannings, now enjoys a substantial cult following, occupies an ambiguous position in the horror movie genre and in the popular consciousness, and Browning himself is no less an ambiguous figure. Vilified by the critics and the public alike—even some of the actors he used in *Freaks* were later reported to have publicly regretted their appearance in a medium that they now perceived as exploitative—Browning retired from filmmaking in 1939 and spent the last 20 years of his life in obscurity. At the same time he is widely credited as the father of freak studies in this century. Brian Rosenberg notes that artists such as Diane Arbus and cultural theorists such as Leslie Fiedler and Robert Bogdan acknowledge Browning as their precursor and his movie, *Freaks*, as the work that most influenced their own thinking in the genre (307).

If both Tod Browning and the movie that is now viewed as his masterpiece occupy an ambiguous position in the history of film, no less can be said for the subject matter of *Freaks* itself. The story of Hans the circus midget's impossible love for the trapeze artist, Cleopatra, her betrayal of him and her punishment at the hands of the circus freaks who band together to visit their inexorable and much vaunted "code of ethics" upon her once beautiful body, is populated with what the Rialto Theatre's 1932 film advertisement lists as "a horde of caricatures of creation—not actors in make-up—but living, breathing creatures as they are and as they were born!"

The use of real circus show "freaks" playing themselves in a movie that proclaims itself sympathetic to the plight of "the abnormal and the unwanted," troubles the borders of reality and illusion, art and artifice, not to mention the always perplexing line between aesthetics and ethics. Elizabeth Grosz views the freak—and, like her, I use this term "freak" instead of more politically correct appellations to encode the act of defiance or gesture of self-determination implicit in its contemporary usage—as an ambiguous being whose very existence imperils normative categories. Freaks, in Browning's movie, throw into confusion the border between discrete human subjects (as in the spectacle of Violet and Daisy Hilton, the conjoined twins), between one sex and another (as in the bearded lady and Joseph/Josephine), between adults and children (as in Hans and Frieda the midgets as well as the childlike trio of pin-heads), between humans and gods (the example here is of Hercules, the strong man, and to a certain extent, Cleopatra of the flying trapeze), between the living and the dead (as in the human skeleton and Prince Randian the human torso), between the "properly" disposed body and its fragmentation in space (Johnny Eck the legless man and Francis the armless woman), and finally, between the human and the animal (a movement that takes into account Cleopatra's shocking transformation from splendid "peacock of the air," as she is initially described, to squawking chicken-woman). The body of the freak in Browning's movie, insofar as it articulates a spectacle of visible difference, draws us as viewers into a space that marks the conceptual excesses of human subjectivity and the degree to which we, as spectators, can tolerate the anomalies that result from this vision of an intolerable because unknowable humanity.

The first half of Browning's movie is devoted to demonstrating the normality of the circus people rather than in exhibiting their freakish characteristics: Madame Tetralini's company of pinheads lead by Schlitze and Elvira play happily in a pastoral meadow, for, as Tetralini explains to the gentleman farmer: "When I get the chance I like to take them into the sunshine and let them play like—children. That is what most of them are—children." The bearded lady gives birth to a baby fathered by the human skeleton. Frieda the midget hangs laundry on the line while chatting to Venus, the apparently "normal" seal trainer. And Violet and Daisy, who are conjoined twins, conduct their separate courtships and engagements with two different suitors. In refusing to represent difference as deviance, Browning demonstrates his resistance to a process of what critic David Hevey has called "enfreakment," the manner in which the extraordinary body is successively silenced, stylized, and commercialized through exhibition (10). At the same time, we as viewers are implicated in the process since the experience of viewing the movie recreates the experience of being a spectator at a so-called carnival freak show with its attendant emotions of ambivalence, since in both cases there is no safe distance from the subjects under scrutiny or from our own disquieting responses.

While Browning's film begins by insisting on the normality and domesticity of the lives of the circus freaks, it rapidly proceeds to break down this earlier perspective by portraying the circus folk—in at least two scenes—as a rabid, undifferentiated mob motivated by infantile aggression and blood lust. The marriage feast between Hans the Midget and Cleopatra the "most beautiful big woman" as he calls her, is almost entirely populated by freaks who cavort, dance, sing, swallow swords, and eat fire for the entertainment of the nuptial couple. At one point a dwarf fills a loving cup and dances round the table offering the assembled guests sips from the communal chalice. As he dances toward the horrified Cleopatra, the guests begin to chant a refrain: "We accept her, one of us . . . one of us, one of us . . . gobble gooble, one of us." The apparently nonsensical phrase "gobble gooble" with its implication of oral pleasures and gabbled speech has the effect of demonizing the freaks who are further vilified by their mass chant which implies that they exist as an undifferentiated, amorphous mass of fragmented bodies and spare parts who nevertheless speak with one voice. The other mob scene, of course, is the nocturnal chase where the freaks slither through mud and slime with knives in their teeth in an effort to capture and mutilate Cleopatra and murder her lover Hercules, the strong man.

Although purporting to treat the enfreaked Other with humanity and empathy, Browning's film, particularly in the last half, traps its carnival subjects securely within the horror mode, thus reinscribing physical difference as a terrifying spectacle. In this context, the fearful refrain "one of us, one of us" is a particularly fraught trope: while it entrenches identification within the community of freaks, it holds up the presumably "normal" or able-bodied viewer as a subject at once cut off from this unified group at the same time that s/he is guiltily implicated in the construction of just such a group identity.

As a way of welcoming the individual into the community, the phrase "one of us" works rather as a battle-cry: the repetitive refrain divides the freaks from the "normals" at the very moment that it articulates an acceptance of otherness. While the refrain works ostensibly to welcome and inaugurate the "most beautiful big woman," Cleopatra, into a company of differently figured but presumably likeminded compatriots, the noisy and strangely nonsensical rhythm of the words clearly menace her as well as our sense of ourselves as detached spectators. As viewers confronted with the repetitive phrase "one of us" we are forced to rethink our normalized identities as members of a bounded or "proper" social category, but whether this, in turn, encourages us to forfeit the essentialized opposition between normal and freakish bodies, or whether it simply confirms the status of all subjects as inherently divided from one another by outward configuration is a question that is not definitively answered. The process by which "one of us" becomes "none of us" is, in any case, a fraught and highly ambiguous act of translation.

One of the ways that Browning more successfully troubles the boundaries between normative and freakish is through his systematic monstering—for want of a better word—of the so-called normal characters in the movie. Browning constantly juxtaposes attractive and extraordinary bodies, as when Phroso the clown compliments Venus' beauty: "Say, you do have a good figure," he tells her, at which point Johnny Eck propels himself into view, thus forcing a contrast between what is constructed as a "good figure" and what may be read as its opposite; a "bad" but clearly not useless body since the man in question is one of the most agile and potent members of the community.

Venus and Phroso are constructed as the normative couple in the movie: both are American—as opposed to Hans and Frieda's Germanic background, Cleopatra's undifferentiated "foreign" accent, and Hercules' Russian heritage—and both appear to be physically intact, even attractive. Venus is the quintessential American girl next door, and Phroso is the good-hearted clown, and both identify with the freaks and attempt to assist their cause. "My people are decent circus folks," Venus affirms, changing allegiance from circus performer to freak, while Phroso wrestles with Hercules in the nocturnal chase sequence. And both feature in the final coda where they escort Frieda to Hans' castle and bring about a reconciliation between the two.

In a fairly early scene, however, this perspective is subtly altered. Venus, who has been living with Hercules the strong man, is angrily removing herself and her belongings from his caravan. On her way to her own caravan she encounters Phroso in full clown make-up. Realizing that he has overheard her altercation with Hercules she lashes out at him, sarcastically remarking, "women are funny, ain't they?" Removing his nose, his wig and his make-up, and in this manner transforming himself from clown into man, Phroso follows her to her wagon where he, in turn, castigates her: "You dames are all alike . . . how you squeal when you get what's coming to you." In light of Cleopatra's later transformation into a squealing, squawking chicken-woman, this comment takes on an oddly misogynistic undertone, and Phroso's apparent normalcy is further undercut by his nonchalant admission of an unspecified operation that, given the sexual tenor of the scene, implies that he has been unmanned or rendered impotent. This impression is confirmed in a later scene with Venus where she flirts boldly with him while he remains crouched within one of his props—a double-bottomed clown bath that gives the impression that he is without limbs and so forces a contrast with Randian the human torso. A contrast, I hasten to add, that is not to his advantage since despite his limb-less condition, Randian is featured as a mature and even manly character whose competence in lighting a cigarette with his mouth far outweighs Phroso's slow-minded sexual fumbling in this scene.

Even more subtly Browning throws normative sexuality and aesthetics into doubt by framing them within a freakish perspective. In one scene, the evil Cleopatra throws herself into the arms of Hercules and as the two embrace the caravan door opens and Joseph/Josephine, the half-man/half-woman gazes in. As the camera swings round to Joseph/Josephine's point of view we realize that it is Cleopatra and Hercules, clasped in their dramatic embrace, who more accurately embody the status of half-man/half-woman and that Joseph/Josephine, far from being half of either sex, comprises instead a doubled sexuality that allows a critical reassessment of the dependent and avaricious relationship between Cleopatra and Hercules.

Of course, the character who is most demonized from the perspective of the freaks is Cleopatra, the "big woman" whom Hans loves and who, in the course of the movie, takes on positively gargantuan proportions. Alternatively dwarfed by the overlarge loving cup or foreshortened on her chaise lounge with Frieda the midget ironically towering over her, she seems to expand in Hans' diminutive cabin, taking on the gigantic proportions of an Alice flailing about after imprudently partaking of the bottle marked "drink me." This effect is further emphasized in her humiliation of Hans at the marriage feast as she piggybacks him around the table, and later carries him off in her arms like a sleeping baby. For Browning, as for a more contemporary imagemaker such as Diane Arbus, the border between the monstrous and the supposedly normal is uneasily navigated. Like Browning, from whom she derived so much inspiration, Arbus too, in her photographic images, elects to enfreak what is most normal so that her pictures of domestic life typically inspire more unease than do her midgets and transvestites.

At the same time, Browning returns us, as viewers, to a final empathetic view of at least two of his freaks by breaking the frame he has so carefully constructed within the side show barker's spiel. As you will recall, the movie begins with the view of a fairground side show, a crowd has gathered around one exhibit and the voice of the ringmaster can be heard asserting the truthfulness and veracity of this particular spectacle: "We didn't lie to you," he declaims. "We told you we had living, breathing monstrosities!" This is the cue to begin the story of how Cleopatra the beautiful peacock of the air was transformed into the pathetic chicken-woman squawking pitifully in her cage. After the horrifying nocturnal chase and implied mutilation we are returned, once again, to the sunlit fairgrounds where the carnival barker dramatically uncovers his exhibit, an unspeakable hybrid of woman and barnyard fowl. This is not, however, the end of the movie: a brief coda follows in which Venus and Phroso escort Frieda to the castle in which, it is implied, Hans has been living his lonely embittered life. As Frieda rushes to him and takes him in her arms offering forgiveness and understanding—presumably for his part in the mutilation of Cleopatra—Venus and Phroso cast knowing glances at one another above the heads of the two sobbing lovers and quietly tiptoe out.

The scene at once reestablishes sympathy for Hans, who has sufficiently repented his part in the demonic midnight chase and for Frieda, who is his means of redemption. Both are singled out and restored to individuality and moral consciousness from the depths of the undifferentiated mob into which all the freaks have been dissolved as autonomous subjects. At the same time, the scene unerringly infantilizes Hans, who is framed sobbing in Frieda's arms in much the same way that he was once helplessly carried off in Cleopatra's arms. Both Hans and Frieda are effectively infantilized in the exaggerated and patronizing manner in which Venus and Phroso tiptoe from the room as if they are parents in the presence of a couple of appealing but sexually inadequate children.

The impression of infantile asexuality is further heightened by the fact that Hans and Frieda are played by Harry and Daisy Earles, a pair of brother and sister circus performers whose resemblance emphasizes their sibling rather than their romantic connection. Like the rest of the movie, Browning's coda is ambiguously framed and ambivalently executed, but it does encourage the viewer to read the movie as a truthful if sentimental exposé of the real lives of a group of unfortunate circus freaks rather than, as we are in danger of doing without the romantic coda, as a mere carnival chimera, a tall tale of boast and bluster serving, in the way of the barker's spiel, only to justify the extraordinary metamorphosis of the once beautiful Cleopatra.

I want to end with the suggestion of another possible way that we, as viewers, can break the frame or at least reframe the narrative of *Freaks*, in a way that Tod Browning in 1932 could not possibly have anticipated. While at first glance Robert Altman's 1992 film, *The Player*, with its satiric interest in the beautiful people of Hollywood, seems to have little to do with Browning's cult movie, it does contain a pivotal scene that refers directly and explicitly to *Freaks*. In *The Player*, Tim Robbins plays a Hollywood producer who has killed a screenwriter—the wrong screenwriter as it turns out—and who is engaged in concealing his crime from the police. In the scene I refer to he is brought into the station for questioning by the police inspector played by Whoopi Goldberg, and the detective, played by Lyle Lovett. Both Goldberg and Lovett seem incongruously distracted, she by the box of tampons she has misplaced and he by the movie he has seen the previous night, nothing less than a re-run of Browning's *Freaks*! As the Goldberg character plays carelessly with an exposed tampon that she maintains is not hers since it is "too small" and hers are jumbo size, the Lovett character repeats the defining phrase of the freak's battle-cry: "one of us, one of us."

Predictably, Robbins becomes more disoriented as the scene progresses—like Cleopatra at the wedding feast, he is clearly out of his element—and the exchange ends with the inspector, her assistant and the detective all laughing uproariously at the bewildered and angry producer who cannot help suspecting that he is being ridiculed at best, entrapped at worst, yet who clearly does not understand the codes that prevail in this alien milieu.

In this scene from *The Player*, a movie that refers obsessively to other movies and is preoccupied with the problem of narrative codes in general, Altman uses *Freaks* as an intertextual allusion to highlight the predicament of his main character. Yet, as may be expected, the other movie emphasizes the ambiguity of the world in which the Tim

Robbins character lives and works. As a killer, Robbins is monsterized and alienated by the crime he has committed, yet in this scene it is the inspector and the detective, the police force, who appear freakish and inscrutable and it is Robbins who mimes our own reaction of helpless bewilderment in the face of their strangely incongruous antics. As such, Robbins is implicitly compared to Cleopatra in the marriage feast, who is plotting to kill the defenseless Hans and yet who appears to be subtly victimized in the course of the scene by the freak's nonsensical and increasingly threatening rants.

Altman introduces this scene with its morally ambivalent undertones as one of many that undermine our certainty in the known and just world and which cumulatively present the ethically unstable milieu of moviemaking and its attendant compulsions. Ambiguity, in the context of Browning's movie, is less a pervasive directoral stance than it is the tenuous result of the director's internal ambivalence about the figure of the freak.

There is another way, however, in which Altman's movie, particularly in the "one of us" scene, addresses Browning's imaginative vision. *The Player*, set as it is in a contemporary Hollywood of film stars and producers, is peopled with well-known and recognizable actors, some playing themselves engaged in moviemaking concerns and others playing characters within a fictionalized and exaggeratedly amoral landscape. Much of the impact of *Freaks*, in terms of its critical history of censorship and limited distribution, centers on the use of so-called "real freaks" like Johnny Eck, Prince Randian, and the Hilton sisters who have real lives outside their circus side show existence yet who come together in Browning's film to play themselves engaged in a fictional and highly fantastic narrative. In effectively blurring the line between what is known to be real and what is assumed to be fictional, Altman follows Browning's lead in *Freaks*, presenting us with the fictionally-real world of Hollywood in much the same way that Browning's barker presented us with the spectacle of the circus side show: as a magnificent and highly duplicitous sleight-of-hand in which what is fictional, narrative, and interpretive is more emotionally and psychologically real than what is merely factual.

Works Cited

Altman, Robert, dir. *The Player*. With Tim Robbins, Whoopi Goldberg, and Lyle Lovett. FineLine Features, 1992.
Browning, Tod, dir. *Freaks*. Metro-Goldwyn-Mayer, 1932.

Davidson, Arnold. "The Horror of Monsters." *The Boundaries of Humanity: Humans, Animals, Machines.* Ed. James J. Sheehan and Morton Sosna. Berkeley: U of California P, 1991. 36-67.

Fiedler, Leslie. *Freaks: Myths and Images of the Secret Self.* New York: Simon and Schuster, 1978.

Garland Thomson, Rosemarie, ed. *Freakery: Cultural Spectacles of the Extraordinary Body.* Ed. Rosemarie Garland Thomson. New York: New York UP, 1996.

---. "Introduction: From Wonder to Error—A Genealogy of Freak Discourse in Modernity." Garland Thomson 1-19.

Grosz, Elizabeth. "Intolerable Ambiguity: Freaks as/at the Limit." Garland Thomson 55-66.

Hawkins, Joan. "'One of Us': Tod Browning's *Freaks*." Garland Thomson. 265-276.

Hevey, David. *The Creatures that Time Forgot: Photography and Disability Imagery.* New York: Routledge, 1992.

Rosenberg, Brian. "Teaching Freaks." Garland Thomson 302-311.

The Horror of Becoming "One of Us": Tod Browning's *Freaks* and Disability

Sally Chivers

Tod Browning's 1932 public relations' nightmare *Freaks* was billed as and continues to be spoken of as a horror film. As Martin F. Norden cites in his *The Cinema of Isolation*, MGM prereleased the film as a "thrillingly gruesome tale" featuring "creatures of the abyss," "strange children of the shadows," and "nightmare shapes in the dark" (116). Montréal's only English repertory cinema recently screened *Freaks* with the supposedly titillating description:

> Now, who says that there aren't any good horror flicks earlier than 1973? Here is the rare gem of an exception, a 1932 scare-a-thon that still eerily works today. *Freaks* is a film with actual circus sideshow freaks ... one of the main reasons why it is so scary (and why it was banned in the US for so many years). You are simultaneously repulsed, attracted, and fascinated (kinda like the way you pick at a scab) by the inhabitants of this film: midgets, people with no arms or no legs (one guy with none of the above), a siamese twin, a hermaphrodite, and stuff that you will never even see on *The X-files*. ("Freaks")

The self-dubbed "Mutant Reviewers from Hell" might just be on to something in their completely off-base description. The bodies of the freaks must be why viewers can be duped into fearing a film which lacks monsters, a threat to normalcy, narrative incoherence, and other typical trappings of horror.

Famous for his innovations in the realm of horror, after Lon Chaney's untimely death forced him to work with Bela Lugosi to create a prototypical *Dracula*, Browning set out to direct "the ultimate horror film" in *Freaks* (Skal 148). Considering this goal, it is strange that rather than following the considerable genre constraints of 1930s Hollywood and presenting a horror film which sacrifices narrative coherence to titillation of viewers, Browning shapes a relatively unified love story whose only recognisable element of horror is that it forces an uncomfortable audience identification. What is stranger still is that 1990s viewers would still be expected to perceive the film as a horror. Where exactly, then, does the horror lie?

The opening of *Freaks* contains fewer typical elements of horror than of melodrama and romance. When Jon and Monsieur Dubois happen upon members of the circus side show on a country estate, there is a hint of their potential for monstrosity in Jon's reaction, "Children! Monsters!", but Madame Tetrallini's instant defense reveals the men's fears to be ungrounded, and the infantilized performers are returned to their idyllic play. Strongman Hercules is set up as an evil character in that he has been a bad lover to Venus and that he punches Joseph of Joseph/Josephine, but there is no clear suggestion of his murderous intent. Although there are suggestions of the evil motives Cleopatra holds towards Hans, especially when she explains to Hercules, "Midgets . . . are not strong . . . . They could get sick," those hints point towards a murder mystery at best, or worst. The introduction to each of the side show actors is perhaps meant to evoke a particular reaction in audience members because of the physical anomalies they might be thought to present, but more so it sets the stage for a later audience identification with the characters those actors portray. The side show members form a coherent group with understandable motivations and common group dynamics, like a general excitement at the birth of a bearded baby to the bearded lady and the human skeleton. For the majority of the film, the elements of horror are muted and exist only in foreshadows and challenges to ableist assumptions.

The turn to more explicit horror occurs during the banquet scene when Cleopatra refuses to participate in the communal ritual which would mark her a freak. Critics attribute the success and memorability of the scene to Browning's capacity with silent film; the banquet was shot silent with sound added subsequently, and, indeed, the only intertitle of the film precedes announcing "The Wedding Feast." Further, Cleopatra's slow, exaggerated revulsion is very recognizably in the style of silent acting. Her gradual recoil shows her to be reacting in fear and even horror to monsters who moments ago were participants in a communal celebration. I suggest that, more than because of the silent method of production, the scene remains in the mind of the viewer and contributes to the horror of the film because it disallows the audience a comfortable identification with the characters possessing what Hollywood most considers to be healthy bodies. Viewers cannot possibly side with Cleopatra even though they share visually her point of view, since she has been shown to be murderous (in most versions[1]), as well as rejecting a generous offering. Viewers' rejection of Cleopatra is made particularly difficult by the point of view shot, since they must actively realign themselves counter to what they are able to see at that moment.

When Robin Wood offers a formula for the horror film in his "An Introduction to the American Horror Film," he very clearly explains that although, in horror, "normality is threatened by the Monster . . . . I use 'normality' here in a strictly non-evaluative sense, to mean simply 'conformity to the dominant social norms'; one must firmly resist the common tendency to treat the word as if it were more or less synonymous with 'health'" (203). In *Freaks*, however, normality can only be perceived in connection with the physical if the horror formula is to apply, which there is every indication it was meant to, from the film's billing to Browning's claims about his goals. Thus, in Browning's configuration, to make *Freaks* a horror film, the normality threatened by the Monster is a challenge, by means of perceptual permutations in physical form, to pervasive understandings of what comprises a healthy body , and how a body signifies moral fortitude.

Hollywood had in the 1930s, and still has, strict standards for what a "healthy" body truly looks like, and deviations from that norm were and are to this day frequently (and ironically) addressed surgically. Arlene Francis' refusal to undergo rhinoplasty prevented her from continuing as a 1930s "scream queen," whereas Dorothy Tree's submission to the procedure allowed her speaking roles and billings where she had previously only held bit parts (Skal 167). In most cases, without such drastic intervention, norms of classic, sleek, contained beauty are impossible to attain and difficult even to imitate. Oddly, self-mutilation is what helps actors to emulate ideals of healthy bodies as promulgated by Hollywood, so that the very transformation that perhaps audiences were meant to fear in viewing different bodies in *Freaks*, and the suggestion of physical pain supposedly invoked by those othered bodies, are precisely what bodies which match circulating notions of perfection actually submit to. What othered bodies signify to an able audience (physical change) is what ideal bodies undergo (in the form of plastic surgery).

Ignoring this actuality, Hollywood film follows a long theatrical tradition in creating certain affinities for audience members based on appearance. Shakespeare's revisionist Richard III continually stands in as an example of how crooked bodies evoke crooked moral subjects. Typically and simply put, film viewers understand the moral leanings of a character based on clothing and physical shape. In a classical Hollywood film, tension builds when two characters with acceptable bodies and suitable clothing vie for the sympathy of the audience. Audience members are then forced to read characters according to actions which are formulaic to the point of being prescriptive. A character transgressing social norms in a classical Hollywood film typically means at least nominally containment—be it death, marriage, or jail. Audiences rarely had a genuine, sustained dilemma in predicting actions, though, since the norms set up in a long-standing theatre tradition play themselves out, and physical anomaly metaphorically predicts immoral action. Threateningly, in *Freaks*, actions do not match appearance, audiences do not know where to situate affinities, and horror ensues.

Two of the supposed "normals" in the film act in ways that predict their certain moral and physical doom, and so audience members cannot choose that obvious site of identification comfortably. Assuming an able audience, as Hollywood usually does, the film renders viewers unable to identify easily with those who look most like them. The unease is further intensified by the refusal of the supposed "freaks" to remain trapped in the narrative roles dictated by their nonconformity with an acceptable body image for identification. They violate Hollywood standards for beautiful and even merely "healthy" bodies. They look like they should act in ways transgressive to social norms. Instead, when motivated, they work together to react to a threat to one of their ranks. Their attack is a frightening ganging up on a woman which could presumably evoke fear in audience members. But even the graphic revenge scene, which could be read as affirmation of the meaning ascribed to their anomalous figures in its brutality and menace, is enacted by bodies other than those the audience has learned to recognise, so that Hans, Frieda, Johnny Eck, and the Hilton Sisters never conform to the expectations created by their deviant physical forms. The "freaks" with whom the audience is most familiar never disallow identification by their actions so that their only threat can be what their bodies signify. In Browning's film, much of the supposed "horror" is muted compared to contemporary depictions of gore and violence and even contemporaneous ravages of women by monsters (King Kong, Dracula, Frankenstein). Yet the central circus side show members in *Freaks* are horrifying, not only because their friends enact a murderous revenge on their attackers, but also because they refuse to remain trapped in a body image that suggests their activities should be restricted or curtailed.

During the banquet scene, audience members are lulled into a comfortable position viewing a celebration amongst friends who at least pretend to feel joy at what Hans considers to be his good fortune. Audience members also remain aware of and visually confront the two "normal"'s murderous intentions. At the moment when Angelino approaches Cleopatra slowly with the loving cup and the side show performers chant "gooble! gobble!" in a nonsense version of what sounds like a bizarre ritual, the audience is placed under their intense and uncomfortable scrutiny. Shifting under their gaze, audience members are explicitly physically aligned with Cleopatra and are, by implication, incited to become one of the group. Cleopatra's outright rejection, then, supposedly mirrors the reaction of an ableist viewership except that to align oneself with her would be to identify with a murderess. Audiences cannot easily feel affinity for the "freaks" since their physical shape dictates moral infirmity and potential nefarious action, and they cannot feel affinity for the "normals" since their actions do not match their physical shape, and so they also present moral infirmity and nefarious action. According to David Bordwell and Kristin Thompson, "the horror genre is most recognizable by its intended emotional effect on the audience. The horror film aims to shock, disgust, repel—in short, to horrify" (58). The titillation of horror and the physical reaction it is meant to evoke crystallize in this moment when audiences cannot gaze comfortably and can presumably only writhe under the uncomfortable and hostile scrutiny of the only possible good guys on screen.

There is no doubt that typical horror elements preside over the revenge scene in *Freaks*. Threatening body shapes loom in dark shadows and slither in mud to, in unexpurgated versions, actually castrate Hercules. Mostly simply read, audiences end up strangely feeling vindicated that the characters which represent a physical threat in the film enact that threat on the character physically most like the audiences' bodies are presumed to be. Although able-bodied, Hercules is characterised as a violent and murderous buffoon to the extent that audiences accustomed to narrative patterns of punishment for moral transgression cannot possibly in fact ally themselves with him. The satisfaction of the bad guy, who physically matches what should be the good guy, meeting his just desserts is unsettling because, by horror conventions, it is achieved by the forces associated with monsters in previous movies rather than by the physical match to health and, by extension, goodness.

The side show artists who defy simple interpretation as monstrosities are continually established as a community which defends its own. Viewers are introduced to a group playing by the stream and during that scene, though infantilized, the characters establish themselves to be tightly associated, with Madame Tetrallini fiercely protecting them. As they become aware as a group of Cleopatra's mistreatment of Hans, but well before they understand its extent, Angelino and Frances articulate the threat they collectively pose:

FRANCES: Cleopatra ain't one of us. Why, we're just filthy things to her. She'd spit on Hans if he wasn't giving her presents.
ANGELINO: Let her try it. Let her try doing anything to one of us.
FRANCES: You're right. She don't know us. But she'll find out.

As the barker warns in the framing narrative, the side show artists have a code: "Offend one, and you offend them all." The power they gain from collectivity allows them to protect Hans from certain death, castrate Hercules, and literally make Cleopatra into one of them, despite, or because of, her vehement earlier rejection.

In Tod Browning's film, the "freaks" are people with disabilities who contemporary viewers hopefully recognise as adopting horror roles rather than representing physical transformation. The characters, in their turn to horror threats, transform Cleopatra into a different kind of "freak," a true physical impossibility. Whereas viewers may be familiar with people physically resembling Johnny Eck, they will likely never have met a woman covered with feathers and capable only of squawking. This transformation is an excess even within a realm of melodramatic excess. The final moment transcends any fear of transformation audience members may have previously held in their necessary identification with a variety of bodies. Cleopatra's final form adheres to narrative dictums as to her fate in relation to her actions. Further, she becomes what she sees when she looks at the circus side show performers—a "dirty," "slimy," "freaky" monster. She is contained, quite literally, not only in a cage, but in a physically impossible state dictated by her prejudicial gaze.

Hers is not the containment, obviously, of the sleek norms of Hollywood health and beauty, however. It is crucial to an evaluation of bodies in the movie to consider that the entire plot revolves around the transformation of a woman's body. Hers, excepting Phroso—who has had that mysterious operation—and Venus, is the only body that could be considered unambiguously not leaning toward physical freakery since Hercules, though visually matching circulating notions of attractiveness or acceptability, is still strangely strong. In discussing body genres, which she calls horror, melodrama, and pornography, Linda Williams explains "even when the pleasure of viewing has traditionally been constructed for masculine spectators . . . it is the female body in the grips of an out-of-control ecstasy that has offered the most sensational sight" (4). The process of ecstasy, from the Greek *ekstasis* standing outside oneself, encapsulates Cleopatra's transformation throughout the movie, but the sensational shudder of fear that its horror should evoke is prevented by her previous actions. The audience may be horrified and curious as to what they will see next, but because they have no comfortable site of identification, they can no longer be relied upon to experience the bodily fear of association with the character transformed. Cleopatra as "other" (in the form of the chicken lady) so transgresses Hollywood notions of classic, contained beauty that her body, and the plot that centers on its mutation, cannot contain the story, and the frame spills over into the final reconciliation between Frieda and Hans.

Although not especially frightening in its lack of depiction of actual violence, the film is still horrific in its demonization of the very "heroes" the audience is encouraged to show compassion for. Instead, the circus characters in the film behave communally as a "normal" character in the way that any victim of mistreatment or abuse might when confronted with an outsider who perpetrates such abuse, especially when the abuse is "justified" by a lack of respect for characters who share "othered" bodies. Creating sympathy and imbuing such bodies with understandable motivation suggests a continuum of body types rather than an ideal and lack. Browning leaves no choice for the viewer but to join the community of people with disabilities and thereby become "one of us."

Notes

[1] Strangely, the only part of the film which was censored shows Cleopatra putting poison into Hans' wine. Authorities feared people would learn methods of crime.

Works Cited

Bordwell, David, and Kristin Thompson. *Film Art: An Introduction.* 5th edition. New York: McGraw Hill, 1997.
Browning, Tod, dir. *Freaks.* Metro-Goldwyn-Mayer, 1932.
"Freaks." *Cinéma du Parc* Monthly Schedule July-August 1999.
Norden, Martin F. *The Cinema of Isolation: A History of Physical Disability in the Movies.* New Brunswick: Rutgers UP, 1994.
Skal, David J. *The Monster Show: A Cultural History of Terror.* New York: Norton, 1993.
Williams, Linda. "Film Bodies: Gender, Genre and Excess." *Film Quarterly* 44.4 (1991): 2-13.
Wood, Robin. "An Introduction to the American Horror Film." *Movies and Methods: An Anthology.* Ed. Bill Nichols. 2 vols. Berkeley: U of California P, 1985. 2: 195-220.

Disabling the Viewer: Perceptions of Disability in Tod Browning's *Freaks*

Nicole Markotic

I wish to discuss, in this essay, Tod Browning's movie *Freaks* (1932), and how that narrative deals with bodies represented, from the title on, as "freaks" of nature, bodies that are, by definition, out of sync with the human, with the "natural" world. I choose, throughout my paper, to use the term "freaks" to speak about bodies either represented in this film or who actually worked in circus side shows. The term accurately conveys a history that has enfreaked disabled or differently abled bodies; at the same time, it celebrates those who have displayed their bodies out of economic necessity, or out of desperation, or for the sheer pleasure of the show. Thus the word "freak" stresses that which both emphasizes and dismisses so-called "atypical" bodies. The word "freak" is both a magical term and a derogatory term that I believe the film questions and manages, at times, to reclaim.

The representation of "freaks" in the film reveals not only how Hollywood views "abnormal" bodies, but also a great deal about the contemporaneous audiences who were so shocked and repelled by the film. In Tod Browning's film, which today has become a cult horror classic, the group of circus freaks who enact revenge upon a murderous acrobatics star and her strongman lover are depicted as a homogenous and identifiable community, as the "us" who chant in unison during "The Wedding Feast" scene.

The depiction of their homogeneity goes a long way to convince audiences that the circus freaks are "all alike" and that they may unite en masse and in horrifying ways. Such scenes as "The Wedding Feast" and the scene where Angelino and Frances hint at the revenge they will enact on anyone who threatens "one of us" are warnings to the audience of the violence to come. The greedy pair, the acrobat Cleopatra and the strongman Hercules, attempt to gain wealth by murdering the midget Hans who is an heir to a great fortune. The plan is for Cleopatra to marry Hans, and then slowly poison him while pretending to care for his illness. They see no obstacles in their way, at least none to worry about. Both believe they are "immune" to the freaks and Hercules, a great oaf, physically threatens the two "normals" who attempt to get in the way of this plan.

In the movie, Browning employs actual circus performers from real 1930s circus acts to play the supporting roles of the circus characters who defend and avenge their wronged friend. This, in itself, is remarkable. Many of the actors made more from this one movie than their (often exploitative) roles in circuses enabled them to earn in their entire lifetimes. What is also remarkable is the film's insistence that the freak characters be front and center of the camera. Though their bodies would be considered commodities to be viewed, such display was, conventionally, a static activity. Contemporaneous audiences (and contemporary audiences, given contemporary reactions to this controversial movie) saw these normally "viewed" bodies as agents in their own actions, and had no choice but to "relate" to the bodies. Thus, being displayed in the film encouraged sympathetic identification, and caused such discomfort and self-consciousness that the film went virtually unseen until the horror film revival in 1962.

The disturbing portrayal of these bodies, until then underrepresented, ensured that the film's director (originally famous for his movie *Dracula* [1931]) would fall out of favor with Hollywood. Typical audience members cannot sympathize with the "freak" protagonists whose lot, in the film, is to be cheated and tormented by the "normal" evil antagonists. The view of such bodies, apparently, is too much for audiences to comprehend on any level except the horrific. How could the hero be a midget? How could "normal-bodied" characters be evil? Audiences felt (and still feel) incomprehension for being placed into a position of spectatorship unable to either relate to, or condemn entirely, the characters coming to life onscreen. Such incomprehension helped push Browning's film underground for thirty years, and still shields Hollywood audiences from viewing any body but the young and "perfect" physique typically displayed onscreen.

Yet can the "freakish" bodies represented onscreen portray "authentic" disabled characters, and is this desire even appropriate, given the genre of "horror"? The phenomenon of the terrifying movie gives permission to audiences to react in particular and scripted ways. Such reactions are encoded into horror films But in Browning's film, such characterizations are reversed, and the bodies "normally" found hideous and evil are portrayed as innocent victims. This reversal causes audiences to reevaluate societal beliefs and prejudices.

The freakish or grotesque body is characteristically portrayed or read as metaphor for emotional or spiritual deficiency. As Paul K. Longmore points out in his essay on the representations of disabled people in literature and film, in most of these representations the deformity of the body symbolizes a deformity of the soul (32). Metaphorical thinking, then, replaces an actual body with an idea behind that body, suggesting what that body means. Longmore points out that what we fear, "we often stigmatize and shun and sometimes seek to destroy" (32). Cleopatra and Hercules loathe and dismiss the side show stars they work with. Destroying Hans, therefore, is defensible and justified. They fear and are disgusted by the freaks, and they have no qualms about killing Hans or stealing him away from his fiancée, Frieda. As Robert Bogdan's son says to a friend who cannot keep straight the good guys and the bad guys in an adventure film, "If they look bad, then they are bad" (6). This child's directive reveals what every moviegoer instinctively already knows: namely, that people who look "different" are different, and that is why "we" the viewing audience are and should be afraid of them.

On the one hand, *Freaks* proposes freakishness to be a superficial defect, curable by medicine and "modern" science. On the other hand, the "code of the freaks" printed at the beginning of the film and the subsequent uprising in obedience of that code, suggests a deeper and significant difference between "normal" people and circus freaks. Shawna Dempsey, in a talk on homophobia in the film *Basic Instinct*, claims that the scenario of lesbians killing asshole-ish men somehow "appeals" to her: "Maybe we shouldn't boycott *Basic Instinct*, maybe we should refer to it as a primer." Maybe there is a similar adage to be discovered in Browning's film. In other words, rather than run from the "insult" such a film proposes, Dempsey suggests that audience members embrace the designation "one of us."

Freaks presents a female character using her body to entice and seduce men. She uses sex as a tool to get her way, to manipulate the male characters into surrendering to her (destructively female) desire. Mary Ann Doane points out: "The very fact that we can speak of a woman 'using' her sex or 'using' her body for particular gains is highly significant—it is not that a man cannot use his body in this way but that he doesn't have to" (82). Traditionally, in the movies, men kill for "bad" reasons—usually revenge, lust, or money. In those movies where women kill (such as *Fatal Attraction* [1987], *Basic Instinct* [1992], *Single White Female* [1992]) these "killer-femmes" attack not so much because of external evil motives, but because women, simply and unambiguously, are essentially evil.

Browning, while invoking this stock view of women through the character of Cleopatra, shows the same essential evil to be ascribed to the disabled bodies in his film. *Freaks* perpetuates simplistic notions of good and evil based on a limited set of narratives that depend on the opposition of what is culturally defined as normal versus horrific. To this end, I insert a question by film theorists Gamman and Marshment: "Can we really assume that audiences identify on the basis of gender (or even sexual orientation) rather than on the basis of other categories that contribute to the construction of our identities?" (7). That audiences do "identify" on the basis of "other categories" is the very reason that "theatre owners, particularly those in rural areas, refused to handle [*Freaks*]" in 1932 (see Hawkins 266).

In narrative, characters with physical impairments are constructed as helpless or pitiful, as merely static, or as metaphorically representing a moral quality expressed through their bodies "lack" of normal functions. Often, the poet is represented as "blind" in much the same way justice is, namely, able to observe or tell the truth, but not able to participate. Physical restrictions, madness, and old age are all "illnesses" which represent groups or individuals as needy of societal care, protection, and assistance. In this way, representations of illness are for the benefit of the able-bodied: there merely to demonstrate the universal power of the human spirit to overcome adversity.

People whose movement or senses are restricted become restricted themselves, at the same time these bodies are being incorporated as metaphor, the metaphor excludes them as integral participants of a universalizing morality. These are not normal bodies, we are told, these are freakish bodies, these are not freaks, these are fallen bodies representing fill-in-the-blank metaphor, these are not fallen bodies, these are ill or diseased bodies, and the disease is visible and noticeable and obvious.

Robert Bogdan, in his book *Freak Show*, states that in the United States, "by the late 1930s the transformation of those with physical and mental anomalies from curiosities to diseased people was complete" (66). Indeed, preceding the action in Browning's film, comes an exceedingly long "prologue" where a written introduction discusses not the film's content, but the medical nature of circus side show displays. This "prologue" was actually inserted by the film's distributor long after the film's release, in the late 1940s. *Freaks* now begins by announcing that "[n]ever again will such a story be filmed, as modern science is rapidly eliminating such blunders of nature from the world." The prologue appears to apologize for its controversial spectacle of the circus freak, at the same time as it reassures audiences that the "horrific" bodies they are about to view will soon be extinct as science works to "perfect" the human physique. Such a reassurance, given that it was offered in the 1940s, can only be reread with a peculiar historical horror.

A prologue which declares that the "ABNORMAL and the UNWANTED" are mere "accidents of abnormal birth" serves a number of purposes. One is to reinscribe the very difference that the prologue purports to annul. The prologue goes on to state: "The majority of freaks are endowed with normal thoughts." Such a sentence only underlines the vast difference laid out between "freak" and "normal." Another purpose of such an introduction to this film is to reassure audiences that the bodies they are about to view are not, in fact, freakish, so much as they are injured or damaged or naturally disabled. The message, then, is one of recovery: with the proper doctors, and the right medical intervention, these bodies can be healed. At the very least, such bodies can be eliminated in future generations, making the ones present both unwelcome and anachronistic. Such a prologue, given the horrific evidence that emerged in the late 1940s about "medical" interventions performed during the Nazi years, is both irresponsible and dangerous. But the attitude towards differently abled bodies is, unfortunately, not restricted to the 1930s and 1940s.

In a recent article on medicine and deformity, Robert Goldwyn writes: "With plastic surgery as well as with the benefits of other medical and surgical specialties, and with the warmth of support groups, many of these unfortunate persons may become active, productive participants in society" (85). This condescending attitude, constructing disability as illness that can be cured, goes a long way to markedly dividing people into two recognizable groups of healthy and disabled. It is an attitude that questions the ability of members of one group to equal the abilities of members of the other.

Rob Budde examines the same behind-the-curtains world as does Browning. Budde's text constantly reminds readers that the circus freakshow is "off to the side," not part of the main show (85). The big tent, in fact, is where normals perform, whereas the side show is where freaks are, and where "normal" people go to reestablish their normal status by staring at what is so obviously "not" normal. Lennard Davis, in his book on the constructions of "normalcy," says that the disabled or racially different are not viewed as "citizen" in the same sense as are the abled-bodied viewers: "That the freak show begins in the same period as we have seen statistics and eugenics begin, indicates a change in the way people thought about the physically different" (91). This change of thought, in the 1930s, shifts the bodies of disabled circus performers from the world of monsters to the world of medicine.

According to Susan Sontag, in *Illness as Metaphor*, a "disease of the lungs is, metaphorically, a disease of the soul" (17). Sontag refers to TB, yet her description can easily be attributed to physical or spiritual "disabilities" of people who do not fit into the world of the abled. Davis says that just as "coded terms signifying skin color . . . are largely produced by a society that fails to characterize 'white' as a hue, so too the categories 'disabled,' 'handicapped,' and 'impaired' are products of a society invested in denying the variability of the body" (xv). This denial of even a small deviance from the accepted body type is what Leslie Fiedler calls the "tyranny of the normal." And whatever their actual bodies, audience members fulfill a cinematic desire to align themselves and their viewing with "normal" viewers indulging in "normal" curiosity and beholding.

Browning's film exploits the binary construction of "healthy" versus "ill" that audience members construct around their own bodies and the bodies of others. The representation of a disabled self relies on the metaphor of illness in that the disabled person, instead of being disabled as a result of a particular past illness or birth, is perceived as actually and continually ill. The signal of this illness is the inability to present a "normal" body, and the manifestation of this disease is any visible bodily variance.

In Browning's portrayal of circus freaks as the center of a narrative, audience members found it impossible to "read" the circus body metaphorically. Such a reading would entail not only seeing those bodies as real and ordinary and present, but also would force viewers to gaze at the "healthy" bodies of the acrobat and her lover as metaphorically ill or diseased.

This movie, in complicated ways, presents disabled and deformed bodies as "merely" a medical challenge, then reverses its benign stance, and represents those same bodies as potentially and essentially vengeful and murderous. Interestingly, none of the freak characters the audience has come to know and sympathize with are shown crawling through the mud with knives in their teeth. For the most part, this scene is reserved for the severely handicapped, such as Randian the Living Torso, rather than the twins Violet and Daisy or Hans and Frieda. The sympathy of the audience, then, shifts from characters who have been shunned or even poisoned to one who may be evil but is still depicted as "normal" and needing protection in this scene. As Joan Hawkins notes: "From the moment [Cleopatra] runs screaming into the night with the band of vengeful freaks behind her, Cleo begins attracting audience sympathy" (269). This sympathy, at the end of the film, turns to morbid curiosity as the final shot of Cleopatra, transformed into a freakish chicken-woman, unveils the hidden and distorted body that the audience has been waiting for since the beginning of the film's frame. But, unlike the circus freaks in the side show, Cleopatra, as Hawkins says, has been "constructed, not born" (270) into this freakish body. The sympathy, then, comes for one who has "lost" her "normality," who has had disability thrust upon her. Cleopatra has become what she most feared and, in the process, her body now displays the inherent evil she previously enacted. In this way, the film reinscribes the essentialism it purports to challenge.

Browning, in depicting real circus performers in his film, shows his audiences that the "normal" body does not, in fact, exist. Although crucial to how they relate to one another and band together against the perceived (and real) threats from "outside," these characters are never merely their bodies. The side show performers suffer the very real disability of being treated unkindly and dangerously by the normal and the beautiful who surround them. But it is not their physical difference that separates them from the rest of the circus performers. It is instead their status of lesser beings within the circus that binds them to the daily struggle to accommodate exploitation of their bodies as freakish, extraordinary, and ceaselessly on display.

Works Cited

Bogdan, Robert. *Freak Show: Presenting Human Oddities for Amusement and Profit.* Chicago: U Chicago P, 1988.

Browning, Tod, dir. *Freaks.* Metro-Goldwyn-Mayer, 1932.

Budde, Rob. *Misshapen.* Edmonton: NeWest, 1997.

Davis, Lennard J. *Enforcing Normalcy: Disability, Deafness, and the Body.* London: Verso, 1995.

Dempsey, Shawna. "On Becoming Fatale." Manitoba Writers' Guild Conference. Manitoba Writers' Guild. Winnipeg, 2 October 1993.

Doane, Mary Ann. "Film and the Masquerade: Theorizing the Female Spectator." *Screen* 23:3-4 (September/October 1982): 74-87.

Donley, Carol, and Sheryl Buckley, eds. *The Tyranny of the Normal: An Anthology.* Kent, OH: Kent State UP, 1996.

Fiedler, Leslie. "The Tyranny of the Normal." Donley and Buckley 3-26.

Gamman, Lorraine, and Margaret Marshment. Introduction. *The Female Gaze: Women as Viewers of Popular Culture.* Ed. Gamman and Marshment. London: The Women's Press, 1988. 1-7.

Goldwyn, Robert. "Deformity and the Humane Ideal of Medicine." Donley and Buckley 85-88.

Hawkins, Joan. "'One of Us': Tod Browning's *Freaks.*" *Freakery: Cultural Spectacles of the Extraordinary Body.* Ed. Rosemarie Garland Thomson. New York: New York UP, 1996. 265-276.

Longmore, Paul K. "Screening Stereotypes: Images of Disabled People." *Social Policy* 16.1 (Summer 1985): 31-37.

Sontag, Susan. *Illness as Metaphor.* New York: Vintage Books, 1979.

Tod Browning and the Monstrosity of Hollywood Style

Oliver Gaycken

The legacy of anomaly that Tod Browning left behind is at least double. On the one hand, his films are remembered as literal anomalies, as the product of a dark current that ran counter to Hollywood's usual stream of sunshine. In the words of a contemporary critic, "Browning is the combination of Edgar Allan Poe and Sax Romer of the cinema. Where every director, save Stroheim, breathes wholesomeness, out-of-door freshness and the healthiness of the clean-limbed, Tod Browning revels in murkiness .... His cinematic mind is a creeping torture chamber, a place of darkness, deviousness and death" (Watts 3; qtd. in Skal and Savada 109). It is no coincidence that what is perhaps Browning's most famous film bears the title *Freaks* (1932). As a consequence Browning's legacy today is a cult following that sees him, as the subtitle of a recent, and to date only, biography puts it, "Hollywood's Master of the Macabre," or, as another nickname would have it, "The Wizard of Odd."

On the other hand, these characterizations of Browning's films are themselves anomalous insofar as they tend to minimize the extent to which Browning was a mainstream artist, a director whose classical pedigree began with his assistant directorship under D. W. Griffith on *Intolerance* (1916) and spanned the rest of the silent period and well into the early sound era, periods during which he worked for major studios. Part of the reason for this oversight is that Browning's work today, like that of many directors who worked in both the silent and sound periods, has been shaped by the inaccessibility of all but a handful of his silent films. While it would be detrimental for an assessment of any director to only have certain films readily available, for Browning the resulting distortion of his career is severe. The films for which he is best known today, *Dracula* (1931) and *Freaks*, are both anomalies in their own right, not only because they come from the last third of his career, but also because each film is marred by Browning's difficulties in adapting to the changes in Hollywood that he faced in this phase of career, in part because he remained stubbornly commited to a silent film aesthetic and a director-unit production style, to say nothing about the problems an increasingly powerful and censorious Production Code effected.[1] In other words, it would only be a slight exaggeration to say that Browning's best known work is the least representative of his overall career. *Dracula*'s status as a Browning film, especially in the form in which it now exists, is questionable at best. Not only was Browning unable to carry out the film as he originally envisaged it because of the terminal illness of his favorite actor, Lon Chaney (he and Chaney had discussed the project and Chaney supposedly had begun experimenting with different make-up ideas), but Universal also reedited the film before its theatrical release "trimming Browning's cut of the film by nearly ten percent—from eighty-four to seventy-five minutes—even while adding new footage" (Skal and Savada 151). And while *Freaks* in a sense represents the apotheosis of his work, it cannot be evaluated without placing it in the context of his previous films. What's more, *Freaks*, whose distribution rights were bought up by Dwain Esper in August of 1947, was one of the first films on the exploitation circuit, and would come to be shown on double bills with George Romero's *Night of the Living Dead* (1969). As a result of this history of midnight exhibitions, *Freaks* has been inscribed into a countercultural discourse that is significantly different from the context in which it originally appeared.[2] *Freaks* has also undergone considerable changes, and its current form, with Esper's prologue and a fair amount of missing footage, makes it into a kind of neither-nor monster in its own right (see Léger 88-90).

In brief, seeing Browning's films as the work of a marginal figure, as memorable anomalies, is problematic. Browning's works fall squarely inside classical Hollywood's definitional boundaries and can be explained in the same terms as other classical films, but at the same time, his films challenge those boundaries at numerous places and open up the Hollywood style from the inside, exposing the freakishness inherent in the classical mode. In other words, his output should be considered not only in terms of its discontinuities from the prevailing style, but also in terms of the equally odd continuities that join his work to the rest of the classical Hollywood style. Through a consideration of Browning's silent period, particularly *The Unknown* (1927), the film that increasingly has been seen as his masterpiece, we can begin to get a better understanding of the peculiar challenge his films pose.[3] An analysis adequate to the task of accounting for Browning's corpus will require a double vision that is able to account for both his singularity as well as his inclusion in the corpus of film that has come to be known as the classical Hollywood cinema. Such a method will allow for both a reassessment of Browning's position vis á vis the classical style and a reassessment of that style itself, especially in its more influential formulation, that of David Bordwell, Janet Staiger, and Kristin Thompson's *The Classical Hollywood Cinema: Film Style and Mode of Production to 1960.*

A crucial aspect of Browning's work that perturbs the prevalent conception of Hollywood cinema is its recurring tendency to "bare the device." This is a phrase David Bordwell uses in his account of an element of the Hollywood style he calls "artistic motivation":

> Normally, any element of a classical film is justified in one or more of these ways [compositional, generic, and realistic motivation]. When it is not, it may be subsumable to yet another sort of motivation, one usually (if awkwardly) called "artistic" motivation. By this term, Russian Formalist critics meant to point out that a component may be justified by its power to call attention to the system within which it operates. This in turn presupposes that calling attention to a work's own artfulness is one aim of many artistic traditions—a presupposition that challenges the notion that Hollywood creates an "invisible" or "transparent" representational regime. Within certain limits, Hollywood films do indeed employ artistic motivation in order, as the Formalists would put it, to make palpable the conventionality of art. (21)

The examples he provides of artistic motivation—the "flagrant technical virtuosity" of lighting effects, camerawork, or special effects (often motivated by genre coventions); the use of parody; and self-referential moments such as one character's description of Ralph

Bellamy in *His Girl Friday* (1940) as someone who "looks like Ralph Bellamy"—all have the ability to cultivate (and in a certain sense rely on) and create "a connoisseurship in the classical spectator" (21-22). This spectator, in other words, would be familiar with genre conventions, technological history, and so on, and can therefore recognize the films' embedded references.

The "certain limits" to which Bordwell refers above are largely a matter of frequency, which becomes most explicit when he writes, "The classical cinema, then, does not use artistic motivation constantly through the film . . . . It does not bare its devices repeatedly and systematically" (23). This argument is made to counter readings that see "self-reflexive" moments in films as *necessarily* rupturing their classicality; instead, in Bordwell's terms, they would be instances of the artistic motivation that is part and parcel of the classical mode of narration. In the footnote appended to the sentence in which Bordwell defines artistic motivation as baring the device ("When an art work uses artistic motivation to call attention to its own particular principles of construction, the process is called 'laying bare the device'" [22]), he adds, "The Russian Formalist concept of baring the device is a marked improvement upon the currently fashionable idea of 'reflexivity'; according to the Formalists, even the most 'realistic' art works find ways to point to their own artificiality, since all art works aim (in different ways) to heighten the viewer's perception of art's specific materials and methods" (417). This move whereby a dismissal of a current that runs counter to Bordwell's definition of classicality at the same time gathers in that current and even enlists it in the service of a generalizing gesture that supports his normative program typifies the argumentative style of the *Hollywood* book. If "all art works" contain self-reflexive moments (and at such a level of generality, the point is easily conceded), then by extension, self-reflexive moments in Hollywood films are only counterclassical if they are constant.

This quantitative argument leaves out precisely what Bordwell addresses only parenthetically, namely, the *difference* of specific self-reflexive moments. It cannot account for the appearance of self-reflexive moments in Browning's work for at least two reasons. First of all, Browning's obsession with what Bordwell would call "artistic motivation," while never sustained to the point of rupture in any one film, is, when viewed across his work, most certainly systematic and repeated. It appears in a great many of his films, and in all of the productions over which he had a large measure of control. It is not only because of its consistent recurrence that Browning's use of this device, or constellation of devices, works against various aspects of the classical mode. What makes Browning remarkable beyond his repeated use of this device is his integration of this "disruptive" element into the fabric of his narrative system, his elevation, in other words, of deception to the level of form and his display of the trickery that is the cornerstone of cinematic storytelling. Instead of producing a classically closed text, Browning's films consistently comment on the freakish nature of cinematic illusion and thereby enable a different, more skeptical spectator.

It is interesting to consider the hyposthesis-testing of the classical spectator that Bordwell describes in this regard. For Bordwell, a significant feature of the Hollywood system is how it requires the spectator to actively perform certain actions in order to engage with the film; the viewer, in other words, "meets the film halfway and completes the illusion" (59). While Browning's films certainly conform to this contruction of a spectator—they utilize the continuity editing system, for instance—they also up the ante by revealing the stakes of completing the illusion. We need to recall here Browning's career before he became involved with film, which was closely tied to the circus and to the American institution of the side show. As a youth, for example, he starred as a "Living Hypnotic Corpse," an act in which he allowed himself to be buried alive for a lengthy period of time (the spectators were not permitted to see the construction of the coffin in detail, which contained a device that supplied him with air). The side show's distinction between the "us" of the exhibition community and the "them" of the paying public hinges on a critique of voyeurism. What Browning's use of the self-reflexive device asks us to consider is how a spectator who is willing to construct a story that is not a seamless reproduction of reality is, in side show parlance, a sucker.

The self-reflexive moments in Browning's films are almost invariably moments that present a side show illusion. The particularity of each of these self-reflexive moments would have to be analyzed in detail in a more comprehensive treatment of this trope in Browning's work, but a cursory survey will be sufficient to indicate the frequency with which it occurs. The earliest instance of this trope that I have come across is in *White Tiger* (1923), whose criminal caper plot includes a detailed exposition of the workings of one of the most famous mechanical illusions of the eighteenth century, Maeltzel's chess player, which the criminals use as a cover for their robberies of the homes of the wealthy. The end of *West of Zanzibar* (1928) presents us with a fascinating instance of the failure of illusionistic spectacle when Lon Chaney, playing an African trader, dies at the hands of African tribesmen who want to sacrifice his daughter. A magician's trick (a coffin with a false back wall that allows her to escape and leaves a fake skeleton in her place) fails to satisfy their "savage" criteria of believability. The staging of the decapitation in *The Show* (1927) contains the same revelation of a side show stunt and the threat of the fictionalized violence becoming actual that marks the end of *The Unknown*. *Mark of the Vampire* (1935), a remake of the lost Browning/Chaney film *London after Midnight* (1927), employs a vampire plot that is debunked at the end of the film as a ploy to trap a criminal into a confession. The con-job setup of *The Unholy Three* (1925), which is repeated in *The Devil-Doll* (1936) involves such side show illusions as ventriloquism, and a small person who poses as a child.

We can consider at a little more length the opening of *Freaks* (not the prologue added later by Dwain Esper for the film's exploitation run, whose pseudoscientific ramble through the history of monstrosity is itself a kind of monstrous appendage). In the original opening, the film's final title credit is riven by a hand, presumably that of the carnival barker who speaks the lines of the opening scene. This impatient, revelatory gesture ruptures the division between title sequence and diegesis, an action that bares the artifice of the titles, literalizing their materiality. Suddenly revealed as paper, the titles are laid bare as something that *conceals* something else, namely, the beginning of the film.

This gesture, which anticipates the film's final unveiling, also functions as an initial warning about the untrustworthiness of appearances that is such a crucial part of the film's logic (i.e. the "beautiful," big people are not good, they are bad; the "ugly," small people are in fact good). This prefatory gesture to my mind goes a long way toward answering the primary complaint lodged against the film, which says that for all its humanizing of the freaks, it ultimately presents them in precisely that demonizing light (when they stalk and mutilate Cleopatra and Hercules in the thunderstorm sequence) that lies at the darkest heart of the prejudices against them. The opening gesture answers that complaint because if we heed its message, it informs us to read the final image of Cleopatra as a human duck as an instance of side show spectacle (in current versions of the film, it is followed by a brief epilogue in which Hans and Frieda are reunited).

Making Cleopatra "one of us" involves making her into a phony exhibit. The physical mutilation that she suffers at the hands of the freaks is not what makes Cleopatra into a freak; rather, it is the mise en scène of her mutilation that allows her to be claimed for the side show community as "one of us," a boundary that she vehemently resisted crossing earlier in the film during the wedding banquet scene. While this reading does not entirely answer the unease people may feel about how the film plays up the freaks' ability to evoke fear, we should also keep in mind that the freaks' revenge is in an important sense as humanizing a gesture as the earlier parts of the film where they are shown going about their daily business. The final sequence allows them to assert an agency that the "big people" have ignored. What this penultimate sequence tells us is that the freaks are just as human as the other revenge-obsessed protagonists of Browning's films.[4]

Browning's recurring fascination with the process of illusion and deceit that stems from his experience with the side show mode of exhibition also involves how the bodies of freaks require deciphering, how they are "divine hieroglyphs" (Davidson 39). The performers in *Freaks*, while forming a *non plus ultra* of Browning's obsession with the unusual body, are also a curious literalization of Browning's work with Lon Chaney, whose protean persona has been described as "a living, breathing assault on the boundaries of human personality, experience, and identity as they were commonly understood" (Skal and Savada 67).

If "the Hollywood cinema uses the human figure as its center of interest" (Bordwell, Staiger, and Thompson 291), then in Browning's films, and especially in those with Chaney, we are witness to an exploration of the limits of the human figure. The "Man of a Thousand Faces," as Chaney was often billed, represents a peculiar kind of star since instead of the classical star's "basic consistency of character traits" (Bordwell, Staiger, and Thompson 15) his persona is consistent only to the extent that it is fundamentally inconsistent from role to role, so much so that when in Browning's and Chaney's *The Big City* (1928), which is believed lost, the attraction was that Chaney would wear "his own face." The Hollywood cinema's peculiar ability to incorporate such a wide range of narrative and performance styles begins to resemble Lon Chaney. Chaney's malleability pushes to a limit the flexibility inherent in the Hollywood cinema and that for the *Hollywood* book is the hallmark of classicality. When considered from the vantage point that Chaney's body offers us, the Hollywood style's flexibility is also the marker of its monstrosity.

The way in which Browning bares the device in *The Unknown* has everything to do with his collaboration with Lon Chaney and Chaney's star persona. The film begins in a typical Browning setting with an establishing long shot of a circus tent. We then see "Alonzo the Armless"'s act, which consists of sharpshooting and knife-throwing with his feet around the body of Joan Crawford. The unveiling of his trick, namely, that he does indeed have arms that he conceals to avoid detection for a murder he committed (he has a tell-tale double thumb on one hand) does not take place until fifteen minutes into the film, a delay that has the effect of fostering spectatorial doubt as to the nature of Chaney's make-up. The original title for the film had been *Alonzo the Armless* and the possibility that Chaney might indeed have gone to the limit, so to speak, of physical modification for this part is registered in the following contemporary review of *The Unknown*: "Despite the popularity of the Chaney distortions, it is rumored that this will be the actor's last film of this sort for some time. The 'don't step on it' jokes, combined with a poisonous Broadway rumor that Chaney's next film would be entitled *Teddy the Torso*, have apparently pierced deeply into Hollywood hearts" (qtd. in Skal and Savada 115).

Beyond this initial, speculative titillation, however, Chaney's subsequent "mutilation" in *The Unknown* is all the more astonishing. After the device has been bared, Browning effects a reversal of this process of unveiling. When Chaney returns from the surgeon he has blackmailed into amputating his arms so that he will be the "perfect" man for Nanon, who has a phobia of being touched by men, the illusion of the film's opening is redoubled. Although we know that he cannot have actually undergone the modification that his part would have required, a certain amount of doubt persists that suggests, impossibly, it might still be so. Even if that particular specter of doubt does not arise, an odd palpability about Chaney's amputation remains.

While *The Unknown*'s evocation of the disabled body taps into a particular vein of the public imagination of the time, namely, the influx of WWI veterans that included a great number of actual amputees, contemporary reviews' references to various operations that involve dismemberment register how the amputation tended to dominate discussions of the film. The *New York Sun* advanced "the suspicion that the picture might have been written by Nero, directed by Lucretia Borgia, constructed by the shade of Edgar Allan Poe and lighted by a well-known vivisectionist" (qtd. in Skal and Savada 114). The reviewer for the *Daily Mirror* wrote, "if you like to tear butterflies apart and see sausage made you may like the climax to *The Unknown*. . . . typical Chaney fare spiced with cannibalism and flavored with the Spanish inquisition" (qtd. in Skal and Savada 115). The *New York Evening Post* wrote, "Mr. Chaney has been twisting joints and lacing himself into strait-jackets for a long time—so long, in fact, that there is almost nothing left for him now but the Headless Horseman. No doubt that will come later . . . . A visit to the dissecting room in a hospital would be quite as pleasant, and at the same time more instructive" (qtd. in Skal and Savada 115). The conservative *Harrison's Reports* also mentioned the Spanish Inquisition and continued, "Of Mr. Chaney's acting it is enough to say it is excellent, of its kind. Similar praise might well be given the work of a skilled surgeon in ripping open the abdomen of a patient. But who wants to see it?" (qtd. in Skal and Savada 115). Who wants to see it, indeed? Or, we might also ask, who does see it, since you do not see the amputation. When Browning bares the device early in the film, showing the illusion of disability, he paradoxically reinforces the believability of the illusion of amputation later on. This is the double edge of Browning's baring of the device. While on the one hand offering the capability to deflate the dramatic power of a certain kind of voyeuristic relation to narratives, Browning's use of artistic motivation in *The Unknown* serves to heighten the film's final impact. Browning's interest in the disabled body, in the unusual body, in the boundary between the human and the animal, in, in other words, the limits of humanity, is not just or simply voyeuristic, it is also heuristic insofar as it contains an implicit critique of Hollywood's obsession with the beauty of perfect bodies, by which I mean not only the bodies of performers but also the perfect body of the classically constructed film. It is in this sense that we should read Browning's peculiar, impeccable classicism as Hollywood's other, as an illuminating shadow of the classical Hollywood style.

An account of melodrama is crucial to any evaluation of Browning's work. To the extent that his films are still available today, they are almost always classified as "horror" films, and while there are certain ways in which Browning's work does cross over into the territory of horror, especially in its focus on the body, any evaluation of Browning's films solely from the vantage point of horror will lack a critical perspective necessary to an appreciation of his work. To quote the programmer of the recent Doc Films series on Browning and the person most responsible for my own interest in the director: "Horror and the supernatural are not Browning's true territory. His work needs to be appreciated not under the horror genre, but from the perspective provided by classical melodrama" (Cucurella). A number of recent writers have recognized melodrama's importance for Browning's films; Stuart Rosenthal notes that the bulk of his output should be classified as "crime melodrama" (8), and Skal and Savada's filmography classifies almost all of Browning's films as melodramas of one type or another (they modify melodrama with the words "crime," "horror," "mystery," and "fantasy").

Since melodrama is far from a unified genre, to classify Browning's work as melodramatic, even in a way that modifies melodrama as above, raises further questions of precisely how to understand the function of melodrama in his films. Recent interest in melodrama has revealed both how complex that mode of literary practice and how complex cinema's involvements with that mode are. The recent work on melodrama that has particular relevance for the present discussion points out how melodrama is a genre particularly attuned to questions of the body. Writing about the Grand Guignol melodramas of André de Lorde, Tom Gunning describes how these plays sought to affect the spectator: "De Lorde wished to produce an explicitly physical sensation of *trac* or *frisson*. Located in the pit of the stomach, it grabs one from within . . . . The Grand Guignol affects the stomach, not the soul" (54). Browning's films often aim to create a similar reaction, and, as we have already seen in the description of the amputation in *The Unknown*, they often achieved this reaction. Indeed, "Grand Guignol" is a term that crops up in reviews to describe various Browning films.

While Browning is often criticized for the Grand Guignol moments of his films, which are often singled out as singular or, depending on the reviewer, offensive, the implausibility of his plots is also frequently a cause for complaint. A story about Herman J. Mankiewicz's collaboration with Browning is illustrative in this regard. According to this story, Browning related an idea for a Chaney film to Mankiewicz in which Chaney is a surgeon who transplants the heads of apes onto female bodies. Browning's request to Mankiewicz was to provide the narrative rationalization for these images (Dietz 160; qtd. in Skal and Savada 101-102). Browning's version of melodrama is an instance of the Hollywood mode being used to provide the scaffolding upon which to hang moments of spectacle.

A final aspect of Browning's particular mode of melodrama is written in Lon Chaney's face in *The Unknown*. Peter Brooks has written of melodrama that it presents an "aesthetics of embodiment," by which he refers to a specific relation to the body that he sees as first appearing in the French Revolution and then appearing later during the silent era of cinema. This bodiliness is characterized by a body that is "seized with meaning," often in moments that are mute (18). Although Brooks' example from the silent era is D. W. Griffith's *Orphans of the Storm* (1921), he might just as well have been writing about the moment in *The Unknown* when Chaney returns to the circus after the amputation and realizes that Nanon will marry Malabar, the strongman. The reaction shot of Chaney's face after this realization is a remarkable performance; his face slowly registers his anguish through laughter that grows in intensity until it is maniacal and indistinguishable from inconsolable grief. It is a moment not only of male hysteria, but also of muteness since Chaney's character cannot reveal the reason for his grief. When Nanon and Malabar do not recognize the emotion on Chaney's face, the scene becomes an arch instance of dramatic irony. Christine Gledhill has noted that in melodrama "the audience is addressed as witness to a staging," that, in other words, there is, as Bordwell has noted as well, a self-reflexive element to the pay-off moment of melodramatic emotion (141). In this case, the spectator is not duped as the characters are (Nanon's intertitle reads "He's laughing because he's happy"), which is another instance of Browning's peculiar, impeccable classicism.

Notes

[1] These films are representative of Browning's difficulties in adapting to Hollywood's change to sound and other factors, such as studio favoritism and the predations of the Production Code. For accounts of the troubles Browning faced in his later career, see Bret Wood, "The Witch, the Devil and the Code: The History of *The Devil-Doll*: Interferences a Filmmaker Had to Contend with in the Age of the Production Code" (52-56), and David Skal and Elias Savada, *Dark Carnival: The Secret World of Tod Browning, Hollywood's Master of the Macabre* (140-205). For an extensive account of *Dracula*'s production, see David Skal, *Hollywood Gothic: The Tangled Web of* Dracula *from Novel to Stage to Screen*.

[2] For an account of *Freaks*' career as an exploitation film, and a reading of the film that is inflected by its exploitation exhibition context, see Jonathan Rosenbaum and J. Hoberman, *Midnight Movies*.

[3] I have not undertaken archival research for this paper, so I cannot take into account all or even most of Browning's films, especially the first five years of his career (1915-1920) when he made a large number of one- and two-reel films. His films available on video are, to my knowledge, *Outside the Law*

(1920), *White Tiger* (1923), *The Unholy Three* (1925), *The Unknown* (1927), *West of Zanzibar* (1928), *Where East is East* (1929), *Dracula* (1931), *Freaks* (1932), *Mark of the Vampire* (1935), and *The Devil-Doll* (1936). Doc Films of the University of Chicago showed a 35mm MGM archive print of *The Show* (1927) as a part of their Browning series in the spring of 1996. For a complete filmography, albeit without information about availability, see Skal and Savada (231-323).

[4] It is worth mentioning here that Rosenbaum and Hoberman see the film as a revolt of the oppressed against the oppressors (295-296 and 306-307).

Works Cited

Bordwell, David, Janet Staiger, and Kristin Thompson. *The Classical Hollywood Cinema: Film Style and Mode of Production to 1960.* New York: Columbia UP, 1985.

Brooks, Peter. "Melodrama, Body, Revolution." *Melodrama: Stage, Picture, Screen.* Ed. Jacky Bratton, Jim Cook, and Christine Gledhill. London: British Film Institute, 1994. 11-24.

Browning, Tod, dir. *Freaks*. Metro-Goldwyn-Mayer, 1932.

---. *The Unknown*. With Lon Chaney and Joan Crawford. Metro-Goldwyn-Mayer, 1927.

Cucurella, Miquel. "Side Show and Crime Melodrama in the Cinema of Tod Browning." *Focus* 2.1 (Spring 1996): np.

Davidson, Arnold. "The Horror of Monsters." *The Boundaries of Humanity: Humans, Animals, Machines.* Ed. James J. Sheehan and Morton Sosna. Berkeley: U of California P, 1991. 36-67.

Dietz, Howard. *Dancing in the Dark: An Autobiography.* New York: Quadrangle/New York Times Book Co., 1974.

Gledhill, Christine. "Between Melodrama and Realism: Anthony Asquith's *Underground* and King Vidor's *The Crowd*." *Classical Hollywood Narrative: The Paradigm Wars.* Ed. Jane Gains. Durham, NC: Duke UP, 1992. 129-167.

Gunning, Tom. "The Horror of Opacity: The Melodrama of Sensation in the Plays of André de Lorde." *Melodrama: Stage, Picture, Screen.* Ed. Jacky Bratton, Jim Cook, and Christine Gledhill. London: British Film Institute, 1994. 50-61.

Léger, Jean-Marie. "Ni fantastique, ni «normal,»" *L'Avant scene du cinema* 160/61 (July/September 1975): 88-90.

Rosenbaum, Jonathan, and J. Hoberman. *Midnight Movies.* New York: Harper and Row, 1983.

Rosenthal, Stuart. *The Hollywood Professionals: Tod Browning.* New York: A. S. Barnes and Co., 1975.

Skal, David. *Hollywood Gothic: The Tangled Web of* Dracula *from Novel to Stage to Screen.* New York: Norton, 1990.

Skal, David, and Elias Savada. *Dark Carnival: The Secret World of Tod*

Browning, Hollywood's Master of the Macabre. New York: Anchor Books, 1995.

Watts, Richard Jr. "A Glance at Tod Browning, an Original of the Cinema." *New York Herald-Tribune* 20 March 1927: sec. 6, 3.

Wood, Bret. "The Witch, the Devil and the Code: The History of *The Devil Doll*: Interferences a Filmmaker Had to Contend with in the Age of the Production Code." *Film Comment* 28 (November/December 1992): 52-56.

Lost and Found in Translation: The Changing Face of Disability in the Film Adaptations of Hugo's *Notre Dame de Paris: 1482*

Laurie E. Harnick

Between July 27, 1829 and January 14, 1830, Victor Hugo (inspired by an ancient inscription found scratched into the wall of Notre Dame) isolated himself in a small room of his house and, from exactly one bottle of ink, wrote *Notre Dame de Paris: 1482*. Or, at least, this is how the story is told. The melodrama that came to be known as *The Hunchback of Notre Dame* (a title that Hugo detested) was an instant success and the first and successive editions sold quickly in France and abroad. Over the years, the story has been reprinted and adapted many times into many forms: children's books, radio plays, stage plays, teleplays, and films. Generations say they know the story. In fact, they are more likely to remember the Lon Chaney, Charles Laughton, Anthony Quinn, or even the Disney version of the tale. Since 1905, 13 films have been made about the deaf, hunchbacked bellringer of Notre Dame, Quasimodo, and many other films have been influenced by the story. Over time, narrative elements of the story have been altered in interesting ways, characters have changed, and the essence of the story has refocused. In successive versions of the text, there is a movement away from a critical discussion of the Church and toward a philosophy of secular humanism. Notably, Quasimodo assumes a greater narrative importance over time and is transformed from a "monstrously-disabled" victim to a "physically-challenged" but morally, artistically and intellectually superior hero. In this essay, I will explore how the treatment and, coincidentally, the perception of disability has changed over time in selected adaptations of *Notre Dame de Paris: 1482*.

In *Notre Dame de Paris: 1482*, Hugo describes the bellringer as a 19 year old man with

> a tetrahedron nose; horseshoe mouth; a small left eye obscured by red bushy eyebrows; a right eye which disappear[s] completely under an enormous wart; jagged teeth with gaps here and there like the battlements of a fortress; that horny lip, over which one of those teeth protruded like the tusk of an elephant; that forked chin, and, above all, the expression on the whole face, a mixture of malice, astonishment, and sadness . . . . His whole person was a grimace. His enormous head bristled with red hair; between his shoulders was an enormous hump, counterbalanced by a protuberance in front he had a framework of thighs and legs so strangely askew that they could touch only at the knees, and, seen from the front, resembled two sickles joined together at the handles. The feet were huge; the hands monstrous. Yet with all that deformity was a certain fearsome appearance of vigour, agility, and courage; a strange exception to the eternal rule prescribing that strength, like beauty, shall result from harmony . . . . He looked like a giant that had been broken and badly repaired. (51-52)

In the novel, when he is seen by Parisians, Quasimodo is greeted with phrases such as: "Let all the pregnant women beware!," "Oh that hideous ape!," "As wicked as he is ugly," "It's the devil," "He casts spells at us down our chimneys," "Oh that ugly hunchback!," and "That vile creature" (52-53). Clearly, Hugo meant to delineate a character who was monstrous, threatening and brutishly indecipherable. Similarly, early film adaptations of the text portray Quasimodo as a grotesquely dangerous creature albeit one who elicits some degree of sympathy.

The first accessible film[1] based on the novel was made in 1923 and directed by Wallace Worsley. This black and white, silent film starred Lon Chaney as Quasimodo and Patsy Ruth Miller as Esmeralda. In her autobiography, *My Hollywood: When Both of Us Were Young*, Miller relates Chaney's description of his preparation for the part. She describes how, following illustrations from Hugo's novel, Chaney attempted to transform himself into a character who was "hunchbacked, knock-kneed, [with] one eye almost entirely closed by a big wart." According to Miller, Chaney wanted to be "altogether repulsive to look at" in order to "get interest in the Hunchback." He told her, "I must get the deepest sympathy for him [Quasimodo] from my audiences, else he fills my onlookers only with revulsion and disgust" (18). For Chaney, physical deformity signalled revulsion and disgust: only by incurring sympathy for the hunchback did he believe he could circumvent the singular disgust of his appearance.

In one scene in the film, Quasimodo must remain on the pillory after he has been whipped. He is separate and isolated from the citizenry: a spectacle for the jeering crowd. Defying the rabble's cruelty, Esmeralda answers Quasimodo's cries for water and comes to his side. In addition to giving him a drink, she exhibits her concern by covering his bloody frame with a ragged shirt. In attempting to hide the young man's form, Esmeralda reinforces the apparent pressures incumbent on Quasimodo as monster/freak to hide his disfigurement from society. Her kindness is manifested not only in satisfying his thirst but in aiding him to conceal his "offending" disfigurement. Here and throughout the film, Quasimodo is portrayed more as an abused animal than an unjustly punished young man. Extraordinarily hairy, grunting in almost unintelligible phrases, he is slumped over on "all fours." Devastated by the attention of the crowd, he seems more embarrassed by his exposure than enraged about his treatment. In this early rendering of Hugo's hunchback, Chaney emphasizes the monstrous nature of the character and pays scant attention to developing a more complex "inner life" for Quasimodo. Ultimately, the audience feels sympathy for the character in the form of shared embarrassment for his exposure and for the injustice of his cruel treatment.

The next adaptation, made in 1939, was directed by William Dieterle for RKO. In this black and white, sound picture, it is easier to "relate" to Charles Laughton's Quasimodo. One of the reasons for this phenomenon is Quasimodo's ability to communicate orally (1939 is the first sound adaptation of the novel). It is also due, in part, to Laughton's performance, which showcases the hunchback's moral and physical dilemmas. Finally, it is because the narrative in this adaptation tends to emphasize Quasimodo's humanity in the face of cruel and arbitrary prejudice.

In one of the most poignant scenes in the film, Quasimodo is falsely accused of assaulting Esmeralda and is taken before a deaf judge. The magistrate is accustomed to the court politely ignoring his hearing loss. Even in Hugo's text, the narrator tells us that "[i]f it so happened that his infirmity disclosed itself here and there by some incoherent apostrophe or unintelligible question, it passed for profundity with some, for stupidity with others. In either case the honor of the magistracy was upheld, for it is better that a judge be considered imbecile or profound, than deaf" (197). Hugo recognizes that disability (in this world) must be hidden even if that disguise takes the form of ignorance. In the film, when the judge's deafness is found out, he is embarrassed and infuriated by its discovery. He doesn't hear the court clerk telling him that Quasimodo is also deaf and, instead of compassionately lessening the man's sentence, the judge appears as if he has heard further mitigating circumstances and sentences Quasimodo to an extra hour on the pillory. By assigning the extra time, the judge attempts to "distance" himself from the hunchback—the embodiment of disability. As well as the public prejudice he must endure, Quasimodo is also punished by the state for his disability. In 1939, this film once again reinforces the sense that physical disability is both a weakness and a cause for embarrassment. Furthermore, it is made clear that while a physically disabling condition can be possessed by both the "highest" and "lowest" elements of society, it can be experienced quite differently and, often, with brutal consequences. In this adaptation and succeeding versions of the story, there is an increased emphasis on the political and unjust pressures of living the life of a disabled person in medieval Paris.

In 1957, Panitalia/Paris Film Productions released *Notre Dame de Paris*. Directed by Jean Delannoy, it stars Anthony Quinn as Quasimodo and Gina Lollobrigida as Esmeralda. Like Chaney's hunchback, Quinn's Quasimodo is identified as an animal. Not only does Quinn's body language suggest the characteristics of a domesticated animal, he is shot in such a way that the mise en scène, lighting and cinematography each contribute to his bestial identity. In his first scene, Quasimodo/Quinn watches the townspeople from what appears to be a pen. He is surrounded by barnyard animals and eats fruit he finds on the ground. Interestingly, while this film explicitly states it is a faithful retelling of Hugo's story, it alters the focus of Quasimodo's disability. Rather than relying on the physical "business" associated with the hunchback seen in the novel and earlier adaptations, Quinn emphasizes the character's mental deficiencies. Indeed, from this adaptation onward, there is an increased emphasis on Quasimodo's emotional and intellectual condition.

In Hugo's book, the final chapter, "Quasimodo's Marriage," describes how Quasimodo goes to the vault of Montfaucon to find Esmeralda's body and lays beside her. The narrator tells us that when the two skeletons are found intertwined years later and an effort is made to separate them, the bones turned to dust. A drawing in the original French edition of the novel shows a skeleton with an arching spine lying on top of a smaller skeleton. The suggestion is that only in death can Esmeralda and Quasimodo form a physical union. The 1957 adaptation of the novel remains provisionally true to this narrative thread. In this film (and only this film), Esmeralda is hung. Quasimodo/Quinn searches for her body and when he finds it, he lays beside her. This is, however, where any suggestion of a post-mortem union ends. In the film, Quasimodo's love for Esmeralda is chaste and any suggestion of a "marriage" between the two (pre or post-death) is, quite simply, out of the question. While the filmmakers attempt to remain reasonably faithful to the novel, in 1957 there are some suggestions which are still forbidden.

Clearly then, from 1923 to 1957, there is a marked movement in Quasimodo's filmic characterization. From Chaney's silent brute to Laughton's more sympathetic victim to Quinn's animalistic but, ultimately, impotent Quasimodo, the portrayal of the hunchback is evolving to reflect the changing perception of disability in society.

In 1982, Michael Tuchner directed the next adaptation, *Hunchback*, based on Hugo's novel. It stars Lesley-Ann Downes as Esmeralda and Anthony Hopkins as Quasimodo. This film begins a trend that is carried through in later adaptations: that is, forms of compensatory characteristics begin to be substituted for the character's physical disability. In this film, Quasimodo's challenges are counterbalanced by increased physical strength and agility and an increasingly self-conscious heroism. Quasimodo is no longer the brutish character who neither comprehends events around him nor truly understands the ramifications of his place in this society. He is an individual with a specific moral compass and an increasing tendency to act with great self-sacrifice.

In one scene, Quasimodo fights a large group of soldiers in order to free Esmeralda from her impending hanging. More Errol Flynn than Quasimodo, Hopkins leaps with graceful agility from the scaffolded walls of Notre Dame and, fighting the men off, he grabs Esmeralda and climbs the edifice to safety. At the end of the film, he leads Esmeralda and Gringoire to a secret tunnel in Notre Dame and distracts the attacking soldiers while they escape. Finally, trapped and hanging precariously from a stone gargoyle on the face of Notre Dame, Quasimodo falls to the ground and presumably dies, giving his life in order that Esmeralda might live.

In 1995, the first of three animated adaptations was released. In *The Hunchback of Notre Dame*, produced by Goodtimes Entertainment, Quasimodo is explicitly punished by society for his disability. For example, in the court scene, the subtleties of the misunderstanding surrounding the deaf judge's ruling are omitted. In this adaptation, the filmmakers emphasize the gulf between the classes, sympathy is increased for Quasimodo, and a direct correlation is established between disability and inhumane treatment at the hands of the state. The film, clearly made for children, sanitizes the story and creates a simplistic black and white/good and evil adaptation of Hugo's complex novel. In fact, the conclusion is drastically altered to this end and Quasimodo and Esmeralda survive to escape to the French countryside and live happily ever after!

In Disney's 1996 adaptation of the text, there are similar narrative sacrifices in the name of a happy ending. This film, more than any other, exhibits the greatest artistic licence in altering Hugo's novel. In the Preface to Disney's companion novel (with drawings by Disney artists), the editors describe Hugo's narrative as their "point of departure" and, clearly, understand the liberties they take in adapting the story for animation. In Disney's film, Quasimodo is no longer deaf. In fact, he can sing! Physically, his appearance has been infantilized: he has large round eyes, a winsome smile and a boyish quality. He is affectionately called "Quasi" by his make-believe gargoyle friends and rather than feeling resentment for his predicament, he meets his fate with a kind of sad resignation. In the film, his disability is uncomfortable shyness rather than any physical impediment. He is portrayed as a kind-hearted but awkward teenager, the underdog who is insecure and worried about his acceptance by society. Following a pattern established in earlier adaptations, "Quasi" is compensated for his disability: he possesses artistic talent and a fine singing voice. A kind of savant, he makes small figurines of the townspeople of Paris (coincidentally available at gift stores and fast food outlets across the continent). He is not a 19 year old man but a prepubescent boy. This, of course, alleviates the "uncomfortable" dilemma when "Quasi" develops a "crush" on Esmeralda. With this narrative alteration, Disney portrays the boy's feelings as "puppy love" and avoids the more complicated implications of portraying a young disabled man's sexual desire for a beautiful young woman.

Other alterations in Disney's adaptation include a less violent pillory scene in which Quasimodo is not whipped but is simply the target of vegetable-wielding Parisians. In fact, throughout the film, Disney's Quasimodo never inflicts pain on another. Unlike other adaptations where the character kills or is killed, at the end of this film, "Quasi" emerges from the darkness of the Cathedral to the sunny square in front of Notre Dame. He meets a welcoming crowd and receives a hug from a small child. The last shot in the film is one in which the townspeople carry him away on their shoulders and cheer for him, the hero who saved Esmeralda and foiled the evil Frollo. In the end, he is not only "one of them": fully accepted by the society around him, his shyness and fear of rejection have been replaced with a heroic sense of purpose.

Perhaps one of the most interesting diversions from Hugo's characterization of Quasimodo occurs in the latest 1997 telefilm adaptation. In this film, starring Mandy Patinkin as Quasimodo and Salma Hayek as Esmeralda, Quasimodo is an accomplished intellect who (like Frankenstein's monster) reads texts such as Plutarch's *Lives* and Cicero. He has a fine sense of aesthetics and there is virtually no emphasis on the character's sexuality: his most passionate love is reserved for knowledge and his "fellow man." In this film, Frollo is an evil, morally-depraved character "disabled" by murderous intentions and his desires for Esmeralda. Esmeralda is "disabled" by her illiteracy: this is exemplified in a scene where she confesses that she has never even seen a book and cannot read. In contrast, Quasimodo is a prodigious reader (having read the entire library of Notre Dame) and writer (writing a book that will be over 600 pages long) and is adept at using the printing press to publish his political tracts. While the "King of the Gypsies," Clopin, says that "we can't get involved," Quasimodo takes action and reacts against injustice. He is not the "overcomer" of Disney's film. In this adaptation, Quasimodo is politicized and assumes a heightened degree of individuality and personal power. He not only understands the inequities of his own situation, he calls the citizens of Paris to arms in defense of individual freedom and against the arbitrary capture and imprisonment of "enemies" of the state. It is interesting that in this adaptation, the printing press (advanced technology in the late 14th century) assumes the role of mechanical facilitation. That is, it is the modern equipment that aids a disabled man to communicate with others without the attendant prejudice related to his appearance or speech patterns.

While, like Chaney, Patinkin's Quasimodo is embarrassed by his physical appearance (indeed, he is thankful to Claude Frollo for "taking him out of the sight of man"), he engenders a greater degree of identification with the audience than has been seen in previous adaptations. In this film, Quasimodo is not only extremely intelligent and articulate, the viewer is encouraged to get "inside" him to a previously inaccessible place. Cinematically, there are more close-ups of Quasimodo combined with point-of-view shots. For example, when he is whipped, the viewer not only identifies with Quasimodo's pain and sense of injustice, she shares the responsibility for the infliction of the abuse. When Patinkin/Quasimodo gazes into the camera, the viewer experiences a sense of shame for the physical and emotional mistreatment the character must endure. This tension, the simultaneous shared pain and guilt, contributes to Quasimodo's heightened status as a martyr. When he tells Esmeralda about his parents, he says he forgives them for abandoning him. Later in the film, he also forgives the murderous deeds of his "father," Frollo. Enduring cruelty and forgiving his persecutors, he increasingly assumes the mantle of a kind of Christ-figure, forgiving the worst and expecting the best.

The final scene of the film is a particularly compelling instance of Quasimodo's deification. Shot from an overhead camera, a mortally-injured Quasimodo lies in an upper room of Notre Dame. While he is lying down, the high angle of the shot makes him appear as if he is hanging upon a cross. His head rests on the books that have enriched his life but that have, in the end, failed him. Candlelight burns around him and gargoyles stand in silent prayer. It seems his bed is both a cross and an altar and he is the sacrifice. While it is a moving scene, there is also a sense that death will be his reward: his freedom from the earthly pain, cruelty and misunderstanding he has always had to endure. With his final breaths, he calls to one of the bells, "Marie!," and then he dies.

More than any other adaptation, this film celebrates Quasimodo's life and death. With this treatment of the hunchback, the movement in film from monster to saint is complete. Ninety-four years after the first film adaptation and 168 years after the first edition of Hugo's book, Quasimodo has evolved into an entirely different character. The perception and portrayal of Quasimodo, the one-named character permanently identified with disability, is no longer the figure imagined by Victor Hugo in 1831. Hugo's story, which dealt with Notre Dame, religion, politics, technology, the freedom and threat of secular power, racism, etc., has become the story of one character. By 1997, the film is a morality play that highlights Quasimodo's physical, social, and psychological predicament. In apology for his abuse, there is increasing compensation: he is refined, heroic . . . a savior.

In examining the film adaptations of Hugo's *Notre Dame de Paris: 1482* and their relationship to the original text and each other, I continue to discover how changes to the narrative are often barometers of their time, reflections of changing perceptions and contemporary historical, cultural, and sociological influences. While disability remains the site of/for punishment in this story, newer films (particularly post-1980) attempt to compensate for this inequity and Quasimodo, increasingly, becomes a martyr, a figure of admiration and sympathy.

Notes

[1] Earlier adaptations of the novel include films made in 1905 (*La Esmeralda*), 1911 (*The Hunchback of Notre Dame*), and 1917 (*The Darling of Paris*). To date, I have been unable to obtain copies of these films.

Works Cited

Hugo, Victor. *The Hunchback of Notre Dame*. New York: Hyperion, 1996.
Medak, Peter, dir. *Hunchback*. With Mandy Patinkin, Salma Hayek, and Richard Harris. TriStar Television, 1997.
Miller, Patsy Ruth. *My Hollywood: When Both of Us Were Young*. West Hanover, Mass.: O'Raghailligh Ltd., 1988.

Disability as Trauma, Mental Illness, and Dysfunction in Post-Vietnam Cinema

Trapped in the Affection-Image: Hollywood's Post-Traumatic Cycle (1970-1976)

Christian Keathley

It has long been commonplace to talk about many American films of the late 1960s and early 1970s as being *about* or *in response to* the Vietnam experience. Even during those years, this seemed to be the case. Asked in a 1972 interview about the curious absence of any films about the Vietnam war, Pauline Kael replied, "Vietnam we experience indirectly in just about every movie we go to. It's one of the reasons we've had so little romance or comedy—because we're all tied up in knots about that rotten war" (Lerman 36).[1] Though any number of films from this period may be discussed in relation to Vietnam, I would like to focus here on a group of deeply pessimistic Hollywood films from the first half of the 1970s (see appended list)—a group that may be dubbed the "post-traumatic cycle," a term I will explain shortly. It is this cycle, I want to suggest, that stands most clearly as America's first round of Vietnam films. Although none is set in and only a few make explicit reference to that war, these films represent and replay, in a displaced fashion, the Vietnam war's defining experience: the onset of trauma resulting from a realization of powerlessness in the face of a world whose systems of organization—both moral and political—have broken down. Or, to use a different set of terms, this cycle of films exemplifies what Gilles Deleuze has described as a "crisis of the action-image."

The Crisis of the Action-Image

In his two volume study—*Cinema 1: The Movement-Image* and *Cinema 2: The Time-Image*—Deleuze borrows the concepts of movement and time articulated by Henri Bergson in *Matter and Memory* and applies them to the history of cinema, developing as he does a typology of images and signs. From this typology, he concludes that, for the first half of its existence (and in most of its product since), the cinema has been content to reproduce human perception of movement; and its plots have largely been driven by movement's corollary: *action*. But, Deleuze argues, at certain points in history, the schema for perception processing was thrown into a state of crisis—thus producing a crisis in cinematic representation. To understand the nature of this crisis, it is necessary to review what Deleuze (via Bergson) defined as the three primary image components of the sensory motor schema: the perception-image, the affection-image, and the action-image. Though it is perhaps something of an oversimplification, one can understand these three components as analogous to the shot sequence in Kuleshovian montage: 1) we see a person looking; 2) we see what he's looking at (perception-image); 3) we see his reaction (affection-image); and this reaction leads him to take some action (action-image). Though he is quick to point out that an individual film shot may include two or even three of these different "images," Deleuze emphasizes that the classical American cinema, which was above all a cinema of action, operated primarily according to the three alternating components of this schema, tightly linking character, narrative, and film form into a standardized sequence. Deleuze summarizes the emergence of the crisis in cinema's representation of this perceptual schema in the following way:

> The cinema of action depicts sensory-motor situations: there are characters, in a certain situation, who act . . . according to how they perceive the situation. Actions are linked to perceptions, and perceptions develop into actions. Now, suppose a character finds himself in a situation, however ordinary or extraordinary, that's beyond any possible action, or to which he can't react. It's too powerful, or too painful, or too beautiful. The sensory motor link's broken. ("On *The Movement-Image*" 51)

It is not that the above described three-shot sequence disappears in post-action-image cinema (though it may indeed become more rare), but rather that the active cause-and-effect chain it implies is disrupted. Broadly speaking, the cinema practice that emerged from the first of these crises was post-WWII European art cinema. As Deleuze explains, for the filmmakers of Italian neo-realism and for many others who followed, the crisis of the action-image marked an *opportunity* that they saw and exploited for an alternative concept of the image. In both style and narrative, post-war European art cinema opened the interval between perception and action—what Bergson referred to as the "interval of thought"—to explore a cinema predicated not on action, but on the possibilities inherent in the interval *between* perception and action. That is, art cinema privileges, expands, and explores the affection-image.

David Bordwell has grouped the formal and narrative characteristics of art cinema under two broad headings: *realism* and *authorial expressivity*. The characteristics of realism include: characters who lack clearly defined goals and thus slide passively from one situation to another; a cause-and-effect narrative structure whose looseness opens space for digressions into "contingent daily reality" or the "subjective reality" of the film's complex characters; and a preoccupation with the conditions—moral and philosophical—of modern life (58-59). Authorial expressivity refers to this film practice's "recurrent violations of the classical norm" of Hollywood filmmaking—that is, the use of formal strategies that call the viewer's attention to the fact that there is a guiding subjectivity behind the construction and arrangement of what they are watching (59-60). One film that is crucial in initiating the strong realist strain in post-war filmmaking is Roberto Rossellini's *Germany Year Zero* (1947). Set in the rubble of that recently defeated nation, the film centers on a young boy, Edmund, who struggles to survive in miserable conditions along with his ailing father, his older sister, and an older brother, a former Nazi who is unable to provide for the family's needs. Edmund, doing whatever he can to help his family, is ultimately led by the advice his former Nazi schoolteacher into poisoning his father. The final act of the film, during which Edmund realizes the enormity of his act, consists of the boy wandering the streets and abandoned buildings of the city; finally, Edmund throws himself out a window and is killed. Deleuze, echoing Bazin, focuses on the "dispersive, elliptical, errant" quality of the film's narrative, especially this final section, which consists of "deliberately weak connections and floating events" (*Cinema 2* 1). He further characterizes Rossellini's immediate postwar films as representative of the crisis of the action-image, as well as pointing to its beyond: "This is a cinema of the seer and no longer of the agent" (2).

Though it is commonly the norm against which art cinema is defined, Hollywood, too, enjoyed a brief period when a surprising number of its films incorporated, in a somewhat diluted form, the formal and thematic characteristics of art cinema. The cultural circumstances of that moment—the late 1960s and early 1970s—further identify Hollywood's art cinema practice as being a response to crisis. Deleuze argues that, in its initial appearance, the crisis of the action-image was precipitated by the host nation's recent *historical* crisis—specifically, the traumatic experience of war. After World War II, Deleuze explains, Italy found itself in a unique situation: as neither victor nor vanquished, that nation saw clearly defining extremes such as those fall away in the face of deep ambiguity. This crisis provoked an interrogation of the established ways of conceiving of and representing the world, especially in the cinema. It was the historical trauma of the Vietnam war which, along with other factors but more so than any of them, provoked American cinema's encounter with a crisis of the action-image.[2]

There is, however, an important distinction to be made between the European and American filmic expressions of this crisis. While Hollywood cinema could face the crisis of the action-image, it could never fully engage with the alternative practice that European cinema did. Indeed, in the six pages of *Cinema 1* in which Deleuze defines the crisis of the action-image, he cites over a dozen films, all but a couple of which are American films from these years. The point here is that, for Deleuze, much American cinema of this period exemplifies the crisis of the action-image without also exemplifying the alternative that European art cinema discovered. Instead, Hollywood represented the opening up of the interval between perception and action as a traumatic event. Further, the perception to which the characters in these films are unable to respond is always the same, for the films of the post-traumatic cycle repeatedly lead their protagonists to the same end: the realization of their total powerlessness.

The Post-Traumatic Cycle

In spite of their status as reasonably budgeted, studio-backed films featuring major stars of the period (Jack Nicholson, Warren Beatty, Gene Hackman) and intended for mainstream distribution and exhibition, the movies of the post-traumatic cycle evince what Robin Wood has called a "major defining factor of Hollywood cinema of the late 60s and 70s": the "breakdown of ideological confidence in American culture and values" (23). This breakdown of confidence, however, was reflected in the cinema of this period in two stages. As David Thomson explains, many of the "naive and liberal revolutionary notions" that had focused the optimistic energy of the counter-culture movement of the 1960s were, in the first half of the 1970s, "confounded by actual experiences" that revealed "the moral bankruptcy of the established order" (45). Along with numerous other "actual experiences," but more powerfully than any of them, America's lengthy involvement in the war in Vietnam, and the impingement of that experience on the national consciousness served as the focus point for this breakdown of confidence. While in the 1960s, the heady energy of college campus protest had been reflected in the counter-culture cycle (see appended list), by the early 1970s, the trauma suffered by soldiers in Vietnam, then by the nation as a whole, was reflected in this second cycle of films whose heroes, like the heroes of Vietnam, are manipulated, exploited, and left paralyzed by the realization of their powerlessness in the face of a corrupt system. The overwhelming feelings of disaffection, alienation, and demoralization that permeate these films are, in a sense, a displaced repetition of the intense trauma suffered by the Vietnam generation.

While there is no neat match between this cycle and any given genre, or any given director's entire output during the period, Robert Altman's films during these years come closest to exemplifying this trend. Robin Wood's description of the "most consistent and recurrent pattern in Altman's films" serves also to describe most films of the post-traumatic cycle: "The protagonist embarks on an undertaking he is confident he can control; the sense of control is progressively revealed as illusory; the protagonist is trapped in a course of events that culminate in disaster (frequently death)" (31). In fact, while the counter-culture films of the late '60s regularly ended with their protagonists' martyrdom (think of *Bonnie and Clyde* [1967], *Easy Rider* [1969], etc.), these films often leave their protagonists not dead, but rather wounded and helpless, disconnected from their surroundings, often muttering to themselves in a catatonic, traumatized state. In Deleuze's schema, this traumatic realization registers as each of the characters finds himself trapped between perception and action in the affection-image. That is, each film concludes with its protagonist literally trapped in a reaction shot that shows not only his devastation at what he has perceived, but also his paralysis as he is unable to respond to it. "The situation [that the protagonist] is in outstrips his motor capacities on all sides, and makes him see and hear what is no longer subject to the rules of a response or an action," Deleuze writes. "He records rather than reacts" (*Cinema 2* 3). As the affection-image finds its purest expression in the face (*Cinema 1* 66), so it is that these films end on a close-up of the protagonist as he registers the full horror of what he is perceiving and of the realization of his own inability to act in response. Two examples:

In *The Candidate* (1972), Bill McKay, an idealistic young lawyer, is encouraged to run for Senator against an unbeatable conservative incumbent. Because he has no chance of winning, McKay is told by his advisors that he needn't follow traditional political standards; he can say whatever he wants, thus bringing attention to the issues he feels need it. As the campaign continues and McKay's popularity grows, he gradually loses this autonomy and begins to succumb to the political system he sought to challenge. Confirmation of this loss of power comes at the film's end when, having scored an upset victory, McKay retreats to a hotel room with his campaign manager and appeals in a stunned voice, "What do we do now?"

In *Chinatown* (1974), private detective Jake Gittes wants to find out not only who killed waterworks engineer Hollis Mulwray, but also who paid a woman to pose as Mulwray's wife and hire Gittes, thus initiating the events that led to Mulwray's death. At the film's conclusion, Jake not only sees his mistress and client, the fragile Evelyn Mulwray, gunned down by police; he is also (again) forced to confront the fact that, in spite of his best and most honorable intentions, he is powerless to help the innocent or bring the guilty to justice. The film's title refers not only to the protagonist's past and his haunted state of mind, but to a world in which "order" is determined by the rich and powerful, regardless of how corrupt they may be. Jake's blank stare and barely audible muttering ("as little as possible") remind us of the warnings that he has repeatedly received: that his power and authority are limited, and that any attempt to exercise what he has inappropriately, especially on moral grounds, will result in complete emasculation.

I am using the term "post-traumatic" here not only because it accurately describes the experience reflected in this cycle of films, but because it was through research and work with mentally and emotionally scarred Vietnam veterans that psychologists came to a more complex and subtle understanding of the condition that had traditionally been called "shell shock." The resulting diagnostic term, "post-traumatic stress disorder" (PTSD), was soon applied not only to those who had experienced battle, but was also used to describe the clinical condition suffered by anyone who exhibits a specific set of symptoms as the result of some intense experience outside normal life patterns (e.g., child or spousal abuse, rape, natural disasters, accidents resulting in serious injury or death). Such a traumatic event might be generally understood as a sudden and violent disruption of the order that defines regular experience of the world and, more importantly, the values (ethical, moral, political) that are taken for granted to lie firmly at the basis of this order.[3] This clinical description of PTSD divides trauma into two categories: the first has to do with a traumatic event that might be described as arbitrary—a random "act of God" event such as a natural disaster or sudden death; the second and often more serious kind of trauma results from betrayal by persons or institutions in positions of authority—that is, those with whom the rules of order are generally associated.

Furthermore, Judith Lewis Herman, a psychiatrist who has conducted comprehensive work on the effects of trauma, has argued that the experience of trauma is not limited individuals; indeed, entire cultures and societies can suffer this tragedy. But if, as Lévi-Strauss has put it, a culture's ideological conflicts regularly find expression and resolution in its myths, the films of the post-traumatic cycle are a unique exception, for they refuse to offer the reassurance of such reconciliation; in this way, they work a complex variation on classical Hollywood cinema's dominant thematic paradigm—a paradigm that, as Robert Ray has argued, seeks to conceal the necessity for choice as a prerequisite to action (70-88). Instead, Andrew Britton has argued that, reflecting the Vietnam experience as they do, films of this period give "evidence of the meaninglessness and ineffectuality of choice" ("Sideshows" 6). That is, these films first foreground the apparent necessity of choice or feature protagonists who believe in the existential responsibility an individual has to make choices (especially moral choices); but they then undercut this notion, showing instead that the privileging of choice implies the opportunity of the individual to gain power and self-determination—something these films reveal to be an impossibility. In *The Conversation* (1974), wiretapper Harry Caul acts initially as a pure professional, interested only in getting a perfect surreptitious recording; but when he suspects that his recording will result in the murder of two people, he takes a stand, refusing to hand over the secret tapes to his client, a wealthy and secretive businessman. This resolve costs Harry and the tables are turned: a murder is committed (not the one he expected), and he becomes the victim of a surveillance that shatters his closely guarded and controlled privacy.

An important characteristic of these films is that their heroes exist in a middle position between the "official hero" and "outlaw hero" positions favored by classical cinema (Ray 58-59). While the films of the counter-culture cycle favored outlaw heroes (*Bonnie and Clyde*, *Butch Cassidy and the Sundance Kind* [1969], etc.), the protagonists of the post-traumatic cycle films are usually marginal establishment figures. For example, although McCabe in *McCabe and Mrs. Miller* (1971) and Charlie in *Mean Streets* (1974) trade in vice and/or have connections to organized crime, both consider themselves businessmen, as are, in a more legitimate way, the men in *Deliverance* (1972). Buddusky in *The Last Detail* (1973) is an unambitious career Navy man; Bobby Dupea in *Five Easy Pieces* (1970) is an oil worker. But the representative figure here is the private investigator, of which there are several in the post-traumatic cycle: Jake Gittes in *Chinatown*, Philip Marlowe in *The Long Goodbye* (1973), Harry Moseby in *Night Moves* (1975), Joe Frady in *The Parallax View* (1974). As unofficial lawman, the investigator identifies himself as being committed to upholding the law, while at the same time residing outside of, and often having a somewhat antagonistic relationship with, its official institutions. While most of these figures do not directly challenge the established system as the figures of the counter-culture cycle did, all are at least partly alienated from it. Nevertheless, each pays this established order—and, more importantly, the values that order represents—a measure of respect, and he assumes that it will do the same for him. This faith is the basis of each man's downfall. Each naively assumes that the combination of his own competence and the larger moral order will not permit any real harm to come to him or those close to him.

Just as these films' narrative, character, and thematic similarities can be understood in terms of art cinema's preoccupation with realism and the conditions of modern life, many of these films also possess certain similar formal and stylistic characteristics that can be understood as authorial expressivity. Rather than employing classic Hollywood's "invisible style," these films use overt stylistic and technical devices—telephoto lenses, zooms, unmotivated pans, oblique camera set-ups, complex editing patterns of both image and sound—all to create a look which is simultaneously more naturalistic and more stylized than dominant cinema's norm. That is, on the one hand, the films often employ the formal codes associated with documentary filmmaking that were disseminated largely by television news; at the time, these codes functioned quite powerfully to evoke an almost wholly unmediated representation of reality, much like Americans encountered in nightly news coverage of Vietnam. On the other hand, the films often also reflect the complex, contradictory, fragmented nature of accounts of trauma regularly offered by those who have suffered it (Herman 1). The opening of *The Parallax View* is a clear example. The cluttered, uncentered shots showing an Independence Day parade, the arrival of a political candidate (who will soon be assassinated), and his interview by a television reporter combine the documentary qualities of television reporting with the formal rigor and complexity of a formalist art cinema. This formal approach is used to comment on the complex nature of perception, particularly in a world where the moral and political landscape that once was so clear has turned opaque, and any misperception can be fatal. Perhaps more than any group of films in Hollywood's history, these films demand a measure of work from the audience; that is, crucial plot and character information is not always underscored, but is rather hidden in an ambiguous world that the viewer, like the protagonists themselves, must attend to with great effort and care.

For the most part, recent film historians have downplayed whatever differences exist between these films of the early 1970s and the films of Hollywood's classical period. For example, in their mammoth study, *The Classical Hollywood Cinema: Film Style and Mode of Production to 1960*, Bordwell, Staiger, and Thompson describe the period since 1960 as marking "the persistence of a mode of film practice" that is commonly called "classical" (367-377). Similarly, in *A Certain Tendency of the Hollywood Cinema, 1930-1980*, Robert B. Ray writes that "the majority of American movies of the 1970s were remarkably similar to those of the 1930s" (68). One exception to this position can be found in Thomas Elsaesser's 1975 essay, "The Pathos of Failure: American Films in the 70s." What is remarkable about this too-little-known piece is not only its perceptive analysis of films in the historical moment, so to speak, but also because it anticipates, in extraordinary ways, Deleuze's discussion of the crisis of the action-image.

In attempting to specify the difference of so many films of this period from their classical predecessors, Elsaesser begins by defining the primary narrative and thematic characteristic of classical cinema. He, like Deleuze, notes that those films, marked by an "implicit causality,"

> were essentially based on a drama of intrigue and strongly accentuated plot, which managed to transform spatial and temporal sequence into consequence, a continuum of cause and effect . . . . Out of conflict, contradiction and contingency the narrative generated order, linearity, and articulated energy . . . . Contradictions were resolved and obstacles overcome by having them played out in dramatic-dynamic terms or by personal initiative: whatever the problem, one can *do* something about it. (13-14)

This schema, which Elsaesser dubs "the affirmative-consequential model," seems to run into problems by the late 1960s, and by the early 1970s, its inversion is underway. Instead of sure, active characters, we get characters who are motiveless or have their motives taken from them and revealed as folly; further, the presentation of the plots in which these characters find themselves "neutralizes goal-directedness and warns one not to expect an affirmation of purposes and meanings" (14). The result is films that, when considered within the history of mainstream or dominant cinema, reveal a certain "experimental" quality (13). Like Deleuze, Elsaesser links the tone and mood of these films to the cultural crisis of the period. Directors of this era, he writes, "opt for a kind of realism of sentiment that tries to be faithful to the negative experiences of [then] recent American history, and the movies reflect the moral and emotional gestures of a defeated generation," foregrounding as they do "the pathos of failure" (17-18).

The fragmented, often oblique style of these films—which Elsaessser sees as symptoms of a "fading confidence in being able to tell a story" (13)—can be linked to trauma in an important way. In "The Modernist Event," Hayden White argues that certain of this century's key events—the Holocaust, the Kennedy assassination, the Vietnam experience—are traumatic occurrences that outstrip the representational capacities of classical or "realist" historiographic practice. Those events "bear little similarity to what earlier historians took as their objects of study and do not, therefore, lend themselves to understanding by the commonsensical techniques utilized in conventional historiographic inquiry nor even to the representation by the techniques of writing typically favored by . . . traditional humanistic historiography" (21). Such events mark the limits and the beyond of the realist discourse that relies on continuity, cause-and-effect, and agency to emplot the events of history. Instead, White argues, such traumatic historical events demand a modernist style of representation, for the formal strategies of fragmentation, discontinuity, chance, and incoherence that are common to modernism are also the characteristics that mark one's experience of a traumatic event. The filmmakers of the post-traumatic cycle seem to have intuited this necessity, for although on the one hand their films reside well within the limits of a realist storytelling practice, on the other hand, they employ modernist formal devices to show that realist practice as strained to the breaking point in even its most sincere attempts to contain the stories of trauma that they offer.

The tragedy of the protagonists of the post-traumatic cycle is, again, that they fail to see this state of affairs that everyone else seems to ignore or already take for granted. Repeatedly, the protagonists are warned that their actions are determined by an archaic set of codes, and that continuing will be fruitless. When, in *The Parallax View*, conspiracy theorist Joe Frady assures the campaign manager of a recently assassinated politician that he "knows the story," the man rebukes him, "Fella, you don't know what this story means." A similar warning is given to Jake Gittes in *Chinatown*: "You may think you know what you're dealing with," Noah Cross tells the private detective, "but believe me, you don't." What the protagonist does not see is that the power of the perpetrator is so great that he alone has the ability to determine what counts as reality, and he can easily discredit any implicating evidence the protagonist might offer (Herman 8). Inevitably, the protagonists ignore the warnings, and their stubborn insistence leads them to that horrible moment when they are faced with the tragic results of their own actions. Refusing as they do to return their characters to the state of quiescence with which they began, the films of the post-traumatic cycle instead leave their characters trapped between perception and action in what Deleuze also called "the centre of indetermination" (*Cinema 1* 65).

A Series of Cycles

To more fully define the characteristics of the films of the post-traumatic cycle, it is helpful to see them in relation to the cycles of films that cluster around them. Various scholars have discussed Hollywood films of this period as being marked by broad "right" and "left" cycles that reflect the ideological polarization that existed in culture at large. Following the counter-culture films of the late 1960s, the post-traumatic cycle clearly stands as the second movement of a key group of left-oriented films (Ray).

On the right, both the nostalgia and disaster cycles sought to offer the ideological reassurance typical of classical Hollywood by featuring films that were either literally or figuratively set before the period of crisis. *American Graffiti* (1973), a film that provoked an extraordinary wave of 1950s nostalgia in the U.S., is set during the earliest days of America's involvement in Vietnam, but it makes no mention of that conflict, save for a cameo at the film's end explaining that one of its protagonists later perished there. Perhaps more than any other in the movie, that closing moment underscores the film's longing for a supposedly simpler time, one associated not only with adolescence, but also one whose future would be bright and fulfilling rather than needlessly wasted. Other nostalgia films offered reassurance by evoking not a historical past so much as a movie past. For example, at a time when films like *The Wild Bunch* (1969) and *Butch Cassidy and the Sundance Kid* were interrogating that most cherished of American myths, the story of the old west, *True Grit* (1969) offered cinema's most recognized and respected cowboy, John Wayne, in his most famous recurring role: as a lawman looking out for respectable folks (Kim Darby as a girl hunting her father's killer) and punishing society's disrespectful, disruptive element (among others, Dennis Hopper, who had starred in and directed *Easy Rider* that same year). In films like *The Towering Inferno* (1974), the disaster cycle also acknowledged society's disruptive element, but did so indirectly, displacing it onto nature; further, those films functioned as sort of reassuring public service announcements, for they suggested that the crisis was still to come and that, if we worked together and prepared, it could all be managed or even averted.[4]

The fascist cop films were those right cycle films that most explicitly staged the ideological conflict in American culture at the time. Like the left cycle films of this period, *Death Wish* (1974) and

Dirty Harry (1971) diagnosed American society as diseased and corrupt, but saw radical liberalism as the problem. What is foregrounded in these films is not a system that is controlled capriciously by a powerful, privileged few, but one that is undone by the legal restrictions placed on law enforcement to protect society, thus rendering police impotent and criminals empowered. As the inverse of the counter-culture cycle of films, the fascist cop movies, too, suggest that the only position of agency available is one outside of existing institutions; but they further show that any such actions are limited in time and scope, for they lack the societal support that would allow them to be extended and to have lasting impact. These films can also be read as Vietnam allegories, for they portray the political right's exasperation at a military involvement marked at every turn by rules and regulations of engagement which implicitly restrict the possibility of success.

The exceptional quality of the films of the post-traumatic cycle becomes even clearer when they are contrasted with the two major film cycles which follow: the Vietnam and blockbuster cycles. If the post-traumatic cycle replays the loss of confidence in American culture and values precipitated by our involvement in Vietnam, then the Vietnam and blockbuster cycles represent a rebuilding, in very different ways, of this lost confidence. Around 1978, the first films to explicitly address the subject of Vietnam began to appear. In films such as *The Deer Hunter* (1978) and *Coming Home* (1978), Hollywood began to directly explore the experience of the Vietnam soldier, both in combat and upon his difficult reentry into American life and culture. While the post-traumatic films can be said to be a replaying or recollection of the process *leading to* the traumatic event, these films represent a more obvious *working through* of the Vietnam trauma. Also, while the post-traumatic films end at the point of trauma, many of the Vietnam films dramatize and attempt to formally represent the symptoms that result from such a trauma: flashbacks, sleeplessness, feelings of guilt, hyper-alertness and hyper-vigilance, memory and concentration problems, and so on.[5]

Around this same time, a group of blockbuster films began to emerge that represent a denial of the trauma the nation had suffered. In fact, these films are in many ways a direct inversion of the post-traumatic films. Rather than heroes who are competent and confident, blockbuster films such as *Rocky* (1976) and *Star Wars* (1977) feature protagonists who are, at the outset, ambitious but uncertain of their abilities; but as the film goes on and they are challenged, they learn that they are indeed competent and able to effect some positive change—that is, to take some decisive, productive *action* in response to what they perceive. The film which is the most obvious turning point into this trend is *Jaws* (1975), a movie which is one of the versions of what Robert Torry calls "therapeutic narrative": an attempt to "diagnose and propose a remedy for the national trauma of the Vietnam era" (27). *Jaws* begins like a post-traumatic film, featuring a protagonist who is, though morally strong, naive with regard to the forces that would seek to control him and determine his actions. When the waters off the small Long Island resort town of Amity are set on by a killer shark, the first instincts of its Sheriff Brody are to protect his citizenry by closing the beaches until the shark is caught. But the mayor and the town council, representing the business interests of the town who are concerned about losing crucial summertime revenue, thwart Brody's honorable efforts at every turn. Ultimately, however, the blockbuster mentality takes over: the deaths continue, the townspeople rebel, and the once sea-fearing sheriff is able to gather his wits and defeat the meance.

As Andrew Britton notes, following the pessimism of the post-traumatic cycle as it does, "*Jaws* might best be described, perhaps, as a rite—a communal exorcism, a ceremony for the restoration of ideological confidence" ("*Jaws*" 27). This move is part of a larger movement in the history of Hollywood cinema that Britton has dubbed "Reaganite entertainment"—a reactionary, conservative cycle of films whose primary functions are repression and reassurance ("Blissing Out"). Further, the films of the blockbuster cycle return to the dominant formal style of Hollywood, underscoring all important narrative components via lighting, camera placement, sound, and editing. These movies present a Manichean world in which good and evil, dangers and safety are always clear, and whatever moral or ethical ambiguities exist are ultimately sorted out.

Though the blockbuster mentality came to dominate Hollywood filmmaking in the late 1970s and beyond, the post-traumatic cycle enjoyed a brief, if commercially disastrous, reprise in the early 1980s. *Blow Out* (1981) and *Winter Kills* (1979), for example, replay some of the post-traumatic cycle's primary themes, but it is Michael Cimino's *Heaven's Gate* (1981) that stands most obviously as the cycle's coda. It seems likely that much of the negative press that greeted *Heaven's Gate* on its release was due, in part, to the fact that the film revisited themes that many viewers and critics simply no longer wanted to face.

The blockbuster cycle was well underway, and there was every initial indication that Cimino's film would participate in the cultural rebuilding of American ideological confidence. First of all, Cimino had already directed the most honored of the Vietnam films, *The Deer Hunter*, and *Heaven's Gate*'s reclaiming of the Western, a genre crucial to the American cinematic mythos but for some time in disrepute, seemed to signal that Cimino's would be a rebuilding of lost confidence. Further, although *The Deer Hunter* possessed some of the characteristics of the post-traumatic cycle, its ending, in which a group of surviving Vietnam veterans and their loved ones sit around a table at their local bar and sing a fragile, tear-stained version of "God Bless America," was ambiguous enough (controversially so) to provide its audience with a measure of reassurance.

But it's hard to imagine a less reassuring Hollywood film than *Heaven's Gate*. Indeed, the story replays the pessimistic theme of the darkest films of the post-traumatic cycle. Set in Johnson County, Wyoming, in the late 1800s, where starving immigrants are forced to steal cattle in order to feed their families, *Heaven's Gate* focuses on the efforts of the local marshall, Jim Averill (Kris Kristofferson), to protect these settlers from the cattle baron Canton (Sam Waterston), who, with the approval of the state government, has drawn up a "death list" bearing the names of suspected rustlers who his bounty hunters will kill. Averill's efforts are, of course, unsuccessful, not only because the government is so thoroughly sided with the interests of big business, but also because of the failure of the members of the threatened community to come together to protect themselves. Instead, they mimic the forces threatening them and concern themselves primarily with individual, rather than collective, self-interest.

In an eloquent and convincing defense of the film, Robin Wood writes that, like the earlier films of the post-traumatic cycle, "*Heaven's Gate* is an epic about failure and catastrophe . . . . It shows the destruction of a possible alternative America (one located in the historic past, but bearing in its values striking resemblance to the radical movement of the 60s and 70s)" (316). Further, Wood notes that the hostile reaction to the film took two forms: "the objection was that the narrative was so muddled that it verged on the incomprehensible, and a vague, troubled murmur about Marxist content (liberal anxiety being by no means aroused exclusively by the *right* wing)" (299-300). These are, indeed, two of the key characteristics of the films of the post-traumatic cycle: complex narrative/representational strategies and a thematic discontent with the dominant order that could best be described as leftist. Further, the film has the standard post-traumatic ending: for the epilogue, the film moves forward some twenty years to a scene in which the wealthy, aging protagonist—the former Wyoming lawman—sits aboard his yacht. He is distant, disengaged, morose, lost in a haze—still trapped between perception and action, still traumatized by his inability to act.

Counter-Culture Cycle	Nostalgia, Vigilante Cop & Disaster Cycles	Post-Traumatic Cycle	Blockbuster & Vietnam Cycles	Post-Traumatic Cycle: Coda
1967-69	1969-75	1970-76	1975-80	1980
Bonnie and Clyde	*True Grit*	*Five Easy Pieces*	*Jaws*	*Winter Kills*
Easy Rider	*Patton*	*McCabe & Mrs Miller*	*Rocky*	*Blow Out*
The Graduate	*Nicholas & Alexandra*	*The Candidate*	*Star Wars*	*Heaven's Gate*
Cool Hand Luke	*American Graffiti*	*Deliverance*	*Close Encounters*	
Butch Cassidy & The Sundance Kid		*The Long Goodbye*	*The Boys in Company C*	
The Wild Bunch	*Death Wish*	*Mean Streets*	*Go Tell the Spartans*	
M*A*S*H	*Dirty Harry*	*The Sugarland Express*	*The Deer Hunter*	
Catch-22	*The French Connection*	*The Conversation*	*Coming Home*	
Alice's Restaurant		*Chinatown*	*Who'll Stop the Rain*	
	Airport	*The Parallax View*	*Apocalypse Now*	
	The Poseidon Adventure	*California Split*	*First Blood*	
	The Towering Inferno	*Night Moves*		
	Earthquake	*Dog Day Afternoon*		
		Shampoo		

Notes

[1] For a discussion of the curious absence of Vietnam films during the years of the war, see Julian Smith's book *Looking Away: Hollywood and Vietnam* and Gilbert Adair's *Hollywood's Vietnam*.

[2] Deleuze acknowledges that the crisis "depended on many factors, . . . some of which were social, economic, political, moral and others more internal to art, to literature, and to the cinema in particular. We might mention, in no particular order," he writes, "the unsteadiness of the 'American Dream' in all its aspects, the new consciousness of minorities, the rise and inflation of images both in the external world and in people's minds, the influence on the cinema of the new modes of narrative with which literature had experimented, the crisis of Hollywood and its old genres" (206).

[3] A fine general study of trauma is to be found in Judith Lewis Herman's book *Trauma and Recovery*. Studies focused more specifically on trauma and the Vietnam war include *Post-Traumatic Stress Disorder and the War Veteran Patient*, edited by William E. Kelly, and Richard A. Kulka et al's *Trauma and the Vietnam War Generation*.

[4] An excellent discussion of the disaster film cycle can be found in Nick Roddick's essay "Only the Stars Survive: Disaster Movies in the Seventies."

[5] For a more detailed description of the most common symptoms of PTSD, see Kulka (31-32).

Works Cited

Adair, Gilbert. *Hollywood's Vietnam*. London: Heinemann, 1989.
Bordwell, David. "The Art Cinemas as a Mode of Film Practice." *Film Criticism* 4.1 (1979): 56-64.
---, Janet Staiger, and Kristin Thompson. *The Classical Hollywood Cinema: Film Style and Mode of Production to 1960*. New York: Columbia UP, 1985.
Britton, Andrew. "Blissing Out: The Politics of Reaganite Entertainment." *Movie* 31/32 (Winter 1986): 1-42.
---. "*Jaws*." *Movie* 23 (Winter 1976/1977): 27-32.
---. "Sideshows: Hollywood in Vietnam." *Movie* 27/28 (Winter 1980/Spring 1981): 2-23.
Deleuze, Gilles. *Cinema 1: The Movement-Image*. Trans. Hugh Tomlinson and Barbara Habberjam. Minneapolis: U of Minnesota P, 1986.
---. *Cinema 2: The Time-Image*. Trans. Hugh Tomlinson and Barbara Habberjam. Minneapolis: U of Minnesota P, 1989.
---. "On *The Movement-Image*." *Negotiations 1972-1990*. Trans. Martin Joughlin. New York: Columbia UP, 1995. 46-56.
Elsaesser, Thomas. "The Pathos of Failure: American Films in the 70s." *Monogram* 6 (October 1975): 13-19.
Herman, Judith Lewis. *Trauma and Recovery*. New York: Basic Books, 1992.
Kelly, William E., ed. *Post-Traumatic Stress Disorder and the War Veteran Patient*. New York: Brunner/Mazel Publishers, 1985.
Kulka, Richard A., et al. *Trauma and the Vietnam War Generation*. New York: Brunner/Mazel Publishers, 1990.
Lerman, Leo. "Pauline Kael Talks About Violence, Sex, Eroticism and Women & Men in the Movies." *Conversations with Pauline Kael*. Ed. Will Brantley. Jackson: UP of Mississippi, 1996. 31-40.
Pakula, Alan J., dir. *The Parallax View*. With Warren Beatty, Paula Prentiss, and William Daniels. Paramount, 1974.
Polanski, Roman, dir. *Chinatown*. With Jack Nicholson, Faye Dunaway, John Hillerman, Burt Young, and John Huston. Paramount, 1974.
Ray, Robert B. *A Certain Tendency of the Hollywood Cinema, 1930-1980*. Princeton: Princeton UP, 1985.
Roddick, Nick. "Only the Stars Survive: Disaster Movies in the Seventies." *Performance and Politics in Popular Drama*. Ed. David Brandby, Louis James, and Bernard Sharratt. New York: Cambridge UP, 1980. 243-269.
Smith, Julian. *Looking Away: Hollywood and Vietnam*. New York: Scribner's, 1975.

Thomson, David. "The Decade When Movies Mattered." *Movieline* (August 1993): 42-47, 80.
Torry, Robert. "Therapeutic Narrative: *The Wild Bunch*, *Jaws*, and Vietnam." *The Velvet Light Trap* 31 (Spring 1993): 27-38.
White, Hayden. "The Modernist Event." *The Persistence of History*. Ed. Vivian Sobchack. New York: Routledge, 1996. 17-38.
Wood, Robin. *Hollywood from Vietnam to Reagan*. New York: Columbia UP, 1986.

The Inner Life of *Ordinary People*

Patrick E. Horrigan

In October of 1989, my best friend and former boyfriend Gary Lucek, then 28 years old, celebrated his tenth year of living in New York City by throwing a party for himself. He sent out a four-page invitation, or as he labeled them, four "panels," filled with text and images marking the years he'd spent in New York, first as a Columbia College engineering-turned-sociology major and then, after graduation, as the bookkeeper for Democratic Socialists of America. On the third panel of the invitation, Gary created a time line from 1979 to 1989 highlighting all the major events of his life during those years. Here's how it begins:

> 1979: enroll in Columbia Engineering School. 1980: come out to a high school friend / fall in love with Conrad Jarrett (Timothy Hutton) after watching *Ordinary People* 5 times. 1981: 1st homosexual experience / shift social circles at Columbia / come out to Columbia Gay group / fail out of Engineering School / 1st NYC gay pride march / fall in love with Bill McCann / accepted to Columbia College (liberal arts). 1982: come out to parents, siblings / fail out of Columbia College and take semester off / a boyfriend tells me about AIDS (Lucek: "amino inquired say what?").

The time line goes on to chart the progress of a gay male reading group that Gary organized in the fall of 1984; a string of unfaithful or disappointing boyfriends (including me); the HIV-related illness and death of Bill McCann (whom Gary had "fallen in love with" the year after falling in love with Timothy Hutton's Conrad Jarrett); and Gary's harrowing struggle with depression—a nervous breakdown requiring hospitalization in 1986, a "3 month depression labeled [the] worst ever" in 1988, first one therapist, then another, then a psychiatrist who "increase[s] [his] drug dosage tenfold."

By the spring of 1991, Gary had become dissatisfied with his life in New York. His older brother had recently moved from Boston to San Diego and seemed happy there, so Gary decided to give San Diego a try. In many ways, Gary's life in San Diego was much like it was in New York—he worked as an accountant for a small corporation, made lots of friends and acquaintances, organized another gay male reading group, and tried but failed to find the kind of psychiatric treatment he needed. On December 6, 1992, Gary disappeared. Eleven days later, the police found his body hanging from a tree in the Armstrong Redwoods Forest near Guerneville, about 60 miles north of San Francisco.

What does it mean that, twelve years before killing himself, Gary "fell in love" with Conrad Jarrett, the suicidal, teenage hero of *Ordinary People* (1980)? What did Gary see in this character? Now I don't remember if Gary and I ever watched *Ordinary People* together, or if we did, what he said about it, but when I think of the film now, one scene in particular reminds me of Gary. It's the scene where Beth Jarrett, played by Mary Tyler Moore, sees her son, Conrad, lying in a lawn chair out on the back patio one cold autumn afternoon and decides to go out and visit with him. (The cold weather, fall turning to winter, is a strong presence in the film, and it makes the action feel all the more sad and valedictory. There's an end of the world feeling about this movie—a feeling that it's time to go underground, to burrow underneath and hold to oneself one's own burning truth, however unsuited for anyone else's eyes or ears that truth may be.) Conrad has recently come out of the hospital where he underwent shock treatment after trying to kill himself. At this point in the film, we don't know exactly why he wanted to kill himself, but we know it has something to do with his older brother Buck, who is dead, and with the never quite invisible tensions grinding away among Conrad, his mother, and dad. "We just don't connect," Conrad later tells his therapist, and this scene, as it turns out, surely is evidence of that:

BETH: It's cold out here. (indicating his jacket) You should put that on, or—or—do you—want a sweater?
CONRAD: Do I need one?
BETH: What are you doing?
CONRAD: Nothing. Thinking.
BETH: About what?
CONRAD: Not about anything.
BETH: Your—your hair—it's starting to grow out—it's looking—looking better.
CONRAD: I was thinking about the pigeon, you know the one that used to hang around the garage? And how it used to get on top of your car and he'd take off when you pulled out of the driveway.
BETH: Yeah, I remember. I remember how scared I used to get if that (imitates the sound of a bird's wings fluttering and waves her hands quickly to suggest flapping wings) *whooosh! fluff fluff fluff fluff fluff*—every time I started the car. (She makes an inward grunting sound as if she gets an uncomfortable chill just to think of it.)
CONRAD: Yeah, that was the closest we ever came to having a pet. You remember Buck asked you—he tried to talk you into getting a dog, do you remember that? And he said, "how 'bout if it's just the size of a little football?"
BETH: You know that animal next door—that Pepper or Pippin—
CONRAD: Pippin—Pippin—Pippin—
BETH: —whatever its name is—is not a very friendly dog— (now overlapping with Conrad's next speech) I—I don't care what Mr. McGreary says, he's really not—he's—and every time that dog comes into this backyard and I try to get him out—
CONRAD: —and what he really wanted was the retriever that was down the street for sale—that's what he wanted— (suddenly barks like a dog) *Aarf! Aarf!*
BETH: (stunned by his outburst and going back into the house) Put that on if you're going to stay out here, OK?[1]

Something about Timothy Hutton's posture as he lies in the lawn chair at the beginning of this scene reminds me of Gary. Timothy Hutton is "piled" into the chair—one of his legs is bent at the knee and sticking up, he's almost but not quite flat on his back, his jacket is draped like a blanket haphazardly over his chest, and he stares off into the sky as if he were reading there some secret message meant for him alone. He doesn't look comfortable, exactly, but he also looks as if seeking comfort is not the reason he's there. (In *The Wizard of Oz* [1939], Dorothy is made to realize by the end of the film that "if I ever go looking for my heart's desire again, I won't look any further than my own backyard; because if it isn't there, I never really lost it to begin with" [Langley 66]. But Conrad faces what Dorothy couldn't afford to admit—that what goes on in one's own backyard can be more disheartening and soul-killing than any greenfaced witch with balls of fire and burning broomstick—that home is the *last* place to go looking for your heart's desire.) At the beginning of the scene, Conrad looks like a vagrant—homeless. He looks tentative, he may get up any minute or he may stay there in that same funny, shapeless heap until the sun goes down, and he won't even have noticed. His mind is elsewhere.

Gary was tall—taller than me. And slender. I guess he had what people call a "tennis player's body"—at any rate, he did play a lot of tennis and he had beautiful, long legs, a lithe torso, long slender arms, not muscle-bound but naturally developed. He often wore clothing that accentuated his limbs—plain, loose-fitting t-shirts, baggy shorts that came down to his knees, and floppy sneakers—the kind of dishevelment that he admired in Timothy Hutton's Conrad. Gary, like Conrad, was too preoccupied with things that were going on inside his head or inside his home to worry about being fashionable or looking like anything other than an ordinary young man. Another reason Gary didn't care much about clothing, I suspect, was that his mother bought most of his clothes for him—packages of shirts, pants, socks, even underwear arrived regularly from Gary's mother. Gary and I would laugh as he opened the packages and laid out the clothing piece by piece on his bed. We laughed both at his mother's bad taste but also, sometimes, at her astonishingly good *gay* taste—sometimes she would hit upon just the right shirt for going to a club, or she would pick up on some latest fashion in blue jeans or a color scheme as fresh as tomorrow. Beth Jarrett, too, buys things for Conrad that he doesn't really want or need. Earlier in the film, while Beth sits pensively in Buck's old bedroom, thinking about her dead son, Conrad walks past the open door not knowing she is there and inadvertently frightens her. She says sharply to him, "don't do that!" Then they make a painful attempt at small talk. After a minute, Beth cuts the conversation short by saying with a brisk, painted-on smile, "I bought you two shirts. They're on your bed." She walks into her own bedroom and shuts the door, leaving Conrad alone in the hallway.

The other thing about the back patio scene in *Ordinary People* that most reminds me of Gary is the climax when Conrad is reduced to barking at his mother. The Jarretts are a good-looking, highly respectable middle-class family from suburban Chicago, but their social standing can't cover up their deeper, baser animal instincts. Gary would have understood that and said, "that's exactly what my family is like." Often he would return to New York after having spent a few days or a holiday at his parents' house in suburban New Jersey, where he grew up, and he would have stories to tell about how they'd be sharing a meal one minute and how the next his mother would be screaming and carrying on at him or his father—"barking" was the word I remember Gary using—"I couldn't stand to have her barking at me when I was talking calmly and quietly and rationally, so I just got up and left right then and there."

"How did you get back to New York?!," I would ask; "how did you get to the train station?"

"I walked."

"You walked? How far is it from your house?"

"About ten miles."

"Ten miles! Gary! It was pouring rain last night! You walked ten miles in the rain?"

"I didn't care, I had to get out of there. I tell you, Patrick, she's so miserable with her own life, the worst thing I could do to punish her was *not* yell back at her, not stay there and play the silent treatment, or take her abuse, but just leave. I even said as I walked out the door, 'thank you for putting me up last night,' like it was a hotel. Like it wasn't even a home where people live. Because it isn't."

The backyard scene from *Ordinary People* is edited so as to emphasize the chasm that suddenly opens up between Beth and Conrad almost as soon as they start talking to one another. Initially, the camera positions them both within the frame, sitting on the patio furniture, talking, until Conrad mentions how his brother wanted a pet. At that point, so uncomfortable has Conrad made her by mentioning Buck's wish for a pet, Beth stands up, now visible only from the waist down, as she tries to overcome what is obviously a mental block about the name of the, to her, wretched next door neighbor's dog ("animal" she calls it—Pepper? Pippin?). Cut to a close-up of Conrad as he angrily reminds her of the dog's name (Pippin), spitting out the name three times in a row like a madman ("Pippin—Pippin—Pippin"). Cut to a close-up of Beth as she obsessively recalls her anger at the "animal next door," how she doesn't trust its owner Mr. McGreary, how she struggles to keep it out of her yard. Adding to the feeling of separateness between Beth and Conrad, they look in opposite directions during these close-ups, not in each other's direction. On both a verbal and visual level, then, as Conrad says later in the film, they "just don't connect."

But the more I look at this scene, the more I see in Beth. She's trying to give Conrad room to breathe, hard as that is for her to do. For the first time in the film since just after the opening credits, we hear the strains of Johann Pachelbel's famous *Canon in D*, music that expresses Beth's good intentions, the promise of a connection between mother and son, and then, as they begin to scratch at each other, the pathos of their inabiltiy to connect. Beth has a rich, complicated interior life that is glimpsed nowhere in the film as palpably as it is here, but even here it is only gestured toward, not really explored in depth. She says she felt "scared" when the pigeon fluttered in the garage: Mary Tyler Moore's best moment in the film comes exactly here when she imitates the sound and movement of the startled pigeon. She, like Timothy Hutton at the beginning of the scene, gets a far-off look in her eyes. She becomes even more tense than she is normally throughout the film when she makes the sound of the pigeon's flapping wings—"whooosh, fluff fluff fluff fluff fluff"—and as she does so, she winces. She momentarily but pointedly contracts her body just after she imitates the pigeon, and she grunts ("unh") as if her imitation of the pigeon has made it uncomfortably present to her again. This is a "window" into Beth's interior life not exactly because she's revealing thoughts that have until now been kept private—for one thing, all through the film she is quite candid in expressing herself in ways that you might think well-mannered, middle-class housewives would not be (for example, she pleads with her husband at one point, "Don't try to change me. For god's sake, I don't want any more changes in my life, Calvin. Let's just hold on to what we've got"), and in any case Beth is not—not consciously—revealing anything directly about herself in this moment. Instead, the sheer existence of an inner life that no one knows anything about is being indicated here by the intensity and elaborateness of her imitation of the pigeon. The pigeon scares her, but it also has her in its thrall—she is momentarily, breathlessly fascinated by it—she identifies with it—she *becomes* it—it expresses her—it expresses, perhaps, her wish to escape (the pigeon is noticed as she's *pulling out* of the garage), just as Conrad, by attempting suicide, tries to escape his family, the world, himself. The "whooosh" that Beth remembers, ultimately, is a gale force escaping *from inside herself.* The "flap flap flap flap flap" is the powerful effect *she* produces on other people, the carrying out of an initial, perhaps youthful burst of energy (in a flashback in the next scene, we see Beth, a younger, prettier woman, laughing flirtatiously with her son Buck) into some other kind of wayward movement (she will, at the end of the film, abandon Calvin and Conrad when she realizes that she can't or won't give them what they want). She winces at her own strength, at her own offhand flamboyance—at her own ungainly animality (we see this elsewhere in the film, for example, when she laughs while talking on the telephone to a friend—an almost wicked laugh—and when she joins her friends in song at a party).

Or perhaps she winces at her *own* suicidal impulse that her imitation of the pigeon has suddenly revealed to her. In his 1989 essay "Suicide of a Schoolteacher," about the suicide of one of his colleagues, Phillip Lopate describes his own lifelong urge to kill himself as the twisted sign of an inner life, a "tenuous flame" (26), he calls it, that one struggles to keep alive inside oneself:

> I would imagine, say, cutting my belly open to relieve the tensions once and for all. Usually, this thought would be enough to keep at bay the temptation to not exist. So I found myself using the threat of suicide for many purposes: it was a superstitious double hex warding off suicide; it was a petulant, spoiled response to not getting my way; and it was my shorthand for an inner life, to which I alone had access—an inner life of furious negation, which paradoxically seemed a source of my creativity as a writer. (22)

His colleague's act of suicide, he argues,

> must have been his attempt to give Pain a body, a representation, to put it outside himself. A need to convert inner torment into some outward tangible wound that all could see. It was almost as though suicide were a last-ditch effort at exorcism, in which the person sacrificed his life in order that the devil inside might die. (41)

While everyone in *Ordinary People* knows that Conrad has tried to kill himself and may still wish to do so, apparently no one knows that Beth may share the same self-destructive urge. Her imitation of the pigeon looks and feels like an attempt at the kind of "exorcism" that Lopate sees in suicide—it's Beth's attempt to give body to her "Pain" (the body of an animal—a rodent with wings, as the Devil is often depicted in traditional Christian iconography), "to convert [her] inner torment into some outward tangible wound that all could see."

I suspect that, whether he knew it or not, my friend Gary saw himself as much in the figure of Beth Jarrett as in the figure of her son Conrad. And if Gary appreciated the film's portrayal of a mother incapable of loving her son the way he wanted to be loved by her, he also understood the extent to which their different depressions were enmeshed with each other (at the gathering at Gary's parents' house after his funeral, Gary's mother sat in a chair by the kitchen door, saying again and again, to anyone who would hear her, "my beautiful baby boy, my beautiful boy"; in her 1995 autobiography entitled *After All*, Mary Tyler Moore concludes a chapter on the death of her twenty-five-year-old son Richie—who may or may not have killed himself—with this meditation addressed to Richie:

> *When I see myself on film, a scene captured from* Dick Van Dyke, *perhaps you were seven or nine or six, as the camera recorded my actions, you, too, are recorded somewhere just offstage. What were you doing then at just those moments? I want that time to be replayed. How frantically I would step through the film, breaking the rules of this rerun to catch you up in my arms. I'd take you to this today I live in and every "Mom, look at this!", "Would you tell me a story?", "What's six times eight?" would be ours again without a thought of tomorrow.* [299-300]).

Conrad isn't looking at Beth when she imitates the pigeon—it's not clear if he even hears what she's saying or the sounds she's making. (No one in this film really knows what Beth goes through, not even director Robert Redford, which may account for what many have called the film's misogynistic blaming of Beth for all her family's ills; even Mary Tyler Moore insists in her autobiography, "it's not that [Beth Jarrett] deserved our sympathy"—why not? —"but," she adds, "I've always resented the meant-to-be compliments of 'I hated you.' 'What a bitch'" [258-259].) Finally, it's *not* clear that Beth is to blame for Conrad's troubles, that something she said set him off (made him bark). If anything, this scene shows the opposite: Conrad has injured Beth, accidentally or intentionally we can't tell, again, because he doesn't look at Beth when he speaks about his brother, but, instead, stares awestruck into space. Beth confesses a fear, exposes her vulnerability (though as I've said, it's also her strength), then Conrad rushes in and stabs her in her open wound.

Gary may have understood all of this—may have identified with ("fallen in love with") Beth's anguish as much as Conrad's. But I don't know for sure. I do know that in his late twenties, he remembered "falling in love" with Conrad Jarrett a decade earlier and that his identification with and desire for Timothy Hutton's Conrad was a primary touchstone of his self-image. I know little about Gary's inner life during his growing up years, but I imagine that, as a teenager, he loved Conrad's suffering as much as the fact that, by the end of the film, Conrad *survives*—survives the death of his brother (in a boating accident some years before, we discover at the climax of the film, Buck drowned while Conrad managed to hang on to the capsized wreck until he was rescued) as well as the breakup of his parents' marriage (at the end of the film, Conrad and Calvin reconcile now that Beth has gone—"haul my ass a little, you know, get after me," Conrad encourages his father, a sure sign, we are meant to believe, of his recovery from the wish to kill himself and from the death-grip of his relationship with his mother).

Conrad survives, but Gary, ultimately, did not. What does it mean? At the very least, it means that whatever inner life Gary kept secret (from his family, his friends, even from himself), whatever of his inner life must remain forever a mystery to me, *Ordinary People*—not Gary's story, but a story proximate to Gary's—may offer some hope of laying bare, and laying to rest.

Notes

[1] Dialogue quoted from the screenplay by Alvin Sargent. Since the screenplay is not in print, I've transcribed the dialogue from videotape.

Works Cited

Langley, Noel, Florence Ryerson, and Edgar Allan Woolf, screenwriters. *The Wizard of Oz: Movie Script*. 1939. Monterey Park, Calif.: O.S.P. Publishing, 1994.

Lopate, Phillip. "Suicide of a Schoolteacher." *On Suicide: Great Writers on the Ultimate Question*. Ed. John Miller. San Francisco: Chronicle Books, 1992. 15-45.

Moore, Mary Tyler. *After All*. New York: Dell Publishing, 1995.

Redford, Robert, dir. *Ordinary People*. With Donald Sutherland, Mary Tyler Moore, Judd Hirsch, and Timothy Hutton. Paramount, 1980.

Disability and the Dysfunctional Family in Wayne Wang's *Smoke*

Lou Ann Thompson

From Chaucer's evil summoner, whose ravaged face frightened children, to Hemingway's Jake Barnes, whose post-bellum impotence represented a lost generation, it has long been an unfortunate literary tradition that physical disabilities are often used as metaphors for an underlying disease of the spirit. In their introduction to *The Body and Physical Differences: Discourses of Disability*, David T. Mitchell and Sharon L. Snyder note, "Historically, the physical surface has existed as a medium that exposes the more abstract and intangible landscape of psychology, morality, and spirituality" (13). Though this "generic convention" of what Mitchell and Snyder call the "ideology of the physical" (15) shows little evidence of disappearing altogether anytime soon, some insightful contemporary artists are treating the subject of disability with greater awareness of the complexity of its implications and with more diverse and innovative approaches. This trend promises to continue as the emergence and subsequent development of Disability Studies remind artists and critics of this long overdue reexamination.

Wayne Wang's 1994 film *Smoke* presents an ensemble of characters who could all be described as having, at the very least, emotional disabilities.[1] The five major characters that make up the film's structural focus—Paul, Rashid, Ruby, Cyrus, and Auggie—are all isolated, lonely, or otherwise troubled individuals—all in large part (but not entirely) because of choices they have made. Three characters in particular are separated from, or have lost, children. Paul Benjamin's wife and unborn child were murdered by crossfire in a bank heist shootout. A writer by profession, Paul's writer's block is something of a disability, a kind of creative impotence, and mirrors his withdrawal from the activity of life.

But physical disabilities are prominent in this film as well. Ruby, Auggie's ex-lover, and Cyrus, Rashid's father, are both estranged from their children and have lost body parts (Ruby an eye and Cyrus an arm), at first glance a stereotypical metaphoric representation of their parental losses. However, rising above literary stereotypes, both characters display intriguing relationships with their disabilities, with both characters ultimately embracing these wounds to an extent in an acceptance of their disability and in a refusal to mask it. Another character, Granny Ethel, who appears at the film's conclusion in Auggie's Christmas story, is blind and is also isolated from family, having been left by her grandson and the rest of the family to spend Christmas alone.

The film's protagonist is Auggie Wren, who works at a tobacco shop in Brooklyn. Ruby, whom Auggie recalls as his "one true love," reappears after more than eighteen years to inform Auggie that he has a daughter named Felicity who is in trouble, pregnant, and hooked on crack (Auster 37).[2]

In the corner tobacco shop, Auggie encounters daily an assortment of people, America's cross section. He has employed Jimmy Rose, a young man who is mentally retarded, and to whom Auggie is uncharacteristically paternal, alternately chiding and affectionate. Paul, a frequent customer and typically inattentive to his surroundings, one day is about to step off a curb into the path of a huge truck, when he is saved by Rashid, a black teenager. Rashid, who has not seen his father in twelve years, is something of a wise-cracker, but he is articulate, artistic, and sensitive. His tough, cool veneer conceals (although not too well) his vulnerability. Despite their emotional defensiveness Paul and Rashid form a bond, a surrogate father/son relationship, which begins to heal the wounds of each. Paul takes Rashid in for a short time, expresses concern for his welfare, and gets him a job in Auggie's shop. When he learns that Rashid has been lying to him—about his name, his family, his home—he scolds him with a distinctively paternal tenderness. In a clever and touching scene in which Rashid and Paul explain to an attractive bookstore clerk that the young man is the older man's father, Rashid indeed assumes the paternal role and arranges a date for the lonely Paul. This bond and its subsequent healing also stimulate Rashid to seek out his real father, who has recently been spotted at a garage outside town.

Not telling Cyrus who he really is (in fact, he uses the name of his new surrogate father, Paul Benjamin), Rashid starts to work at the garage. Cyrus wears a prosthetic arm with a hook. He has purchased a garage and repairs cars, but when he has some difficulty with the ostensibly simple task of opening a soda can, Rashid, in a considerate and surprisingly intimate gesture, and again in a kind of father/son role reversal, opens the can for Cyrus. This gesture is preceded by Rashid's asking Cyrus how he lost his arm. Cyrus explains that he had an accident while driving drunk with a woman who loved him (Rashid's mother) in the car. She was killed, he explains, but Cyrus was doomed to live out his life. It is clear that it is not the loss of the arm, however, which Cyrus regrets. Rather it is the guilt he feels for being responsible for the woman's death. The missing arm is a reminder of two important truths for Cyrus: first, that of God's mercy; and second, of Cyrus' own sinful past. God was merciful, he explains, in that He could have taken both of his arms or both of his legs. God didn't even take his right arm, he adds. (It is an interesting parallel that when Paul is beaten by The Creeper, the criminal who is looking for Rashid, it is his left arm that is injured—a wound common to Rashid's "fathers"?) In a curious way, Cyrus embraces his prosthetic arm as the reminder that has enabled him to turn his life around. It has, in essence, saved him, and it continues to "save" him everyday.

Cyrus clearly sees his injury as a form of punishment. Rashid's Aunt Em agrees. "Cyrus lived, but he came out of it a cripple," she tells Paul. "His left arm was so mangled, the doctors had to cut it off. Small punishment for what he did, if you ask me" (61). Paul, no stranger to survivor's guilt, is more sympathetic. "It can't have been easy on him. Walking around with that on his conscience all these years," he responds (61). But Paul shares some sense of the balance of cause and effect, of deeds going rewarded and punished. When Rashid saves his life, Paul insists that he be allowed to do something for him. "It's a law of the universe. If I let you walk away, the moon will spin out of orbit . . . pestilence will reign over the city for a hundred years" (20). The irony is that Paul unwittingly brings about his own healing by taking on Rashid's cause.

Similarly, Ruby's lost eye could be viewed as a punishment for past sins, and it is perceived in just that way by Auggie, who is incidentally reading *Crime and Punishment* when Ruby appears. In their past relationship, Ruby talked Auggie into stealing a necklace for her, and when he was caught, the judge gave him two options: go to prison or enlist in the armed forces (this would have been during the Vietnam war). Auggie chose the latter, and while he was away—"I watch men lose their arms and legs, I nearly get my head blown off"— Ruby married someone else (72). That husband was abusive and poked out her eye in a fight. After the war Ruby and Auggie were reunited for a time, but Auggie was disturbed by her glass eye: "Every time we got into a clinch," he tells his boss, "I'd start thinking about that hole in her head, that empty socket with the glass eye in it. An eye that couldn't see, an eye that couldn't shed any tears. The minute I started thinking about it, Mr. Johnson would get all soft and small" (38).

When Ruby returns to Auggie eighteen years later, she is wearing an eye patch. She claims that she lost what Auggie calls "that old blue marble," but then explains that she never liked it anyway. "If you really want to know, I lost it. And I'm not sorry I did. That eye was cursed, Auggie, and it never gave me nothing but grief" (49). The patch becomes something of an Achilles heel for Ruby: Auggie tells her she looks like Captain Hook; her daughter Felicity calls her "Hawkeye." The first comment is an example of Auggie's insensitivity and his anger towards Ruby; the second is a vicious, painful wound inflicted by a terrified and angry daughter. But it is important to consider that these comments reveal volumes about the speakers and really nothing about Ruby.

One critic, Hayden Bixby Nichols, has complained that *Smoke* is a sexist film, noting that women are excluded from the smoking ritual and "are limited . . . by their rigidly feminine names" (51). Nichols continues, "Other misrepresentations of women, however, bypass disappointing and approach shocking," particularly in their lack of physical sight, which renders them "passive subjects of a man's representation" (51). This critic's attempts to point out sexism in the film results in ableist assumptions about Ruby's missing eye and Granny Ethel's blindness. But it's important to note that Ruby is not the one who has trouble with her missing eye. It is Auggie who is bothered by it. He is rendered impotent by the glass eye and he is the one who makes the connection between Ruby's injury and her betrayal of him. He notes that the artificial eye cannot shed tears, but the directions in the screenplay note that "[w]e see tears falling from her one good eye" (73). Ruby is one of the few characters in the film who, from its beginning, can admit her feelings. She tells Auggie she thought she could handle the problem with Felicity herself, but she has realized that she needs help. Unlike Cyrus' prosthesis, Ruby's prosthetic eye serves no real function. It merely allows her to "pass" as able-bodied and it perhaps lessens the discomfort of others. Her decision to forego the prosthesis and wear the more visible eye patch, then, is a gesture of acknowledging her wound and a statement of vulnerability; but that vulnerability should not be mistaken for weakness. The other characters in the film have to learn to admit these vulnerabilities, and to admit they need the support of relationships with other people.[3] Ruby has already learned this lesson.

As for Granny Ethel, her blindness does not make her susceptible to Auggie's deception that he is her grandson. "I mean, that woman knew I wasn't her grandson," he tells Paul. "She was old and dotty, but she wasn't so far gone that she couldn't tell the difference between a stranger and her own flesh and blood" (144). Granny Ethel's blindness allows her (and him) to pretend that she is deceived, so that the two of them will not have to spend Christmas alone. Auggie explains that it made both of them happy to play the game.

Though in *The Cinema of Isolation: A History of Physical Disability in the Movies* Martin F. Norden acknowledges that some improvement in the cinematic depiction of people with disabilities has been evident since the 1990 American Disabilities Act, he sadly acknowledges the persistence of certain stereotypical figures who are disabled. A typical use of disability is still "to suggest some element of a person's character" (5). I suspect that this will always be the case, to some extent. After all, stereotypes of men and women, of lawyers and schoolteachers and blondes and redheads and so on, persist. And even without stereotypes, writers will always use literary devices like physical attributes or names to enhance characterization. But we are seeing some improvement in the portrayal of disability in some films.

I think films like *Smoke* break away from stereotypes and even some of the conventions. The characters with physical disabilities are not different, no less able in a human sense, than those without. Without discounting the uniqueness of their situations, *Smoke* presents these characters as much more than their disabilities. And while making the point that, after all, all of us are flawed, not all disabilities are physical or visible, nor do they define the totality of the self.

Notes

[1] In an interview, Wang explained that when he and writer Paul Auster "talked about it initially, we wanted all the characters to be wounded in some emotional or physical way. So there's[Ruby] without the eye, there's [Cyrus] without the arm, there's [Rashid] without the father, there's [Paul] without the wife. It was a movie about wounded animals" (Rennert).

[2] Direct quotations are taken from the screenplay for accuracy and will be hereafter cited in the text by page number. In addition, I am using the screenplay here to provide a look at directions and at scenes that were later cut from the film.

[3] Indeed a rhetoric of disability permeates even in the directions in the screenplay. Ruby's car has "a defective muffler and a dented body" (83); the car Auggie borrows has bald tires and drives "limping into the [Cyrus'] station with a flat tire" (127); the door to Felicity's apartment is "scarred" (86).

Works Cited

Auster, Paul. *Smoke and Blue in the Face*. New York: Hyperion Miramax Books, 1995.

Mitchell, David T., and Sharon L. Snyder. "Introduction: Disability Studies and the Double Bind of Representation." *The Body and Physical Differences: Discourses of Disability*. Ed. Mitchell and Snyder. Ann Arbor: U of Michigan P, 1997. 1-31.

Nichols, Hayden Bixby. "*Smoke.*" *Film Quarterly* 51.3 (1998): 45-51.

Norden, Martin F. *The Cinema of Isolation: A History of Physical Disability in the Movies*. New Brunswick: Rutgers UP, 1994.

Rennert, Amy. "Smoke Screen." 1 June 1999 <http://www.diablopubs.com/focus/aRCHIVES/INTERVIEWS/wang.html>.

Wang, Wayne, dir. *Smoke*. With William Hurt, Harvey Keitel, Stockard Channing, and Forest Whitaker. Miramax, 1994.

Disability as Spectacle in Contemporary Cinema

The Noble Ruined Body: Blindness and Visual Prosthetics in Three Science Fiction Films

Susan Crutchfield

> Cinematic perception is primordial to the very extent that it is monstrously prosthetic.
>
> —*Stephen Shaviro*, The Cinematic Body

> The cyborg is a matter of fiction and lived experience that changes what counts as . . . experience in the late twentieth century. This is a struggle over life and death, but the boundary between science fiction and social reality is an optical illusion.[1]
>
> —*Donna J. Haraway, "A Cyborg Manifesto: Science, Technology, and Socialist-Feminism in the Late Twentieth Century"*

Media-ted Vision

In the fall of 1995, Detroit's Channel 7 News ran a story about a new technology in visual prosthetics that promises to "restore sight to the blind" ("A New Featherweight"). The incredulous local newscaster likened this breakthrough to something more likely to appear on an episode of *Star Trek* than in one's living room, explaining that it involves "floating" a tiny computer chip in the retina to "receive an invisible laser beam from two glasses mounted with TV cameras."[2]

The newscaster did not show nor describe what kind of image the blind would see with this device, but I am not interested here in probing, in the popular manner of Oliver Sacks, the details of exactly what blind people see when vision is restored to them in one way or another.[3] Rather, I am interested in something akin to the *Star Trek* program to which the newscaster referred, namely, three science fiction films: Roger Corman's *X: The Man with the X-Ray Eyes* (1963), Bertrand Tavernier's *Death Watch* (1979), and Wim Wenders' *Until the End of the World* (1991).[4]

X: The Man with the X-Ray Eyes, Death Watch, and *Until the End of the World* portray blindness within science fiction's postmodern tradition of critiquing our scientific-technological information society, and they do so with a keen interest in prosthetic visual technology.[5] In these films, blindness is a subversive alternative to the postmodern ideologies and power systems symbolized by prosthetically enhanced bodies. At the same time, however, the films suggest that physical disability is a product of capitulation *to* those postmodern ideals, with the difference between revolutionary and reactionary forms of blindness involving, respectively, a refusal and a willingness (even a desire) to compensate one's vision through prosthetic technologies. While the films critique a particular vision that is enhanced through technology, they nevertheless also suggest that no vision can escape the influence and inflection of visual technology—not even the filmgoer's vision. Furthermore, all technological visual prostheses, including film, are *monstrous*. There is no natural or so-called normal vision, only remarkable extremes: prosthetically enhanced, *media-ted* vision or its alternative, *blindness*.

Bringing their critiques to bear directly on the spectator's experience of media-ted vision, these films depict prostheses of the eye in such a way that their characters' prosthetic vision is aligned with the film spectator's viewpoint, much in the way this Detroit television news story projected simultaneously the perspective and the prospect of television as a visual prosthesis. Watching this news story, the living room audience's vision was mediated by televisual technology, similar to how that of the blind would be with their prosthetic mini-cameras trained on the newsworthy world. Donna J. Haraway's remark captures precisely the uncanny sense of how this media bite, like the prosthetic device it described, places viewers in confrontation with science fiction special effects turned into reality. The optical illusion this story and the films considered here project and examine is the illusion that viewers are—or more precisely that their *vision* is—autonomous from visual media as they watch them. Moreover, the films explore the concomitant illusion that spectators are autonomous from the specific ideals those prosthetic media serve. *X: The Man with the X-Ray Eyes, Death Watch,* and *Until the End of the World* are primarily concerned with the transcendent ideals of health, visual ability, and youth, in other words, *physical wellness.* As these films propose, glued to our sets, we sighted spectators of technologically produced images *are* Haraway's cyborgs just as much as the blind person whose eyes are implanted with a floating computer chip. And if the stakes of this prosthetic interface are as high for the spectators as they are for the films' characters, then this is indeed a "struggle over life and death."

Seeing Well

> XAVIER: Sam, we are virtually blind, all of us. You tell me that my eyes are perfect. Well, they're not. I'm blind to all but a tenth of the universe.
> SAM: My dear friend, only the gods see everything.
> XAVIER: My dear doctor, I'm closing in on the gods.

Dr. James Xavier (Ray Milland), the eponymous protagonist of Roger Corman's *X: The Man with the X-Ray Eyes,* experiments upon his own eyes in an attempt to outperform the x-ray machine. In the film's opening discussion between Xavier and another ophthalmologist, Xavier formulaically explains the disabled status of normal vision in the face of modern scientific innovation: "we are virtually blind." A Dr. Frankenstein for the nuclear age, Xavier closes in on the gods with the prosthetic aid of a chemical liquid he has developed, which corrects this vision problem when dropped into the eye, enabling him to see through the surface of things and uncover truths invisible to normal human eyes. Xavier's dream is to surpass the visualizing capabilities of machines (particularly the x-ray machine) through the human capacity for a motivated, dynamic point of view. Indeed, his powers are initially godlike when he saves a young girl from unnecessary surgery, rediagnosing her after visually penetrating through her skin and muscles to view the afflicted organs. His x-ray eyes re-envision the human body as antiseptically open, completely readable and understandable, a transparent text for medical science's intervention.

Visual prosthetics function similarly in Bertrand Tavernier's *Death Watch,* a brooding, existentialist critique of the television industry and the ravaging nature of image production and consumption in the information age. The narrative takes place in a futuristic Britain where, thanks to advances in medicine, people no longer die young nor publicly but instead mysteriously go away to die. Our protagonists are Katherine (Romy Schneider) and Roddy (Harvey Keitel). Katherine is dying of some undisclosed ailment at an uncharacteristically young age, and because she is unique in dying "the old way," she has become the target of a television network program called "Death Watch," for which Roddy is a cameraman. Literally a camera-*man*, Roddy has had surgery on his eye, which has been implanted with a microcamera, allowing him surreptitiously to film and transmit images of Katherine, whom he follows on her trek to Land's End after she breaks her contract with the network and goes on the lam during her final days alive.

Similar to Xavier's hopes for his prosthetic vision, Roddy's vision is designed to objectify and control the threat of an abject body. I am calling this abject adversary of prosthetic vision a *body in ruins*, primarily for the phrase's indication of a diminished physiology,[6] but also for its connotations of an atavistic throwback, of a historical past now considered obsolete and therefore undesirable. The latter conceptualization I take from Walter Benjamin's work on German tragic drama, or *Trauerspiel*, in which he describes the architectural ruin as a disturbing historical remnant:

> When . . . history becomes part of the setting, it does so as script . . . The allegorical physiognomy of the nature-history, which is put on the stage in the *Trauerspiel*, is present in reality in the form of the ruin. In the ruin history has physically merged into the setting. And in this guise history does not assume the form of the process of eternal life so much as that of irresistible decay. (*The Origin of German Tragic Drama* 177-178)

For "Death Watch"'s viewers, Katherine's ruined body, the material proof of her anachronistic disease and impending death, reveals the "irresistible decay" of history from which their culture collectively flees while nevertheless hungering for its corresponding invigoration of the senses. Katherine is thus made their sacrificial lamb on the altar of modern progress and "eternal life." As a journalist puts it to Katherine, she is about to become a celebrity because

[w]e need it . . . tragedy . . . or at least to come close to someone dying. There's a certain sad fame about it, in dying the old way. Not in flames in a clash or a border war—we've had that up to here. I mean in the way it's . . . happening to you. We miss the real thing.

Broadcast to the citizenry via satellite, the tragic drama of Katherine's impending death, recorded by Roddy's microcamera, will provide a cathartic experience necessary to the healthy functioning of the populace at large. Able to experience vicariously the fragility of human life and health, the television viewers will nevertheless remain secure in their position as healthy, whole, and truly contemporary subjects.

Updating this narrative pattern for the digital age, Wim Wenders' *Until the End of the World* also portrays the curative powers of the prosthesis. Made in 1991, the film takes place on the cusp of the year 2000, a then-future world in which surveillance and other information and visual technologies have proliferated to a point seemingly beyond human management—case in point, an Indian nuclear satellite spinning out of control and threatening world-wide nuclear disaster. The film follows Sam Farber (William Hurt) as he travels the globe gathering images on a special photographic apparatus developed by his father, Dr. Henry Farber (Max von Sydow), who has stolen the technology from the US government. Sam hopes the camera will enable his blind mother, Edith (Jeanne Moreau), to see. As in *X: The Man with the X-Ray Eyes* and *Death Watch*, the value of the prosthesis is directly related to its ability to stave off physical disability or vulnerability, and in this case, Edith's blindness. These apparatuses will help their users *see well*, both because they will see more and better than they could without the devices, and because what they view will (ideally) make and keep them healthy.

Dis/enabled Vision

To reiterate, each film's narrative revolves around its protagonist's desire for, or complicity in, maintaining some sort of control over bodily disease and decay through a prosthetically enhanced scientific or medical gaze. Visually penetrating, videotaping, and otherwise optically recording bodies in ruins, these techno-humans serve the cultural prerogatives of staving off disease, halting the decaying effects of time, and, importantly, reversing blindness.[7] It is especially curious, therefore, that these visual prostheses compromise the visual abilities of their users, literally disabling them. This violent diminishment of the prosthesis-users' vision is represented as a vicious catch-22 visited upon them for their naive, uncritical participation in the society of the spectacle, with its concomitant ideal of a subject transcending physical limitations.

For example, as *X: The Man with the X-Ray Eyes* progresses, Xavier's own body takes on qualities antithetical to his own rational, medical gaze: his becomes an illogical, erratic body governed by unstable emotions and by the unpredictable effects of the sight-enhancing drug. After inadvertently killing a colleague, Xavier escapes into the hands of an unscrupulous carnival side show agent (Don Rickles), who exploits Xavier's powers in a mind-reading act before graduating him into a more lucrative and illegal role as medical fortune-teller. But Xavier sinks to even greater depths, eventually fleeing the police in a desperate attempt to win enough gambling money to finance his own cure. As he increases the number of drops in his eyes in preparation to cheat at cards, his eyes turn black, their opacity symbolic of the increasing uselessness and pain of his x-ray vision. His eyes penetrate so far beneath the surfaces of objects that it becomes difficult for him to see anything at all; only the sinister skeletal outlines of bodies and buildings remain in his field of vision. The horror of this so-called enhanced vision leads Xavier to blind himself. Having fled the gambling casino, he staggers into a Christian revival tent meeting where he ends the torturous consequences of his desire to be God by following the preacher's counsel that, "If thine eye offends thee, pluck it out!"

In *Death Watch* Roddy's technologically enhanced body likewise is decaying, seeming more and more like Katherine's fleshy, vulnerable body. To avoid the naturally degenerative effects of the microcamera upon his eyesight, Roddy must shine a light into his eye in dark conditions. He also must not sleep and is prescribed pills to stay awake. So, while the camera device may extend Roddy's vision, it nevertheless makes him physically weak. Both Roddy and Katherine are vulnerable to the microcamera and the powerful media and medical systems it represents: her vulnerability is marked by her objectification by the camera, his by an integration with it. Acknowledging their similar experiences of dehumanization (both physiological and spiritual) at the hands of the television studio, Roddy eventually blinds himself when he can no longer abide his role in Katherine's exploitation.

Until the End of the World complicates this paradoxical relationship of technological prosthetics to the material body by depicting two different scenarios of blindness: Sam's progressive visual impairment from use of the special camera, and Edith's complete physical blindness. Sam's vision, like Xavier's and Roddy's, is ironically *dis/enabled* by prosthetic visual technology: he is rendered virtually blind from recording extensively on his father's machine. However, unlike Xavier and Roddy, Sam does not use the special camera to extend his *own* vision. Widening the scope of *X: The Man with the X-Ray Eyes'* and *Death Watch's* critiques, the physical and mental discipline Sam needs to perform the recording symbolizes the degree to which the health of the larger human Body is made vulnerable, and even dis/enabled, by ideologies of prosthetic vision. *Until the End of the World* sharpens this critique further by developing the psychological significance of Sam's willful masochism. Sam's choice to don the special camera and suffer its detrimental physical effects grows out of his personal *emotional* vulnerability; the visual sacrifices he makes will, he hopes, not only help his mother regain sight, but also prove his devotion and self-worth to his cold, overly demanding father.

A fantastic example of Michel Foucault's disciplines of the body, the sado-masochistic relationship between the special camera and its user expresses what is repressed in any dialectical opposition of ability to disability, namely, the fact that ability is gained through disciplines which amount to physical restrictions in themselves. This situation encapsulates a crucial logic of the prosthesis: others' bodies are the unlucky standard bearers against which prosthetic abilities can be considered *abilities* as such. Sam's body literally degenerates so that Edith may see, or be more whole. But her body is more whole only in comparison to bodies decaying at the hands of the technological innovations that would help her see. Likewise the bodies of Dr. Xavier's medical patients provide the touchstone against which his new abilities are meaningful and necessary; and Roddy's camera-vision technology is developed and deployed only when his society is faced with its own antithesis—Katherine's diseased and dying body. However, this able/disabled dialectic—with its accompanying notion that the prosthetically enabled subject is more healthy and whole than the body divorced of technological enhancements—is an imaginary construct (an optical illusion) that our films dis/enable, dashing it to ruins.

The Noble Ruined Body

Nevertheless, the films do preserve another ideological dialectic, that between the simulational technologies and immaterial body rhetorics of postmodernity and the more authentic, primal physicality of postmodernity's imagined past. Sam's ocular exhaustion in *Until the End of the World* proposes a fundamental incompatibility between prostheticized vision and the body's normal processes of vision. The film's critical irony is not subtle: staving off blindness through technology causes blindness. Perhaps an even greater irony is that Sam's visual sacrifice does enable his mother to see, but that experience would seem to be the cause of her death. Edith's character—more specifically, her *noble ruined body*—thus stands in opposition to the assumed curative value of technological visual prosthetics, revealing this culture's ideology of *seeing well* to be short-sighted.

Exemplary of the noble ruined body's postmodern martyrdom, Edith's demise deserves detailed examination. Exactly how the laboratory procedure produces vision in her is rather mysterious, a feat made possible only through Wenders' science-fictional imagination. The images gathered with the camera are but one component in an elaborate technique that marries human and machine in startling ways. Voice-over narration from Claire's ex-lover, Gene (Sam Neill), explains the process:

> It wasn't as simple as just putting in a tape and playing it back. Whoever had initially recorded the images had to see them again. The first time the computer had recorded the act of seeing. Now it was reading the act of remembering. In theory, these two grids of information, together with the actual video-recordings of the event, enable the computer to translate these images into brainwaves again, and to reproduce them in the blind person's visual cortex.

The special camera records the psychosomatic experience of seeing, not just the images seen. Memory and repetition are integral to the technique producing images in Edith's brain.

While the spectators' own memories may color in some of the gaps between Edith's visual experience and their own, the spectators still cannot know what the images generated through this camera/computer/human conglomerate represent for Edith. On the lab's bed, she reacts ambiguously, placing her hands over her eyes as if to cover them while simultaneously exclaiming how beautiful her daughter is (as pictured with her granddaughter). Perhaps this shielding of the eyes is an effort to guard against the image. Perhaps Edith is expressing a pain similar to Sam's, be it emotional or physical. Perhaps it is a reflexive gesture of awe and humility before the projected vision of her daughter. Formally capturing Edith's stimulating and uncanny experience for the viewers, the image on the film screen is rendered in spectacular, unrealistic photography. Edith is seeing again, but not in any way she (nor the spectators) has seen before. Furthermore, what she sees, and the spectators with her, is visually overwhelming—the image's abstract expressionism is in tension with the unemotive, graphic hard-edge of its pixeled video medium. Double- and triple-exposed images create an experience that is visually overdetermined and beautifully confusing for it. The spectators' celebratory awe that the system works is thus corroborated by their aesthetic pleasure in the cinematography.

However, these delights are counterpoised against the prosthetic recordings' message of a world decaying in the hands of technology. In one recorded scene, Edith's daughter harps on her own ugliness and the detrimental effects of time upon her body. Embodying two generations of female descendants after Edith, her daughter and granddaughter represent both life and mortality, symbolizing the uncanniness of the familiar made strange by the passing of time. Another daughter extends the theme of decay to the landscape itself: "I wish you didn't have to see me in such an ugly place, but I'm afraid this is what the world looks like." Perhaps this ugliness and transitoriness are the horrors to which Edith covers her eyes, for the convolutions of passing time visualized in these images strongly and irreversibly affect her, as Gene, somehow divining Edith's thoughts, explains:

> Edith Isner had been eight years old when she'd lost her sight. The experience of seeing the world again was exhilarating, but it was also confusing and disorientating and unpredictably sad. Her childhood friends aged fifty years in a minute. The world they moved in was darker and uglier than she could possibly have imagined. It would have been ungracious for her to have mentioned these things. Her grief was only there for those with eyes to see it.

Contrary to the visual prosthetics' ideologies of health, ability, and youth, Edith's prosthetic gaze does not halt nor even provisionally circumscribe the debilitating effects of temporal progression and physical decay. Instead, it immerses her once again into the vicissitudes of time and its material effects on the surface of landscapes and bodies—including her own. Edith dies on the eve of the twenty-first century, aligning her unhappy experience of prosthetic sight with the passing of time and the mortality of the material body, and fashioning her death as an allegory for the tragic death of the past in postmodernity.

Prosthetic technology reveals to Edith what it has created in the others: debility and pain. As I have noted, it is ironic that Xavier's, Roddy's, and Sam's ability to practice their specific prosthesis' ideology of seeing well is dis/enabled by the unhealthy effects of the apparatus upon their own bodies (the abilities of which the prosthesis supposedly extends and protects). This irony is crucial to these films' critiques of visual technology, in that it reveals, within the prostheticized subject, the repressed and undervalued content of humanity that technology attempts to control, and even efface, from that supposedly ideal body. The disappearance of this index of humanity through technological constructions of the body is the threat these films simultaneously represent and work to dissuade, and the rhetorical embodiment and hero of their oppositional ideology is their blind characters. Evoking a profound nostalgia for the past (as in Edith's essentially suicidal nostalgia for a time before the present as well as a time before she regained her sight), the films enact a postmodern fantasy of the return to the noble ruined body, which is every-body, once stripped of modern technology's prosthetics.

The narratives of *X: The Man with the X-Ray Eyes, Death Watch,* and *Until the End of the World* portray worlds in which prosthetic technologies save human lives, simultaneously ensuring and justifying their existence. Furthermore, this prosthetic interface *enables* the existence and continued purposefulness of a human body which has become, in the technologically mediated realm of postmodern experience, a liability. While disability is symbolic of the subjective duress entailed by the body's interpolation with technology and its various ideologies, the disabled body with prosthetic extensions nevertheless becomes a rhetorical figure for the postmodern *norm* of human/technology interfaces. In the worlds of these films, the culturally acceptable body cannot be imagined and does not properly function outside of its relationship to technology. Without technology, it resides with-out the dominant culture of health and ability, and it will (in *X: The Man with the X-Ray Eyes*) suffer a dangerous and unnecessary surgery; (in *Death Watch*) die prematurely, a freakish object of prurient social interest; and (in *Until the End of the World*) be blind and reside on the margins of society.

Critical of such prosthetic ideologies, these films incite a revolution of categories in opposition to those considered normal in their narratives' futuristic worlds. Instead of embracing the cyborg as a liberatory figure transgressing boundaries in the face of oppressive political constructs (to paraphrase Haraway), the prosthetically enhanced protagonists of these films feel more and more oppressed as they realize an interface with visual technology. Rather than capitulate to the abusive power systems that use technology to suture their subjects to an ideology of health and visual ability, these characters embrace the revolutionary position of the abject, a-technological material body by blinding themselves. For these characters, there is no material body without disability, and the body's disability constitutes its humanness. The blinded body is lionized as a noble ruined body: a body marking and privileging a nostalgic return to the subject before technology and, more particularly, before postmodernity, when the Subject has come to be understood as a construction of discourses, as immaterial, as, in a word, inauthentic.

Film as Prosthesis and the Media-ted Spectator

The mad scientists at the heart of these science-fiction dystopias (Dr. Xavier, the "Death Watch" program's producers and hired medical staff, and Dr. Henry Farber) engineer creatures of technological and human parts that represent exaggerated versions of film spectators in our contemporary age. This meta-filmic reference to the viewers' experience watching film is achieved, more or less explicitly, through narrative allegory and through aligning the prosthetic vision of the protagonists with the spectators' vision by providing a prosthetic point of view. In *Death Watch,* for instance, Roddy's visual prosthesis legitimates within the narrative the film spectators' ability to accompany Katherine and Roddy on their adventure. Whereas Roddy's prosthetic travelogue is filmed predominantly in realistic-style cinematography with some prosthetic points of view visually altered to look like low definition video, in *X: The Man with the X-Ray Eyes* the spectators' travelogue is depicted from Xavier's iris-framed point of view using a special effects technology called "SPECTARAMA,"[8] further insinuating film technique within an ideology of prosthetics. While the spectators do not actually *have* the characters' points of view, the films' formal structuring of point of view pointedly reminds viewers of their similarity to the characters in their relationship to film's media-ting vision.

Stephen Shaviro is not the first film theorist to proclaim film's prosthetic quality, though no other terms it "monstrous." Christian Metz's cinematic apparatus deeply embeds the viewer's body (sitting in the dark, dream-space of the movie theater) within a prosthetic circuitry of human, machine, and screen. He describes the cinema screen as "a veritable psychical substitute, a prosthesis for our primally dislocated limbs" (4). Walter Benjamin also notes how film elicits the tactile *involvement* of the viewer, creating in her a "shock effect" that "distracts" and confuses in a manner comparable, but not equatable, to the prosthetic effects of visual technology on Xavier, Roddy, and Sam ("The Work of Art" 237-241). On a less menacing note, Benjamin observes film's power to "extend" human perception and experience:

> By close-ups of the things around us, by focusing on hidden details of familiar objects, by exploring commonplace milieus under the ingenious guidance of the camera, the film, on the one hand, *extends* our comprehension of the necessities which rule our lives; on the other hand, it manages to assure us of an immense and unexpected field of action. Our taverns and our metropolitan streets, our offices and furnished rooms, our railroad stations and our factories appeared to have us locked up hopelessly. Then came the film and burst this prison-world asunder by the dynamite of the tenth of a second, so that now, *in the midst of its far-flung ruins and debris*, we calmly and adventurously go traveling. With the close-up, space expands; with slow motion, movement is extended. The enlargement of a snap-shot does not simply render more precise what in any case was visible, though unclear: it reveals entirely new structural formations of the subject. ("The Work of Art" 236; emphasis added)

Here Benjamin articulates the interrelation of film as prosthesis with the ruins of our culture's claustrophobic ocular history. Prosthetically guarding viewers against the boredom and ignorance of an outmoded past, film simultaneously effects that past's ruination. In essence, film dis/enables the modern subject, creating a lack where one had not been felt, only immediately to supply its compensation.

Most pertinent to the themes of our science fiction films is Anne Friedberg's argument for film as prosthesis. In her essay "Cinema and the Postmodern Condition," Friedberg maintains that the particular attributes of film as prosthesis are components of postmodern subjectivity in general, explaining that postmodernity is marked by "the growing cultural feature that is integral to both cinema and television: a mobilized virtual gaze" (60). This mobilized virtual gaze is a compelling metaphor for the prosthetic properties of film, as its prosthetic effect is related to cinema's ability imaginatively to enable the spectators' "pleasures [in] escaping [their] physically bound subjectivity" (65). Film provides the illusion of a spectatorial body unbound by time and space, in other words, unbound by the realities of physiology—such as race, gender, sexual identity, and, more important to my argument, mortality, physical mutability, and the postmodern constraints on physical mobility (such as economics, time, and differences of ability). Friedberg's formulation brings the prosthetic ideology of film into direct agreement with the prosthetic ideologies of *seeing well* so integral to our science fiction films' worlds.

Indeed, the science fiction and travelogue film genres are paradigmatic of film's capacity for enabling the spectator imaginatively to take leave of the restrictions of space, time, and their physiological effects on the body. Science fiction re-imagines the body as well as our conventional sense of time by re-imagining the present in the form of a future past. Meanwhile, the travelogue film takes its audience to faraway places without the annoyance of having to move a material body through space or having to expend time or money getting it there. Aside from belonging to the science fiction genre, *X: The Man with the X-Ray Eyes, Death Watch,* and *Until the End of the World* also incorporate elements of travelogue, road-movie, and chase films, all of which feature narrative structures designed to marry narrative impetus with the capacity to show a variety of scenes, landscapes, and places. All of these genres are predicated on film's ability to beam viewers to an "elsewhere and elsewhen" (Friedberg's phrase).

Until the End of the World most profoundly literalizes this film-as-prosthesis simile in that its travelogue form and narrative are propelled by a desire to stave off blindness. Advertised as the "ultimate road movie," the film is a sprawling spectacle of glossy cinematography interspersed with SONY-developed high definition video effects, which stylistically mark the special camera's recordings. The narrative follows Sam, chased by a bounty hunter as well as by Claire and her hired detective, as he travels through Europe, the USSR, Japan, and the United States among other countries, taking motion photographs on this camera to bring back to his mother at his father's lab in the Australian outback. Claire also records a visual travelogue of sorts on a handheld video camera as she chases Sam through numerous countries and landscapes. She even video-faxes her footage to Gene in Paris. The ubiquity of this sort of motion-picture recording and vicarious, prosthetic travel illuminates how Edith's prosthetic vision is an integral component of a culture that values visual mobility. By having Edith reject the purpose and pleasures of prosthetic vision, having her choose to die rather than to see, Wenders disputes the values of her postmodern culture while suggesting that the promise of film's prosthetic properties, as Friedberg describes them, is an empty one.

Creating a blind ideal and a dis/enabled norm, the films examined here investigate the meaning and value of *seeing well*. Positioned on the extreme margins of postmodern society, the blind body symbolizes for these films a cultural anxiety about the contemporary body's relationship to visual technology, a relationship that can be pared down to the double-bind of technology as prosthetic extension of the body and technology as alien threat to the body. As a specific symbol for the film medium, the blind character incarnates for spectators the physical and psychological dangers of film and other media-ting technologies, even as those viewers are seduced by the unique pleasures of film's prosthetic properties.

Certainly, their idealization of blindness leaves these films open to accusations that they are merely metaphorizing disability, essentializing the experience of blindness in order to construct a compelling mythology of sighted culture's fears. I suggest, however, that *X: The Man with the X-Ray Eyes, Death Watch,* and *Until the End of the World* cogently critique the postmodern notion that to see more is to be healthier and to have more pleasure and power. In drawing attention to the fluidity of the category of disability and to the transcendent nature of the noble ruined body, these films expose the constructed, un-transcendent nature of bodies that *see well*—most notably those prosthetically extended film viewers who would throw off the constraints of their own physicality in the interest of entertaining a blind point of view.

Notes

[1] Haraway's passage reads, "The cyborg is a matter of fiction and lived experience that changes what counts as women's experience in the late twentieth century. This is a struggle over life and death, but the boundary between science fiction and social reality is an optical illusion" (149).

[2] This technology received more attention in 1999, when a collection of news reports heralded a promising future for the "intraocular retinal prosthesis" (Curry), for which "large-scale human clinical trials could begin [in] two to five years" (Di Christina).

[3] Sacks' 1993 *New Yorker* story about a blind man whose sight is restored spawned a 1999 Hollywood film adaptation, *At First Sight*.

[4] *X: The Man with the X-Ray Eyes, Death Watch*, and *Until the End of the World* represent disparate moments in film and history—1963, 1979, 1991. Nevertheless, the three science fiction films are strikingly similar in their treatment of visual prostheses and blindness, and that is why I bring them together here.

[5] Before this postmodern turn, science fiction films lionized the potential of new technologies to create a more efficient, productive, accessible, and equable world.

[6] In choosing this phrase, I have been most directly influenced by Catherine Richards' artwork, "Body in Ruins" (Kroker and Kroker 263-270). This multipaneled piece features the photographed figure of a disabled man with wheelchair and computer prostheses and provocatively juxtaposes his body to two others taken from a NASA diagram: a typically "able" body covered from head to toe in a virtual interface suit, and the anthropomorphic body of that suit's virtually-controlled robot.

[7] I may seem to stretch the term "techno-humans" a bit when I use it to designate Xavier's relationship with his sight-enhancing chemical, but the relationship of technology to chemical medicine in the field of prosthetics is so enmeshed that naming Xavier's drug a "prosthesis" does not seem a misnomer. Also, his model for heightened physical powers of vision is the x-ray machine, suggesting that the drug's effects are comparable to bio-mechanical interfacing.

[8] SPECTARAMA is a low-budget technique using "tinted color and negative reversals" (Morris 82).

Works Cited

Benjamin, Walter. *The Origin of German Tragic Drama.* Trans. John Osborne. New York: Verso, 1994.

---. "The Work of Art in the Age of Mechanical Reproduction." *Illuminations.* Trans. Harry Zohn. Ed. Hannah Arendt. New York: Schocken Books, 1969. 217-251.

Corman, Roger, dir. *X: The Man with the X-Ray Eyes.* With Ray Milland, Diana Van Der Vlis, Harold Stone, and Don Rickles. American International, 1963.

Curry, Nathalie. "Health." *The Independent—London* 9 December 1999: Features Section. Archived at: <http://library.northernlight.com/PN19991213030028351.html>.

Di Christina, Mariette. "The Eyes Have It." *Popular Science* October 1999 <http://new.popsci.com/scitech/features/eyes/index.html>.

Friedberg, Anne. "Cinema and the Postmodern Condition." *Viewing Positions: Ways of Seeing Film.* Ed. Linda Williams. New Brunswick: Rutgers UP, 1995.

Haraway, Donna J. "A Cyborg Manifesto: Science, Technology, and Socialist-Feminism in the Late Twentieth Century." *Simians, Cyborgs and Women: The Reinvention of Nature.* New York: Routledge, 1991.

Kroker, Arthur, and Marilouise Kroker, eds. *Body Invaders: Panic Sex in America.* New York: St. Martin's Press, 1987.

Metz, Christian. *The Imaginary Signifier: Psychoanalysis and the Cinema.* Trans. Celia Britton, Annwyl Williams, Ben Brewster, and Alfred Guzzetti. Bloomington: Indiana UP, 1982.

"A New Featherweight Computer Chip." 6 pm News Broadcast. ABC. WXYZ, Detroit. 12 October 1995.

Sacks, Oliver. "A Neurologist's Notebook: To See and Not to See." *The New Yorker* 10 May 1993: 59-73.

Shaviro, Stephen. *The Cinematic Body.* Minneapolis: U of Minnesota P, 1993.

Tavernier, Bertrand, dir. *Death Watch.* With Harvey Keitel, Romy Schneider, Harry Dean Stanton, and Max von Sydow. Quartet-Films, 1979.

Wenders, Wim, dir. *Until the End of the World.* With William Hurt, Solveig Dommartin, Sam Neill, Max von Sydow, and Jeanne Moreau. Entertainment, 1991.

Winkler, Irwin, dir. *At First Sight.* With Val Kilmer, Mira Sorvino, and Kelly McGillis. Metro-Goldwyn-Mayer, 1999.

The Spectacle of Disabled Masculinity in John Woo's "Heroic Bloodshed" Films

Anthony Enns

Between 1986 and 1992 John Woo, the celebrated Hong Kong filmmaker, made a series of films which have become known as the "heroic bloodshed" films. These films were distinctive for their extreme violence, their rapid editing, and their nostalgia for medieval Chinese chivalry. While the narratives of the "heroic bloodshed" films typically involve the struggles between cops and gangsters in modern-day Hong Kong, the heroes all adhere to a chivalric code of honor in which the sacred bonds of friendship and loyalty are far more important than law and justice. The tremendous success of these films in America has led to a growing interest in Hong Kong cinema and it has also enabled Woo to emigrate and become part of the Hollywood motion picture industry. One reason this assimilation was so easy, as Tony Williams points out, is that these films already show the influence of American Westerns (67). However, Williams also sees these films as reflecting a particular historical crisis concerning the reunification of Hong Kong with China in 1997 (71). The nostalgia for an older system of honor and loyalty has been read as a direct response to the anxiety of Hong Kong citizens in the wake of the Tiananmen Square protests in 1989. By evoking this nostalgia within a climate of impending doom, Woo's films have been read as offering a potentially radical image of masculinity which incorporates both physical prowess and emotional intimacy.

This new masculinity has been interpreted as a direct response to the crisis facing Hong Kong, but no attention has yet been paid to the possible connection between this new masculinity and the frequent presence of figures of disability in Woo's films. Disability appears constantly in this film cycle, always as the result of bullet wounds: characters frequently lose the use of their legs, hands, or sometimes even entire limbs or eyes. These representations of disabled people fulfill many of the stereotypes seen in American films: the disabled are often portrayed as angry because of their inability to accept their own limitations, and death is often shown as a merciful way to deal with the "problem" of disability. Film and disability scholars have already shown that these clichés allow the audience to not have to look at themselves and their own behavior, and thus they put all the responsibility of assimilation onto the disabled person. However, it would be reductive to simply examine these images only in terms of how realistic their portrayals of disability are; rather, an analysis of the function of disability in Woo's films will reveal that it also has potentially positive effects. While the disabled are often weak characters who need to be protected or avenged, they are also depicted as wounded men who have become empowered by their wounds and their suffering. Disability also enables a new kind of masculinity by predicating difference on the figure of disability rather than gender. The primary relationship in each of these films is not between a male and a female, but rather between a disabled and an able-bodied person, and even secondary relationships, relationships between able-bodied characters, are mediated through a third, disabled person. A closer examination of the role of disability in these films will not only reveal a more complex picture of how disabled masculinity might operate within these narratives but also how this role is related to a specific cultural and historical moment.

In order to explain how the figure of disability operates in place of the figure of gender, it is necessary to begin with Laura Mulvey's definitions of narrative and spectacle. In her groundbreaking essay "Visual Pleasure and Narrative Cinema," Mulvey uses Freudian psychoanalysis to argue that there are two pleasures inherent to the viewing of cinema: scopophilia, or objectification, and narcissism, or ego formation. These two pleasures are in contradiction: the first comes from a separation between the viewer and the object, while the second comes from an identification with the object. Mulvey links scopophilia to the cinematic spectacle: "The presence of woman is an indispensable element of spectacle in normal narrative film, yet her visual presence tends to work against the development of a story line, to freeze the flow of action in moments of erotic contemplation" (11). This interruption is brought back into the narrative of the film through the male look, and therefore "the split between spectacle and narrative supports the man's role as the active one of forwarding the story, making things happen" (12). However, Mulvey complicates this model by returning to Freud once again: "[I]n psychoanalytic terms, the female figure . . . also connotes something that the look continually circles around but disavows: her lack of penis, implying a threat of castration and hence unpleasure. Ultimately, the meaning of woman is sexual difference" (13). The male ego has two different options for dealing with the threat that the female figure imposes: voyeurism, the "preoccupation with the reenactment of the original trauma," or fetishistic scopophilia, the "complete disavowal of castration by the substitution of a fetish object" (13-14). Voyeurism, a technique which Mulvey claims is typified by the film noir genre, "has associations with sadism: pleasure lies in ascertaining guilt (immediately associated with castration), asserting control and subjecting the guilty person through punishment . . . . This sadistic side fits in well with narrative. Sadism demands a story, depends on making something happen, forcing a change in another person, a battle of will and strength, victory/defeat" (14). The presence of the female figure thus invokes both pleasure and unpleasure, and it is the narrative which works to transform the unpleasurable aspect of the spectacle back into pure pleasure.

Mulvey notes the emergence of the "buddy movie" genre in the early '70s, "in which the active homosexual eroticism of the central male figures can carry the story without distraction" (11). In this genre, according to Mulvey, the spectacle is completely removed in favor of pure narrative. It would be tempting to place Woo's "heroic bloodshed" films in this category, because they have few female characters and these characters rarely hold any sexual stimulation for the males; however, Mulvey's categories of female spectacle and male narrative have been the source of much debate over the past two decades. Many theorists have attempted to dissect Mulvey's model in order to account for the pleasure of the female or gay male spectator. Paul Willemen, for example, complicates Mulvey's definition of identification by suggesting that there are films in which men occupy both spectacle and narrative simultaneously; they are both passive figures to be looked at and characters who forward the action. To illustrate this point he analyzes the films of Anthony Mann, in which "[t]he viewer's experience is predicated on the pleasure of seeing the male 'exist' . . . [a]nd on the unquiet pleasure of seeing the male mutilated . . . and restored through violent brutality" (16). In Mann's films, the pleasure behind this look clearly has a homoerotic quality, but Willemen adds that the "look at the male produces just as much anxiety as the look at the female" (16). The reason for the violence and mutilation in Mann's films, Willemen suggests, is the need to repress the homosexual desire latent in this look.

Steve Neale, in his article "Masculinity as Spectacle" (1983), reiterates Willemen's notion that identification is not as simple as Mulvey makes it out to be by pointing out that the spectacle of the shoot-out in the Western genre does not halt the narrative but actually propels it forward: "[Shoot-outs] are . . . points at which the drama is finally resolved, a suspense in the culmination of narrative drive" (18). The line between spectacle and narrative is therefore not as clear as Mulvey suggests, and the notion that spectacle is reserved exclusively for women is also brought into question. Neale takes this argument one step further by reexamining Mulvey's notions of voyeurism and fetishism. Neale points out that the sadistic properties associated with voyeurism can be applied to the male as well as the female, and that the source of this sado-masochism is inherently tied to the "repression of any explicit avowal of eroticism in the act of looking at the male" (16). According to Neale, the key difference between the female spectacle and the male spectacle is this "refusal to acknowledge or make explicit an eroticism" (18). Like the female, therefore, the image of the male is a source of unpleasure for the viewer because it evokes an anxiety, not of castration, but of homosexuality, and because this homosexuality must be repressed, the male, like the female, is tortured and mutilated through voyeurism.

Recent scholarship on the representation of masculinity in Woo's films have read them as much more complicated than Mulvey's notion of the "buddy movie," and most Woo scholars also acknowledge that even Neale's model is too simple. Jillian Sandell, for example, uses Neale's theory of "spectacular masculinity" to account for the way in which Woo's films are able to contain moments of spectacle without women, moments in which men look at each other but which also forward the action of the narrative. However, Sandell points out a key flaw in Neale's argument: "For Neale, any objectification automatically means feminization, and feminization automatically means disempowerment. Yet, rather than being a process of disempowerment, masculinity frequently derives considerable social and sexual power from being represented as castrated and wounded" (27). Here Sandell changes the terms of the argument by not defining spectacular masculinity in terms of homosexual repression and sadistic voyeurism, but rather in terms of intimacy and friendship. By showing men who are able to express their emotions without being feminized, Woo's films "valorize a model of masculinity that . . . celebrates both strength and intimacy," and they show relationships where "male bonding can suggest an erotic charge without the associated anxiety such relationships often trigger within the Hollywood action genre" (24).

Julian Stringer builds on this idea by connecting Woo's reinvention of masculinity to the historical crisis of Hong Kong's reunification with China in 1997. Stringer claims that Woo's films are

> caught up in the instabilities of a historically specific conception of patriarchal masculinity. . . . [T]he Hong Kong social environment of [these] films is marked by an ambivalent treatment of male subjectivity. This contradiction within male identity is achieved by what might be regarded as the mixing of two film genres . . . male action or 'doing' genres (the Western, war films) and female 'suffering' genres (melodrama, the woman's film). . . . Woo's films collapse these two paradigms of masculinity into one. They combine simultaneously doing and suffering heroes. (29-30)

Just as Sandell pointed out that the males in these films occupy both passive spectacle and active narrative, Stringer suggests that these films combine the male "doing" genre and the female "suffering" genre. He also agrees with Neale by pointing out that moments of suffering, or spectacle, do not interrupt but rather fuel the narrative: "The emotionally intense suffering . . . is there in order to provide the strength needed for the superhuman acts of heroism and violence" (32). Stringer then connects this combination of doing and suffering to the historical situation of Hong Kong: "The male melodrama of doing and suffering is perfectly in keeping with the situation of a city caught in this impossible position, wanting to both acknowledge its real, impotent position, and also storm its way out of it" (35).

Given the graphic violence of Woo's films and his intense interest in male relationships, it would seem easy to apply Willemen and Neale's notions of spectacular masculinity to these films by arguing that the violence and mutilation were simply caused by the need to repress a homosexual desire latent in the male look. However, Sandell and Stringer both point out that the male look in Woo's films does not have the anxiety associated with it that a Hollywood action film would. In the absence of any homosexual anxiety, however, what is missing from this scholarship is an explanation for the violent, sadomasochistic content of the films. Stringer's argument is useful in that it connects the reinvention of masculinity to a historical crisis, but in the end his definitions of male "doing" and female "suffering" genres merely replicates the problem with Neale's argument: because they are suffering heroes, Woo's characters are therefore feminized, and this again becomes the reason why they must be subject to a sadistic voyeurism.

A possible solution to this problem lies in an examination of disability. What these theories seem to ignore is that the spectacle of the female has not simply been replaced in these films by spectacular masculinity, but rather by the spectacle of disabled masculinity. Disabled men are the focus of the male look, and it is the suffering of these individuals which in turn forwards the narrative. The males in Woo's films are able to occupy both spectacle and narrative because they are able to move back and forth between abled and disabled, often quite freely, and the spectacle of disabled masculinity is a signifier for difference that does not produce the anxiety associated with homosexuality. It is also important to note that the disabled male is not simply feminized. While the image of disabled masculinity does evoke the anxiety of castration, an anxiety which is clearly related to the impotency of Hong Kong in the face of the impending reunification with China, it is also an image of castration that is empowering and heroic.

The spectacle of disabled masculinity can be seen in Woo's first "heroic bloodshed" film, *A Better Tomorrow* (1986). This film tells the story of three men who are able to bond with each other through disability. Ho (Ti Lung) and Mark (Chow Yun-Fat) work for a counterfeiting syndicate and Ho's brother, Kit (Leslie Cheung), is training to be a cop. When Ho is arrested after a counterfeiting deal goes bad, Kit finds out that his brother is a criminal and vows to defeat him. Mark avenges Ho by killing the men who double-crossed him; in the process, however, Mark is shot in the leg and is forced to wear a brace, a disability which causes him to lose his job. Three years later, Ho is released from prison and returns to find Mark working as a janitor. He is visibly moved by the sight of Mark limping and wiping windshields, an occupation which is treated in the film as a fate worse than death itself. When the two finally meet, Ho says, "I didn't realize things had gotten this bad." Mark seems humiliated and ashamed of his disability, and later, as they are drinking in a bar, he ridicules himself by lifting his brace onto the table, making a toast to it in front of his ex-boss, and then pouring the drink over his leg.

As a portrayal of disability, Mark displays many of the clichés which have become familiar to disability scholars; for example, his inability to assimilate back into the community is shown as the result of his own self-contempt. As Paul Longmore points out, in his analysis of portrayals of the "maladjusted disabled person," "[t]hese portrayals suggest that disability is a problem of psychological self-acceptance, of emotional adjustment. Social prejudice rarely intrudes" (34). This is identical to what Lauri Klobas has called "devaluation": "People with disabilities are illustrated as hating themselves and their limitations," and she adds that these characters "require help and aid to regain full personhood status. They are subordinated to characters without disabilities who help turn their lives around" (xiv). Klobas refers to this as "non-disabled catalyst syndrome," a feature common to many disability films. Mark's anger is clearly linked to his inability to accept his own personal limitations, and thus the film is able to avoid the question of whether his anger could be the result of larger social problems, such as prejudice and discrimination, and like the maladjusted disabled person, Mark requires Ho, a non-disabled catalyst, to help him adjust. Ho attempts to help Mark by devising a scheme to rob the counterfeiting syndicate; Ho intends for his brother to arrest him, which he hopes will repair their relationship, and he wants Mark to be able to escape with the money and start a new life. Although his plan does not work out as he intended, Ho's attempts to help Mark and to sacrifice for Mark's welfare do result in Mark's recuperation. In the climactic gunfight, when the two brothers are surrounded, Mark's disability miraculously disappears; he is not only able to walk, but also to run and fight with the same strength and agility as before, if not more. However, Mark does not simply represent a disabled person who is brought back into the community by the help of a non-disabled catalyst; rather, he is also able to help the catalyst in return. Through his own self-sacrifice in battle, Mark is able to convince Kit that his brother loves him and is trying to help him. Ho and Mark develop an intimacy between them because of Mark's disability, and Mark's disability, in turn, is a spectacle which is able to bridge the rift between the two brothers.

The spectacle of disabled masculinity is even more prevalent in Woo's next film, *The Killer* (1989). In this film the relationship between two enemies, a hit man named Jeff (Chow Yun-Fat) and a cop named Lee (Danny Lee), is mediated by Jeff's disabled contractor, Sydney (Chu Kong). Sydney once worked as a hit man himself but was forced to quit after being shot in the hand. Jeff seems to be particularly fascinated by Sydney's disability, and he mentions it in nearly every interaction between the two men. Jeff attempts to test the strength of Sydney's wounded hand by making him grab hold of objects, such as a beer can, and he encourages Sydney to exercise it: "You should use it more often." But, like Mark, Sydney has a problem with low self-esteem. "A one-handed killer is useless," he replies. When Jeff's last hit goes wrong, however, and his employer attempts to kill him, Sydney intervenes by insisting that Jeff should be paid. Sydney is so insistent that the boss beats him and is about to kill him when Sydney, like Mark, has a miraculous recuperation and regains the use of his hand. Even though he has been brutally beaten, Sydney is able to escape with the money after killing dozens of men and taking the boss hostage. When Sydney manages to get back to Jeff with the money, he is too wounded to survive and asks Jeff to kill him; Jeff's act of shooting Sydney is not portrayed in the film as callous but rather as an act of kindness and mercy.

This merciful death is another trope in many disability films which Longmore has spoken about most emphatically. Longmore claims that films in which disabled characters choose to commit suicide "present death as the only logical and humane solution" (33). While the non-disabled audience is asked to feel good about itself for being so compassionate, Longmore argues, these films actually allow the audience "to avoid confronting its own fears and prejudices," and the audience is actually "urged to compliment itself for its compassion in supporting death" (33). Disability is thus represented as making "membership in the community and meaningful life itself impossible, and death is preferable. Better dead than disabled" (34). This criticism could certainly be leveled at *The Killer*: in a community where everyone carries a gun there is certainly no meaningful life for someone with a disabled hand. However, such a reading would devalue the radically new and positive image of masculinity illustrated in Sydney's relationship to Jeff, as well as the tremendous impact this relationship has on the other characters. Lee is so moved by Sydney's sacrifice, for example, that he makes a sacred vow of friendship with Jeff, and therefore the spectacle of Sydney's disability enables the intimacy between Jeff and Lee.

The scene where Sydney asks Jeff to kill him is repeated in an even more dark and somber way in Woo's next film, *A Bullet in the Head* (1990). This film is set in 1967 and depicts several street protests which are brutally suppressed by the police, an obvious allegory for the Tiananmen Square massacre of 1989. The film tells the story of three friends growing up in Hong Kong: Ben (Tony Leung), Paul (Waise Lee), and Frank (Jacky Cheung). When Ben accidentally kills a gang leader in revenge for beating Frank, the three friends are forced to flee to Vietnam, where they hope to earn money as smugglers. After teaming up with a fourth man, a cool, French-speaking Eurasian named Luke (Simon Yam), the group robs another gang leader of a box of gold and attempt to escape. The intimacy of their friendship is threatened, however, after Paul, overcome by greed, betrays the other two and shoots Frank in the head. The bullet doesn't kill Frank but rather becomes lodged in his skull, causing him excruciating pain which eventually drives him to become a morphine addict. When Ben discovers what has happened to Frank, the two men share long looks at each other and then Frank, like Sydney, asks Ben to kill him. Ben complies with Frank's request, and the rest of the film is devoted to Ben seeking revenge for Paul's betrayal. In many ways this film seems to reverse the narrative trajectory of the previous two, moving instead from intimacy to alienation, but such a reading ignores the fact that the primary relationship in the film is not between the original three friends but rather between Ben and Luke. The relationship between these two men becomes increasingly intimate during the course of the film, and this relationship is mediated through Frank, the figure of disabled masculinity. Perhaps what makes this film darker than the previous two is the absence of any miraculous recuperation of Frank's disability, an absence which is made even more explicit by the fact that Ben keeps Frank's punctured skull as a reminder of Paul's betrayal.

The spectacle of disabled masculinity is perhaps most significant in this last film, not only because Frank's disability is also the title of the film, but also because it shows a direct connection between disability and the historical crisis facing Hong Kong in the early '90s. The bullet in the head is not merely a symbol of Paul's betrayal, a betrayal so deep it can never be healed or forgotten, but it also becomes a symbol of the Tiananmen Square massacre, which remains a vivid backdrop throughout the film. This event was an obvious focus for Hong Kong's anxiety over its impending return to Chinese sovereignty in 1997, and while the new image of masculinity presented in Woo's films is clearly related to this sense of impending doom, it is only through disability that this reinvention of masculinity is made possible. It is the spectacle of disabled masculinity which looms over these films as a reminder of the impossible situation in which this city is caught, as Stringer points out, "wanting to both acknowledge its real, impotent position, and also storm its way out of it" (35). The anxiety this spectacle produces is not the anxiety of a repressed homosexuality but rather it is an historically-grounded anxiety of impotence, and like the anxiety of castration, it can only be assuaged through the violence and sadism associated with the voyeuristic look.

While most critics mark the end of Woo's "heroic bloodshed" cycle with *Hard Boiled* (1992), it is significant that during this period he also made *Once a Thief* (1991), a comedy-thriller which has received relatively little attention. Although the narrative of this film is much lighter than the previous films, at times even combining violent action with slapstick comedy, it still emphasizes many of the same values, particularly the importance of male intimacy. The spectacle of disabled masculinity also features a central role in this film, and its portrayal of disability is particularly interesting for the ways in which it breaks with Woo's earlier clichés. The film concerns three orphans, Joe (Chow Yun-Fat), James (Leslie Cheung), and Cherie (Cherie Cheung), who were raised together by Mr. Chow, an abusive man who trained them to be professional art thieves. As adults, the three thieves continue to live and work together, although Joe and James are essentially partners; Cherie's involvement in the operation seems limited to translating French. Cherie is also Joe's girlfriend, but from the beginning of the film it is clear that they are having difficulties in their relationship: Cherie seems desperate to get married, while Joe prefers to remain "footloose and carefree." It later becomes clear that the primary relationship in the film is not between Joe and Cherie, but rather between Joe and James. Joe repeatedly risks his life to save James, and after escaping from a castle with a stolen painting, Joe and James even pause on the side of a road while Joe tends to James' wounds, which is a familiar scene of male bonding that echoes both *A Better Tomorrow* and *The Killer*. Eventually Joe sacrifices himself to save James' life by driving his car into an enemy gunboat.

Two years later, Joe reappears in a wheelchair to find that James and Cherie are now a couple. He chooses to confront James first, but rather than explain what happened to him or where he has been for two years, the two men simply stare at each other for several seconds while the camera moves back and forth between them. This moment of silence is a perfect example of how disabled masculinity becomes spectacularized in Woo's films; it does not forward the narrative at all, but merely pauses and allows the characters and the audience to simply gaze. This scene even has a greater emotional intensity than the gaze shared by Ho and Mark in *A Better Tomorrow* because it remains entirely uninterrupted by dialogue. Joe's disability is also similar to Mark's in that it facilitates the relationship between the two able-bodied characters. If Joe had returned from his accident unscathed, the relationship between James and Cherie would not have been possible, and it is their mutual consideration for Joe and their gratitude for the sacrifice he made for them which becomes the focus of their romance; there is even a dream sequence in which Cherie imagines she is kissing Joe, but Joe gradually transforms into James. Unlike Mark, however, Joe does not seem to have any resentment for his disability or for the fact that he has lost his girlfriend to James; on the contrary, he seems to support their relationship and appears worried that his presence might jeopardize it. Joe's portrayal of disability also differs radically from Woo's previous portrayals in that Joe is depicted as a victim of prejudice. Soon after his reappearance, Joe pays a visit to his first father, Mr. Chow, and begs him for charity. Joe had always been Chow's favorite son, but upon seeing him in a wheelchair, Chow kicks him down a flight of stairs. There is also a scene where James is locked inside a vault and Joe has difficulty rescuing him because the building's front stairs have no access ramp. Scenes such as these emphasize that the problems faced by disabled people are largely problems created by society, and when free of these obstacles, Joe appears to be as happy and well-adjusted as before his accident; there is even a ballroom scene where Joe is shown dancing with Cherie, an act which would have been inconceivable for the disabled males in Woo's previous films.

However, the positive aspects of Joe's portrayal of disability are somewhat undercut in the climactic battle, where Joe is able to save James' life once again by leaping from his chair and performing a series of martial arts kicks on their mutual attacker, Mr. Chow. This miraculous recuperation is obviously similar to Mark's in *A Better Tomorrow* and Sydney's in *The Killer*, except for the fact that Joe has only been pretending to be disabled rather than actually overcoming his disability through force of will, as the other characters had done. In some ways, this deception undermines the progressive aspects of Joe's portrayal of disability. For example, Joe's positive self-image could then be explained by the fact that he is not actually disabled, and in the final scene, where Joe and James manage to achieve a comic revenge over Mr. Chow by placing his wounded body in Joe's wheelchair, disability once again becomes a source of shame and humiliation. However, by depicting the discrimination and the difficulties that disabled people actually face, Woo is able to use the spectacle of disabled masculinity in this film as a way of not only achieving a new kind of masculinity but also addressing the realities of disability, which his previous films largely ignored.

Despite the fact that most of these films clearly do not contain politically correct representations of disabled people, they still represent a world where people constantly move back and forth between disability and ability and where disabled people have a particularly significant function in the community. While they are often assisted by non-disabled catalysts, these disabled characters frequently enable their able-bodied companions to have more emotionally intimate relationships through a reconfiguration of masculinity which bridges the realms of intimacy and action. It is the spectacle of disabled masculinity in these films, therefore, which simultaneously represents and works to alleviate the anxieties facing Hong Kong in the late 1980s and early 1990s.

Works Cited

Klobas, Lauri E. *Disability Drama in Television and Film.* Jefferson, NC: McFarland, 1988.

Longmore, Paul K. "Screening Stereotypes: Images of Disabled People." *Social Policy* 16.1 (Summer 1985): 31-37.

Mulvey, Laura. "Visual Pleasure and Narrative Cinema." *Screen* 16.3 (1975): 6-18.

Neale, Steve. "Masculinity as Spectacle: Reflections on Men and Mainstream Cinema." *Screening the Male: Exploring Masculinities in Hollywood Cinema.* Ed. Steven Cohan and Ina Rae Hark. New York: Routledge, 1993. 9-20.

Sandell, Jillian. "Reinventing Masculinity: The Spectacle of Male Intimacy in the Films of John Woo." *Film Quarterly* 49.4 (Summer 1996): 23-34.

Stringer, Julian. "'Your Tender Smiles Give Me Strength': Paradigms of Masculinity in John Woo's *A Better Tomorrow* and *The Killer*." *Screen* 38.1 (Spring 1997): 25-41.

Willemen, Paul. "Anthony Mann: Looking at the Male." *Framework* 15-17 (1981): 16-20.

Williams, Tony. "Space, Place, and Spectacle: The Crisis Cinema of John Woo." *Cinema Journal* 36.2 (Winter 1997): 67-84.

Woo, John, dir. *A Better Tomorrow*. With Ti Lung, Chow Yun-Fat, and Leslie Cheung. Cinema City Co. Ltd., 1986.

---, dir. *A Bullet in the Head*. With Tony Leung, Waise Lee, and Jacky Cheung. Golden Princess Film Production Ltd., 1990.

---, dir. *The Killer*. With Chow Yun-Fat, Danny Lee, and Chu Kong. Circle Films, 1989.

---, dir. *Once a Thief*. With Chow Yun-Fat, Leslie Cheung, and Cherie Cheung. Golden Princess Film Production Ltd., 1991.

Sexy Cyborgs: Disability and Erotic Politics in Cronenberg's *Crash*

James L. Cherney

> We are the Sexual Other.
>
> —*Barbara Faye Waxman*

In our ableist culture, people with disabilities often encounter barriers to being sexy, having sex, and expressing sexuality. Throughout North America and Europe they face prohibitive sexual laws, codes, and values that unconscionably restrict many accessible forms of sexual expression (Waxman; Shakespeare, Gillespie-Sells, and Davies). While able-bodied observers might ignore such restrictions, or bracket them as the work of an overzealous religious right, disability activists have long argued that sexual taboos are a central component of the ableist establishment. Anne Finger struck a nerve in many people with disabilities when she called sexuality "the source of our deepest oppression . . . the source of our deepest pain" ("Forbidden" 9). Nowhere is our culture's tendency toward ableism more evident than in the way it discounts and degrades the sexuality of people with disabilities. Anthropologist Robert F. Murphy observed that our society tends to construct and (en)vision people with disabilities in sexually prohibitive ways, as "either malignantly sexual, like libidinous dwarfs, or more commonly, completely asexual, an attribute frequently applied to the elderly as well" (97). Just as sexism employs a masculine perspective of sex to subordinate the feminine, ableism constructs an able-bodied perspective that isolates the disabled as sexual others.

Mary Douglas' famous work on purity and danger provides a basic explanation for this relationship between sexuality and ableism. In the context of her work, de-eroticizing the disabled body signals the oppressive ableist hierarchy of contemporary society. Douglas writes: "[M]any ideas about sexual dangers are better interpreted as symbols of the relation between parts of society, as mirroring designs of hierarchy or symmetry which apply in the larger social system" (4). In this analysis, cultures stigmatize "polluted sex" to gratify such impulses as "the desire to keep the body (physical and social) intact" and "the desire to keep straight the internal lines of the social system" (141). Viewing the disabled body as asexual or as "malignantly sexual" extends a marginalizing wall protecting ableist views of the disabled body as other, and protecting ableism as a legitimate social practice.

Such a wall seeks to obscure ableist thinking, but it reveals an important point: sex lies at the core of the ableist imagination. The ableist perspective denies viewing the disabled body as sexy, and often views the sex shared with or between people with disabilities as abnormal itself, but it is easy to read a voyeuristic impulse behind these prohibitions. As both Freud and Foucault have noted, attention to sex is always more apparent when denied. Finger's work suggests that the ableist focus on sex pervades ableist thinking, and she notes that sex-based distinctions even form subsets in its discriminatory apparatus. Like Murphy, she identifies the two primary ableist views of people with disabilities as asexual or infected by libido, but she further notes that the divergent associations are organized around gender divisions: disabled *women* are asexual, while disabled *men* are "filled with diseased lusts" ("Claiming" 282, 291-92; qtd. in Norden 316). Ableist attention to sex borders on obsessive when even the stereotypes are sexually categorized. Certainly sexual mores alone cannot explain ableism, but the pervasiveness of sexual distinctions and sexual taboos in ableist thinking demands further analysis.

To do so, I propose that we invert the conventional perspective on ableist impulses and their targets. Based on Douglas' explanation, we could (and often do) understand restrictions on sexual expression of people with disabilities as simple extensions of ableist oppression. In this perspective, the ableist identifies actions associated with the disenfranchised Other and creates policy to discipline and punish those activities. But reversing this perspective sheds new light on ableist thinking. In this second perspective, the need to restrict certain actions promotes disenfranchisement and oppression of the other. The first analysis sees disabled sex as polluted because it involves the already soiled body of the disabled person; the second identifies oppressing the disabled body as an attempt to make disabled sex polluted and, by extension, repulsive. The simplicity of this move belies its significance, for the two perspectives indicate different origins, motives, and patterns behind ableist practices. Indeed, the first perspective obscures ableist motives while the second suggests that ableism arises in part from a need to repress sexual attraction to disability. This second perspective rests on Freud's theory that disgust masks secret attraction, which Lennard J. Davis argues is necessary to understanding negative views of disability (*Enforcing* 12). Viewed as sublimated attraction, learned repulsion to the disabled body can be understood as socially-conditioned psychosis, just as intense latent homoerotic desires are understood to generate the psychosis homophobia. Society protects itself from recognizing ableism as such a psychosis by making sexual attraction to disability taboo. As Leslie Fiedler argued in his famous study *Freaks*: "All Freaks are perceived to one degree or another as erotic. Indeed, abnormality arouses in some 'normal' beholders a temptation to go beyond looking to *knowing* in the full carnal sense the ultimate other. That desire is itself felt as freaky, however, since it implies not only a longing for degradation but a dream of breaching the last taboo against miscegenation" (137). In this analysis, revaluing and rethinking sex becomes a project capable of deconstructing ableist views. Just as ableist views of sex politically and socially promote the ideology of ableism, challenging those views can undermine ableist hegemony.

Images of sex and disability in film are critically important at this juncture. Sex in our society has coupled furiously with the visual imagination (in everything from the erotic power of the image, to the myths that inform beauty, to the primarily visual appeal of the fashion world) and given enormous power to its offspring, the cinema. We look to film to learn what is sexy, we look to film to realize our erotic fantasies, and we look to film to validate our beliefs. Similarly, film plays a substantial role in the construction of the able-bodied imagination of disability. Unless we ourselves are born disabled, we form our first impression of disability from images of disability in our homes, our communities, and in the media. Erving Goffman argued that it is "through our sense of sight that the stigma of others most frequently becomes evident" (42). Although our current understanding identifies stigma as a social construct rather than as a visible characteristic, sight continues to play a significant role in its development. We learn who and what to stigmatize by witnessing discriminatory treatment of people with disabilities. Note the emphasis on the visual—and its control—in Murphy's description of a typical episode of ableist social education: "Children are quite understandably curious about disabled people and often stare at them, only to have their parents yank their arms and say, 'Don't look.' Nothing could better communicate to a child a sense of horror for disability; the condition is so terrible that one cannot speak about it or even look at it" (130). Seeing disability so dominates the development, production, and structures of ableism that Davis declares unequivocally: "Disability is a specular moment" (*Enforcing* 12). In this context, images of disability in American cinema, which Martin F. Norden has aptly labeled "the cinema of isolation," have protected ableist foundations by burying and visually denying the repressed erotic impulse that inflames ableism. Insofar as ableism springs from attraction to disability, cinematic isolation protects ableists from confronting their desire. In typical films of the cinema of isolation, ableists are able to enjoy the voyeuristic erotic pleasure of seeing the other displayed against a background that allows them to deny their desire. The stock movie characters Norden identifies as the "Sweet Innocent" and the "Obsessive Avenger" correspond roughly with the asexual disabled female and the disabled male infected with "diseased lusts" (314-23). Films displaying these characterizations reinforce ableist sexual stereotypes while allowing the ableist to enjoy "safely" the erotic pleasure of watching the disabled body in action. Ableism, the repressed attraction turned repulsion temporarily able-bodied persons (TABs) project on people with disabilities, thrives in this environment as the erotic nature of the gaze is protected from recognition by blatantly desexualized images. In the remainder of this paper, I read David Cronenberg's 1996 film *Crash* as a challenge to this regime perpetuated by the cinema of isolation. By exploring the intersection of sexuality, disability, and cyborgs, *Crash* confronts the ableist gaze. To explain this function of the film, the next section introduces the political theory of the cyborg.

Disability and the Cyborg

Unleashed by Donna Haraway in her "Manifesto for Cyborgs," the cyborg has become a radically new figure reshaping the political landscape. Many early cyborg theorists have suggested that people with disabilities should celebrate a cyborg existence and engage in cyborg politics. Penley and Ross, for instance, assert that "the highly developed technoculture of the handicapped and the complexity of their discussions around appropriate levels of technology" is an important area for future study of cyborg theory (xvi). Likewise, Haraway recognizes that "[p]erhaps paraplegics and other severely handicapped people can (and sometimes do) have the most intense experiences of complex hybridization with other communication devices" (*Simians* 178). People with disabilities have always had a complicated relationship with technology. As technology is built for and by bodies, many technological advances reify and affirm notions of normalcy that disable people who do not have "normal" bodies. On the other hand, technology can provide aids and prostheses which allow many people with disabilities to accomplish many of the tasks associated with "normal" life and access to areas that had previously excluded the disabled. Finally, the medical community often seeks to "solve" the "problem of disability" through tech fixes (such as therapeutic machines, surgical procedures, and drug regimens) that attempt to make disabled persons into normals. The variety of intimate roles technology plays in the lives of people with disabilities suggests the need for a closer examination of the potential benefits of cyborg theory in Disability Studies. This is not to argue that we should uncritically accept cyborg thinking, or to conclude that cyborg politics is the most viable option for people with disabilities. In some contexts, the cyborg has been seen as a detrimental construct. The Deaf rejection of the cochlear implant, for example, implicated both the cyborgian impact of the disputed technology and the status of identity politics in cyborg political theory (Cherney).

Nevertheless, the cyborg and cyborgian sex offer unique avenues for rethinking normal society, normal bodies, and normal relationships with technology. Essentially, cyborg politics rearranges the foundation of equality by recognizing that interaction between humans and machines have made us all cyborgs. The "normal human body" has become so dependent on technology, and integrated with it in so many ways, that the root binary division between human and machine has been weakened. This blasphemous transgression makes the biological fact of distinctiveness between different kinds of humans seem practically irrelevant. By blurring the line between human and technology, the cyborg denies the value of the distinction between these historic opposites. Once violated, the foundational border separating machines and humans becomes increasingly leaky and imprecise, and the fluid that escapes through the holes simply washes away the finer distinctions based on gender, or race, or ability. On what grounds can I claim to be different from any other technology dependent organism if I cannot clearly distinguish myself from my toaster? As cyborgs, we are all hybrids and all bordercrossers. Our common violation of the human/machine divide unites us and becomes the only "pure" foundation of identity. This context renders distinctions based on bodily ability senseless, for how do we separate one cyborg from another? A cyborg who depends on a car is not qualitatively different from a cyborg who depends on a wheelchair. As cyborgs, biologically distinct bodies become irrelevant, so socially constructed disability becomes an artificial abstraction.

While the presence of the cyborg belittles the distinctions we make between different humans, cyborg theory undermines the ideological foundations of ableist culture. The line dividing normal/abnormal, which Davis labels "the modern binary," and virtually any extension thereof, is less visible in the cyborg context. Such root opposing divisions form the basis of ableism. Davis locates the impetus for the normal/abnormal divide in "the desire to split bodies into two immutable categories—whole and incomplete, abled and disabled, normal and abnormal, functional and dysfunctional." As Davis put it, cultures construct themselves through an act of splitting, equivalent to Freud's process of *Spaltung*. Splitting protects the social order: the division of good from bad creates and protects the notion of good. Inability to craft a clean break between desired and undesirable creates social anxiety and confusion. As culture wields biopower by splitting bodies into good and bad parts ("good: hair, face, lips, eyes, hands; bad: sexual organs, excretory organs, underarms"), the unification of these parts in a single body creates something of a psychological crisis, making *Spaltung* a social imperative. Davis concludes: "The division neatly seals off the frightening writing on the wall that reminds the hallucinated whole being that its wholeness is in fact a hallucination, a developmental fiction. The primitive reaction creates the absolute categories of abled and disabled, with the concomitant defenses against the fragmented body" ("Nude Venuses" 53-54). As the emblem of unification, the cyborg implicitly denies the power of division, problematizing any act of *Spaltung* and collapsing these fundamental divides that shape the ableist view of the world.

Images of cyborgs abound in American cinema and television. Indeed, the most readily recognizable cyborg characters all appear in these fora: the Terminator, RoboCop, and the 'Borg in television's *Star Trek: The Next Generation* (1987-1994). Like portrayals of the disabled body, most depictions of the cyborg are sexually isolated, as the cyborg is generally imagined as sterilized or unacceptably aberrant because of its mechanical components. Generally speaking, the Terminator or the 'Borg are presented as asexuals, often more machine than human, and incapable of true human emotions. The cyborgs of *Crash* are displayed much differently. In *Crash*, the collision of human and machine is literalized in the automobile accident and celebrated as a sexual event. Both the recurring theme of the film and the characters explode the traditional view of the cyborg, and the disabled body, as asexual constructs, repeatedly displaying these figures in an erotic context.

Crash, Cyborgs, Sex, and Disability

David Cronenberg's controversial *Crash* directly engages the intersection of sex, cyborg theory, and disability. A rather faithful adaptation of J.G. Ballard's 1973 erotic novel by the same name, its display of sexual acts was explicit enough to win the film a NC-17 rating in this country and became the focus of many critics.[1] Jack Matthews described the film in *Newsday* as containing "some of the most graphic and unconventional sex scenes this side of a triple-X rating" (B3), and Janet Maslin wrote for the *New York Times* that "Cronenberg's cool and rigorous film explores a link between sex and car crashes" (C11).

Less discussed is the film's examination of cyborgs, which is somewhat surprising given the presence of the cyborg theme in J. G. Ballard's original novel and in Cronenberg's work. The union of dichotomous pairs (the basic action of the cyborg) appears at some level in most of Cronenberg's films to date. Steven Shaviro argues that in Cronenberg's major films released prior to 1991:

> New arrangements of the flesh break down traditional binary oppositions between mind and matter, image and object, self and other, inside and outside, male and female, nature and culture, human

and inhuman, organic and mechanical. Indeed, systematic undoing of these distinctions, on every possible level, is the major structural principle of all of Cronenberg's films. (130)

While *Crash* was made well after Shaviro's critique, the argument retains its cogency rather well, as the film continues the tradition of collapsing distinctions by reveling in the synthesis of body and machine in its erotic exploration of the automobile accident. Likewise, Shaviro's claim that "[e]verything in [Cronenberg's] films is corporeal, grounded in the monstrous intersection of physiology and technology" continues to cogently explain the central dynamic in *Crash* (129).

The film's plot erupts out of a car accident between film producer James Ballard, played by James Spader, and Dr. Helen Remington, played by Holly Hunter. While Dr. Remington's husband is killed in the accident, both she and Ballard survive with serious injuries. While recovering, the two meet and eventually become involved with the enigmatic character Vaughn, played by Elias Koteas, a former international traffic control specialist who has become enamored with the erotic implications of the car accident. The remainder of the film explores the predominantly sexual relationships of these major characters along with Ballard's wife Catherine, played by Deborah Kara Unger, Vaughn's assistant Colin Seagrave, played by Peter MacNeill, and Gabrielle, an earlier crash victim who has joined Vaughn's circle, played by Rosanna Arquette. Throughout, these encounters occur in the context of Vaughn's project that he initially describes in terms familiar to cyborg theorists. "It's something we are all—intimately—involved in," he says. "The reshaping of the human body by modern technology." Displaying the film's sex scenes in environments dominated by technological devices visually reinforces the cyborg theme. Most of the sex acts occur in spaces exquisitely shaped by technological concerns: in the seats of cars, pressed against the nose of an airplane in a hanger, and in a camera room (with the "camera girl") on the set of the film Ballard is producing. Even those sex scenes located in more traditional environments are generally marked by technology's conspicuous presence. Ballard and Catherine engage in sex while watching cars on the highway, they talk about Vaughn's car ("it's like a bed on wheels") while having intercourse in bed, and Catherine meticulously describes the remains of Ballard's wrecked vehicle while masturbating Ballard in the hospital. Out of the film's numerous sex scenes, only one does not directly engage modern technology in some way. This brief, dialogue-free transition scene of

Ballard and Catherine having face-to-face sex in a chair seems remarkably conventional, and its obvious ill-fitness in the film as a whole makes one immediately aware of technology's near omnipresence in the sex scenes. Against the large amount of time spent rigorously detailing sexual adventurousness, the extremely short duration granted this glimpse of typical sexual behavior announces that such everyday acts are simply unworthy of attention. Common sexual activity has not been overlooked; it is viciously ignored. The erotic potential of Vaughn's project is underscored by his restatement of its terms to Ballard in the following conversation:

> VAUGHN: That's the future, Ballard, and you're already a part of it. You're beginning to see that, for the first time, there's a benevolent psychopathology that beckons towards us. For example, the car crash is a fertilizing rather than a destructive event. A liberation of sexual energy, mediating the sexuality of those who have died with an intensity that's impossible in any other form. To experience that, to live that . . . that's my project.
> BALLARD: What about the reshaping of the human body by modern technology. I thought *that* was your project.
> VAUGHN: That's just a crude sci-fi concept. It kinda floats on the surface and doesn't threaten anybody. I use it to test the resilience of my potential partners in psychopathology.

Vaughn's interest, in short, makes cyborg theory seem almost conventional, as he explores the more controversial dimensions of the sexual power of the penetration of the body by machine.

Crash is also about disability. At one point or another, all of the major characters are displayed as disabled, disfigured, or scarred, except Ballard's wife Catherine. Ballard uses a wheelchair and crutches, Vaughn sports a heavily scarred face, Dr. Remington has facial scars and walks with her head resting on her shoulder, Seagrave has a concussion, and Gabrielle wears leg braces, a body brace, and walks with canes. Catherine herself seems to feel excluded from this club. She proudly displays large bruises she receives while having sex with Vaughn, and, at the end of the final sequence of the film—where Ballard intentionally involves her in a car accident so she can experience her own cyborgian side—Catherine is dismayed to find that she has "escaped" unscathed. The film focuses on disability and sex throughout, forever entwining them and exploring places where they overlap. In the following analysis I closely read a few scenes that most explicitly depict the interpenetration of these themes and focus on the erotic potential of the disabled body, scars, and finally, tattoos.

In the first scene I examine, Gabrielle, alluringly dressed in a matching black leather ensemble of jacket, short skirt, cane, and leg braces accented by fishnet hose, visits a Mercedes Benz showroom with Ballard. The salesman who approaches as she leans over the trunk of a large black and gray convertible is clearly caught by her appearance. As she hugs the car, the camera focuses on the inverted vee of the back of her legs, her skirt riding slowly up to expose a large scar on the upper left thigh. The camera quickly flicks its gaze to the tall and well-groomed salesman, whose eyes focus on her legs, struggle to make eye contact, and finally return to rest on her exposed thighs. He asks if anything interests her. "This interests me," she replies. Continuing to fondle the vehicle, she calls attention to her disability, coyly saying: "I'd like to see if I can fit into a car designed for a normal body. Could you help me into it please?" As she sits in the car, she exposes the crotch of her hose, hands the salesman her cane, and sultrily declares "I'm caught." While entering the car, placing first one leg into position before shifting weight to allow her to raise the other, a metal ring attached to her left brace has penetrated the edge of the leather seat. The salesman looks away furtively, a small smile on his face, checking to see whether he will be noticed. He grabs her leg and tugs, pulling progressively harder when his efforts fail to free her leg. As the salesman struggles, the camera directs us to Gabrielle's fingers busily stroking the crotch of Ballard's jeans. Gabrielle's heavy breathing accented by small moans becomes audible, and the sex act progresses until its orgasmic release when the salesman finally frees her leg from the seat with an audible rip.

The erotic display of Gabrielle's disabled body, the titillating flash of the scar on her thigh, and the sexual implications of the salesman's attempt to assist her, clearly alter the conventional views of disability. In direct contrast to the ableist perspective, Gabrielle is beautiful, erotic, and desired. Ballard and Gabrielle carry the sexual tension into the next scene, where they proceed to have sex in the front seat of Ballard's car. The leg braces again play a specific role, as Ballard struggles to lift her leg beyond the steering wheel. The frustrated fumbling with Gabrielle's disabled body reminds one of the passionate but inexperienced sexual experimentation of teenagers in the back seat of a car. Conventional expectations might see the braces as posing unwanted difficulty, but it is clear from facial expressions and audible groans that this is sex*play*. Finally lifting Gabrielle's leg, Ballard tears the hose away from her thigh scar, sensuously running his fingers along its length and kissing it passionately.[2]

Scars are typically assumed to be unsexy, disfiguring blemishes. In *Stigma*, Goffman cites numerous stories of people with scarred faces as prototypes of the stigmatized body (1, 10, 45). In a sex scene from Eric Red's 1991 film *Body Parts*, a man recovering from a serious operation after a car accident wonderingly asks his wife, "It doesn't bother you to touch the scars?" His wife seems surprised at her own willingness to stroke him, replying "I thought it would . . . ." Scars denote wounds, sites of leakage, places where the boundaries of the body have been breached. Like cyborgs, scars suggest the impermanence, fluidity, and instability of the body. Scars violate the precise outlines of the proper human form. To find scars sexy is to find the "normal" human body boring, to admit that beauty can be located elsewhere than in the perfection of idealized form. Scars also imply cyborgian influence. Scars are often created by contact with technology, and scarred people often know what it is like to experience a cyborg existence. Scars can identify the location of direct human/technology interfaces, where metal meets skin and leaves a permanent impression.

Tattoos can be read as a special kind of scar in this context. Recognized as decoration, and displaying the influence of technology on the body, tattoos have long been associated with certain ideas of beauty and sex. It is not uncommon to find people willing to admit that they find tattoos sexy, and the popular use of breasts, thighs, and buttocks as locations for tattoos reinforce their sexual implications. Tattoos also mark the exotic, suggesting the mysteriousness of Bradbury's *Illustrated Man*, the heavily tattooed bodies of the Orient, or the tribal markings of pre-colonized peoples. By extension, tattoo wearing carries somewhat naughty connotations, as violations of social orders of display, reserved for seafarers, toughs, and bad kids. Tattoos, too, indicate cyborgian action, the penetration of the artist's needle or tool and the resulting permanent placement of pigment in an artificial pattern under the epidermis. *Crash* conflates the role of the scar with the tattoo, leading us to see both in the same erotic role. This association is apparent in the sexual power that scars play in the film, but it is strongly reinforced by a scene where Vaughn and Ballard both receive "medical" tattoos detailing the impact of automobile parts upon their bodies.

This scene preludes Vaughn and Ballard's only direct sexual encounter in the film. Vaughn contacts Ballard at work, telling him that he needs to "talk to him about the project," casting what follows into an explicitly cyborg context. Ballard arrives in a long dark room with a row of padded reclining chairs along the side. Each identical chair has an identical lamp alongside it, and retracted privacy screens are waiting between each chair attached to the adjoining walls. The setting is disorienting: it is not easily identifiable as any conventional location, and seems to combine elements of the living room or massage parlor with the institutional regimen of the hospital or prison. The camera cuts to focus on Vaughn, reclining on one of the chairs as a woman in a white coat leans over his half-nude body. At first it appears that she is drawing on his chest, but the buzzing sound emitted by the tool she wields and the slight grunts of pain we hear from Vaughn make it clear that he is receiving a tattoo. The tattoo is the outline of a steering wheel impressed upon his abdomen. As she works, Vaughn tells her she is making it "too clean." She objects that "medical tattoos are supposed to be clean." His reply highlights both the futuristic implications of his work and suggests its sexual undertone. "This is not a *medical* tattoo, this is a *prophetic* tattoo, and prophecy is ragged and dirty. So. Make it ragged and dirty." Not stopping her work she responds: "Prophetic? Is this personal prophecy or global prophecy?" Vaughn confidently rejoins: "There's no difference."

The prophetic nature of the cyborg project, Vaughn's insistence that we are all, essentially, but awaiting our own collision, may be too radical for many to accept. But it echoes the inevitable collapse of our own bodies, the necessity that everyone will someday become disabled, that has led to the term "temporarily able-bodied persons," or TABs. On this level, as the simple reminder of our all-too-human frailty, Vaughn's tattooing can be recognized as a political statement. It is a statement, the film makes clear, with definite erotic potential. After Ballard gets his own tattoo, the impression of a car hood ornament on his thigh, the two rendezvous in Vaughn's car and engage in sex. The tattoos, just as the scars a few scenes before, are critical sites of contact in this lovemaking. Revealing Ballard's new tattoo from under its gauze bandage receives as much attention as any striptease, and they each kiss the other's tattoos. In *Crash*, this politically charged reminder of the limits of the human body is not rejected or hidden, it is embraced and sexually celebrated as the peak of erotic expression.

Conclusion

> I want to be seen as beautiful because of my disability, not in spite of it.
>
> —*Aimee Mullins*

This paper examined David Cronenberg's controversial film *Crash* in the context of the political matrix formed by the intersection of disability, sexuality, and technology. As I read the film, *Crash* (re)visions these issues in ways that powerfully contrast with their typical treatment by Norden's "Cinema of Isolation." In *Crash*, the erotic takes on both sexual and political implications as characters embrace the cyborgian project of investigating how the machine has (re)made the body. The film destabilizes traditional associations of normalcy and disability, especially questioning assumptions of erotic appeal generated by such categories, rejecting the ableist way of seeing in favor of a radically altered vision. Just as the disabled model Aimee Mullins seeks to reconfigure our gaze with her claim "I want to be seen as beautiful because of my disability, not in spite of it" ("People" 125), *Crash* forces ableist viewers to rethink their erotic gaze.

Films which violate the rules of the isolationist cinema offer a politically charged corrective to the ableist impulse. They offer the opportunity to accept the desire implicit in the gaze, to come out of the ableist closet and into contact with people with disabilities. I find the controversial *Crash* just such a film, pregnant with the potential to make TABs conscious of their ableist assumptions. While the film's controversial public reception raises many questions of the effectivity of rejecting the rules of the cinema of isolation, the attempt itself deserves attention. In *Crash*, the cyborg and disabled bodies are erotically displayed as sexy, and the viewer is led to recognize the desire implicit in the gaze. Many viewers were offended by this blatant violation of their ableist sensibilities, finding Vaughn's "ragged and dirty" prophesy too disturbing to accept. When I first screened the film in Bloomington, Indiana, an usher announced the theater's offer that anyone overly disturbed by the film would be granted a refund if they left prior to its midpoint. I do not know which surprised me more: the offer itself, or the large number of viewers who left the film early to apparently take advantage of it. There should be no doubt that *Crash* is a disturbing film, but as long as cinematic vision protects ableists from recognizing the desire that motivates their repulsion, this center of ableist thinking will remain intact. Confronting this desire, recognizing it, and dealing with it in films like *Crash*, can be a critical counter to ableism. Embracing the erotic potential of disability and welcoming the sexy side of cyborgs is nothing if not a direct assault on the conventions of ableism. It is this collision of sexuality and cyborg that makes the loudest noise in Cronenberg's *Crash*.

The combination of disabled and cyborg sex appears also to have masked the film's implications for Disability Studies. A number of colleagues have commented that, while they understood labeling *Crash* a cyborg film, and certainly agreed that it was about sex, they did not see it as a film about disability. To such viewers, the disability displayed by the characters was so insignificant compared to the wider exploration of the erotic crossing of the machine/human divide that it was almost forgotten. Frankly, I feel that such a response reinforces the significance of the film, for when even such noticeably disabled characters as Gabrielle are hardly remembered as anything but erotic figures, the typical ableist view has been distracted, undermined, and derailed. This does, however, signal the possibility of erasure, the eliminating of disability from the visual field, and it is worth noting that one possible critique of *Crash* is that it combines the uncombinable to such an extent that the categories necessary for interpreting its political impact dissolve while the film is viewed.

Another concern worth raising is that *Crash* risks involving the disabled body in sexual objectification or fetishization. By prominently displaying disabled characters as sexy, erotic figures, Cronenberg relies on the already sexual conventions of cinema (e.g. nudity, etc.) to make viewers see the characters in this way. As with any erotic display of the body, the film allows viewers to see the characters as sex objects. While I do not mean to suggest that people with disabilities should accept such objectification, I do feel that the principal erotic political action of *Crash* makes such risks acceptable. It is enough for me that the film boldly challenges the conventions of the objectifying gaze, especially as that gaze typically sees the disabled body as either asexual or malignantly sexual, yet I sympathize with those who would rather free movies from the objectifying (and typically male) gaze. Such a move, however, might best be made in a piecemeal fashion, making *Crash* an important step in the right direction.

Crash exemplifies Cronenberg's project to show "the true beauty in some things that others find repulsive" (Rodley 66). Forcing the ableist to recognize this beauty, to question and confront repulsion of the disabled body, and to accept the sexuality of even the sterile cyborg, Cronenberg's film works to undermine the political power of the ableist repression of sexual desire for the other. So far, ableism has withstood the attack, and it is likely to do so for a while. But if we are to change the way our culture treats, sees, and interacts with people with disabilities, films taking such a radical approach are useful tools for expanding awareness. As Cronenberg puts it: "We have to continue to try and wrest control from the world, from the universe, from reality, even though it might be hopeless. I think the more inventive and extreme we are, the better off we are. I know that is a dangerous route to take, so I am also exploring the dangers of going that particular route" (Rodley 67). As a visual iteration of this belief, and as one of the most radical displays of the intersection of disability, sexuality, and cyborg imagery, I conclude that *Crash* makes an important assault on ableism. It is the kind of erotic politics we need to practice if we are ever to make our ableist society more aware of the damage caused—and motives obscured—by restrictions on the sexuality of people with disabilities.

Notes

[1] To avoid potential confusion between James Ballard, the character, and J. G. Ballard, the author of the book, I will always include the initials when referring to the latter. Any reference to "Ballard" identifies the character.

[2] Although ambiguously displayed in the film, J.G. Ballard's novel makes it clear that the sex act in this scene actually involves intercourse with Gabrielle's scar tissue. Ballard describes the scar as "more exciting than the membrane of a vagina" and orgasms "within the deep wound on her thigh." Later sexual encounters between the two involve other scars on Gabrielle's body, and these "sexual apertures formed by . . . high-speed impact" lead Ballard to have erotic fantasies about "other accidents that might enlarge this repertory of orifices" (176-179).

Works Cited

Ballard, J. G. *Crash*. 1973. New York: Noonday, 1994.
Bradbury, Ray. *The Illustrated Man*. Garden City, NY: Doubleday, 1951.
Cherney, James L. "Deaf Culture and the Cochlear Implant Debate: Cyborg Politics and the Identity of People with Disabilities." *Argumentation and Advocacy* 36 (1999): 22-34.
Cronenberg, David, dir. *Crash*. With James Spader, Holly Hunter, Elias Koteas, Deborah Kara Unger, and Rosanna Arquette. FineLine Features, 1996.

Davis, Lennard J. *Enforcing Normalcy: Disability, Deafness, and the Body.* London: Verso, 1995.
---. "Nude Venuses, Medusa's Body, and Phantom Limbs: Disability and Visuality." *The Body and Physical Difference: Discourses of Disability.* Ed. David T. Mitchell and Sharon L. Snyder. Ann Arbor: U of Michigan P, 1997. 51-70.
Douglas, Mary. *Purity and Danger: An Analysis of the Concepts of Pollution and Taboo.* 1966. London: Routledge, 1995.
Fiedler, Leslie. *Freaks: Myths and Images of the Secret Self.* 1978. New York: Touchstone-Simon, 1979.
Finger, Anne. "Claiming *All* of Our Bodies: Reproductive Rights and Disability." *Test-Tube Women.* Ed. Rita Arditti, Renate Klein, and Shelley Minden. London: Pandora Press, 1984. 281-297.
---. "Forbidden Fruit." *New Internationalist* July 1992: 8-10.
Goffman, Erving. *Stigma: Notes on the Management of Spoiled Identity.* 1963. New York: Touchstone-Simon, 1986.
Haraway, Donna J. "Manifesto for Cyborgs: Science, Technology, and Socialist Feminism in the 1980s." *Socialist Review* 80 (1985): 65-108.
---. *Simians, Cyborgs, and Women: The Reinvention of Nature.* New York: Routledge, 1991.
Maslin, Janet. "Cannes Finally Gets a Noisy Controversy." *New York Times* 20 May 1996: C11.
Matthews, Jack. "A 'Crash' Test: Cronenberg Film Draws Walkouts, Boos at Cannes." *Newsday* 20 May 1996: B3.
Murphy, Robert F. *The Body Silent.* 1987. New York: W. W. Norton, 1990.
Norden, Martin F. *The Cinema of Isolation: A History of Physical Disability in the Movies.* New Brunswick: Rutgers UP, 1994.
Penley, Constance, and Andrew Ross. Introduction. *Technoculture.* Ed. Penley and Ross. Minneapolis: U of Minnesota P, 1991. viii-xvii.
"People." *Time* 12 October 1998: 125.
Red, Eric, dir. *Body Parts.* With Jeff Fahey. Paramount, 1991.
Rodley, Chris, ed. *Cronenberg on Cronenberg.* 1992. London: Faber, 1997.
Shakespeare, Tom, Kath Gillespie-Sells, and Dominic Davies, eds. *The Sexual Politics of Disability: Untold Desires.* London: Cassell, 1996
Shaviro, Steven. *The Cinematic Body.* Minneapolis: U of Minnesota P, 1993.
Waxman, Barbara Faye. "It's Time to Politicize Our Sexual Oppression." *Disability Rag* March-April 1991. Rpt. in *The Ragged Edge.* Ed. Barrett Shaw. Louisville, KY: Advocato, 1994. 82-87.

Index

ABC 15
ADAPT xiv
Act of Love, An 6, 11
African-American Studies 34
Adorno, Theodor xi
Alice (television series) 14
Althusser, Louis xi
Altman, Robert xv, 54-55, 103
American Graffiti 110
Americans with Disabilities Act x, 131
Arbus, Diane 48, 53
Arquette, Rosanna 172

Ballard, J. G. 171
Barthes, Roland 25-26
Basic Instinct 67-68
Bazin, André 101
Beatty, Warren 103
Bellamy, Ralph 76
Benjamin, Walter 138, 146
Bergson, Henri 100-101
Best Years of Our Lives, The 1, 8, 12, 23

Better Tomorrow, A 156, 160-161
Big City, The 79
Big Parade, The 1, 27
Black Bird, The 11
Blow Out 112
Body Parts 175
Bogdan, Robert 24, 48, 67, 69
Bogdonavich, Peter 39
Bonnie and Clyde 103, 106
Boone (television series) 8
Bordwell, David xiv, 61, 75-77, 83, 101, 107
Born on the Fourth of July 23, 27
Bradbury, Ray 175
Britton, Andrew 105, 112
Brock, Walter 24
Brooks, Peter 82-83
Brown, Christy 40-41
Browning, Tod xii-xiv, 22, 36, 47-55, 57-59, 61-63, 65-71, 73-83
Bryan, Willie 24
Budde, Rob 70

Bullet in the Head, A 159
Butch Cassidy and the Sundance Kid 106, 110

CBS 14-15
Calendar Girl 27
California Foundation on Employment and Disability 12; Media Access Office 12
Campbell, Arthur Jr. 24
Canby, Vincent 27
Candidate, The 104
Carney, Bill 13
Cassuto, Leonard 19
Chaney, Lon xiv, 22, 58, 74, 78-83, 87-91, 94
Chaplin, Charles 22
Chaucer, Geoffrey 127
Cherney, James L. xvii
Cheung, Jackie 159
Cheung, Leslie 156, 160
Cheung, Cherie 160
Chinatown 104, 106, 109
Chivers, Sally xiii
Chronicle of Higher Education 19
Cimino, Michael 112-113
City Lights 22
Coming Home 1, 12, 23, 111
Cook, Méira xii
Connors, Chuck 3
Conversation, The 106
Coppola, Francis Ford xv, 35
Corman, Roger 136-137
Crash (1973) 171
Crash (1996) xvii, 168, 171-179
Crawford, Joan 80

Cronenberg, David xvii, 168, 171, 178-179
Crutchfield, Susan xvi
Cutter's Way 23

Darby, Kim 110
Davidson, Arnold 47
Davis, Lennard x, 70, 167-168, 170
de Lorde, André (See Lorde, André de)
Death Watch 136-141, 144-145, 147-148
Death Wish 110
Deer Hunter, The 111
Delannoy, Jean 90
Deleuze, Gilles xv, 100-104, 108-109
Deliverance (1919) 27
Deliverance (1972) 106
Dempsey, Shawna 67-68
Dennis, Rocky 39
Devil-Doll,The 22, 78
Dick, Bernard F. 33
Dieterle, William 89
Directors Guild of America 29
Dirty Harry 111
Disability Research 28
Disability Studies x-xi, 19-20, 29, 34-36, 39-43, 127, 169, 178
Disability Studies in the Humanities 28
Disney 28, 87, 92-93
Douglas, Mary 166
Downes, Lesley-Ann 91
Dracula 58, 66, 74
Dunn, Michael 3

Earles, Daisy 53

Earles, Harry 53
Easy Rider 103, 110
Elephant Man, The 7, 14, 35, 39-40
Ellis, John 38
Elsaesser, Thomas 107-108
Enns, Anthony xvi-xvii
Esper, Dwain 74, 78

Facts of Life (television series) 12
Fatal Attraction 68
Fiedler, Leslie 24, 48, 70, 167
Film Studies ix-xi, 19-20, 29, 35-36, 39-40, 42
Finger, Anne 165-166
Five Easy Pieces 106
Flynn, Errol 91
Foucault, Michel xvi, 141, 166
Francis, Arlene 59
Freaks xii-xiv, 20, 36, 47-48, 54-55, 57-61, 65-71, 73-74, 78-79
Freud, Sigmund 153, 166-167, 170
Friedberg, Anne 147
Fugitive, The (television series) 3

Gamman, Lorraine 68
Gaycken, Oliver xiv
Germany Year Zero 101
Godfather, The 35
Goffman, Erving 5, 167, 175
Goldberg, Whoopi 54
Goldwyn, Robert 69
Golfus, Billy 28, 34
Good Times Entertainment 92
Graduate, The 35
Griffith, D. W. xiv, 22, 73, 83

Grosz, Elizabeth 49
Gunning, Tom 82

Hackman, Gene 103
Hall, Stuart 22
Harnick, Laurie E. xiv
Haraway, Donna J. xvi, 135-137, 145, 169
Hard Boiled 160
Hawaii Five-O (television series) 3
Hawkins, Joan 68, 71
Hayek, Selma 93
Hemingway, Ernest 127
Henderson, George 24
Herman, Judith Lewis 105
Hevey, David 50
Highway to Heaven (television series) 12
His Girl Friday 76
Hoeksema, Thomas B. xii
Hook 23
Hopkins, Anthony 91
Hopper, Dennis 110
Horrigan, Patrick xv
Hot Pursuit (television series) 3
Hour Magazine (television series) 10
Hugo, Victor xiv, 87-95
Hunchback 91
Hunchback of Notre Dame, The (1923) 4-5, 11, 22, 88
Hunchback of Notre Dame, The (1995) 92
Hunchback of Notre Dame, The (1996) 28, 92
Hunter, Holly 172
Hurt, William 139

Hutton, Timothy xv, 117-119, 125

Ice Castles 23
If I Can't Do It 24
Inside Moves 23
International Leadership Forum for Women with Disabilities 27
Interrupted Melody 23
Intolerance xiv
Ironside (television series) 8

Jaws 112
Jewel in the Crown, The (television miniseries) 4
Jewell, Geri 12
Jimenez, Neal 27

Kael, Pauline 99
Kawin, Bruce 25
Keathley, Christian xv
Keitel, Harvey 138
Killer, The 158, 160-161
Kinmont, Jill 13
Klobas, Lauri 157
Kong, Chu 158
Koteas, Elias 172
Kovic, Ron 27
Kristofferson, Kris 113

Last Detail, The 106
Laughton, Charles 87, 89, 91
Lee, Danny 158
Lee, Waise 159
Leung, Tony 159
Lévi-Strauss, Claude 105
Little House on the Prairie (television series) 8, 10, 14

Lollobrigida, Gina 90
London After Midnight 78
Long Goodbye,The 106
Longmore, Paul K. x-xiii, 33-34, 67, 157-158
Lopate, Phillip 123
Lorde, André de 82
Lovett, Lyle 54
Lugosi, Bela 58
Lung, Ti 156
Lynch, David 35, 40

MacNeill, Peter 172
McCabe and Mrs. Miller 106
Mairs, Nancy 21
Mankiewicz, Herman J. 82
Mann, Anthony 154
Mark of the Vampire, The 78
Markotic, Nicole xiii
Marshment, Margaret 68
Mask 14, 39
Maslin, Janet 171
Mast, Gerald 25
Matthews, Jack 171
Mean Streets 106
Men, The 8, 23
Metro-Goldwyn-Mayer 48, 57
Metz, Christian 37, 146
Milland, Ray 137
Miller, Patsy Ruth 88-89
Mitchell, David T. 33-34, 127
Moore, Mary Tyler xv, 118, 122, 124
Monroe, Marilyn 27
Moreau, Jeanne 139
Mr. Magoo 28
Mullins, Aimee 177
Mulvey, Laura x-xi, 152-154
Murphy, Robert F. 165-166, 168

My Left Foot 39-41

Neale, Steve 154-156
Neill, Sam 142
Nevis Mountain Dew 6, 11
Nichols, Hayden Bixby 130
Nicholson, Jack 103
Night Moves 106
Night of the Living Dead 74
Norden, Martin F. x, xii, xiv, xvii, 19-20, 22, 33-34, 43, 57, 131, 168, 177
Notre Dame de Paris 90

Of Mice and Men 5, 11
Once a Thief 160
One Flew Over the Cuckoo's Nest 35
Ordeal of Bill Carney, The 13
Ordinary People xv, 117-125
Orphans of the Storm 22, 83
Other Side of the Mountain, The 13, 23
Other Side of the Mountain Part II, The 13, 23

PBS 24
Pakula, Alan J. xv
Panitalia/Paris Productions 90
Parallax View, The 106-107, 109
Patinkin, Mandy 93-94
Passion Fish 23
Penley, Constance xi, 169
Penalty, The 22
Phantom of the Opera, The 4, 11
Player, The 54-55
Poe, Edgar Allan 73
Pride of the Marines 23

Quincy (television series) 13-14
Quinn, Anthony 87, 90-91

Raisch, Bill 3
Ray, Robert B. 105, 107
Real People (television series) 8
Red, Eric 175
Redford, Robert xv, 124
Rickles, Don 140
Ripley's Believe It Or Not (television series) 8
Robbins, Tim 54-55
Rocky 111
Romer, Sax 73
Romero, George 74
Rose, Jacquelin xi
Rosenberg, Brian 48
Rosenthal, Stuart 82
Ross, Andrew 169
Ross, Steven 21
Rossellini, Roberto 101-102

Sacks, Oliver 136
Sandell, Jillian 154-156
Schneider, Romy 138
Screening Disability conference 19, 28
Sebian, Carol 26
Shakespeare, William 60
Shaviro, Stephen 135, 146, 171-172
Show, The 78
Single White Female 68
Smit, Christopher R. xii
Smoke 127-131
Snyder, Sharon L. 33-34, 127
Sontag, Susan 70
Spader, James 172
Speed 23

Spudich, Paul 28
Staiger, Janet 75, 107
Star Trek (television series) 135-136
Star Trek: Next Generation (television series) 171
Star Wars 111
Stone, Oliver 27
Stratton Story, The 23
Stringer, Julian 156, 160
Stubbins, Joseph 25
Sunrise at Campobello 23
Sydow, Max von 139

T. J. Hooker (television series) 3
Tavernier, Bertrand 136, 138
That's Incredible (television series) 8
Thompson, Kristin 61, 75, 107
Thompson, Lou Ann xv
Thomson, David 103
Thomson, Rosemarie Garland 24, 47
Til the End of Time 23
Torry, Robert 112
Towering Inferno, The 110
Tree, Dorothy 59
True Grit 110
Tuchner, Michael 91

Unger, Deborah Kara 172
Universal 74
Unholy Three, The 78
Unknown, The 22, 75, 78, 80-83
Until the End of the World 136-137, 139, 141-142, 144-145, 147-148

Vietnam War xiv-xv, 99-114; veterans 23, 27
von Sydow, Max (See Sydow, Max von)

Wang, Wayne 127
Waterdance, The 23, 27
Watergate xv
Waterston, Sam 113
Waxman, Barbara Faye 165
Wayne, John 110
Weinberg, Nancy 26-27
Wenders, Wim 136, 139
West of Zanzibar 22, 77
When Billy Broke His Head... And Other Tales of Wonder 28, 34
White, Hayden 108
White Tiger 77
Whose Life Is It, Anyway? 6, 11
Wild Bunch, The 110
Wild Wild West 23
Wild Wild West, The (television series) 3, 11
Willeman, Paul 153-155
Williams, Linda 63
Williams, Tony 151
Winter Kills 112
With a Song in My Heart 23
Wizard of Oz, The 119
Women's Studies 34
Woo, John xvi-xvii, 151-156, 158-162
Wood, Michael 1-2
Wood, Robin 59, 103, 113
World War I veterans 80
World War II 8, 22, 24-25, 102
Worsley, Wallace 88

Writers Guild of America 29

X: The Man with the X-Ray Eyes 136-137, 139-141, 144-145, 147-148
X-files, The (television series) 57

Yam, Simon 159
Yamamoto, Kaoru 26
Yellow Rose, The (television series) 3
Yun-Fat, Chow 156, 158, 160

About the Contributors

JAMES L. CHERNEY is a Ph.D. candidate in the Department of Communication and Culture at Indiana University and currently teaches at Westminster College. He completed his M.A. in Rhetoric at Indiana University with a critique of the legal foundations of the Americans with Disabilities Act. Through Indiana University's department of Extended Studies, he developed and taught an award-winning course on "Americans with Disabilities" in addition to teaching courses in public speaking, argumentation, and interpersonal communication. He is currently writing his dissertation titled "Rhetorical Norms of Ableist Culture."

SALLY CHIVERS recently completed her Ph.D. at McGill University and is currently a postdoctoral fellow at the University of British Columbia where she is researching depictions of aging in literature. She has presented her work at conferences in Canada, the United States, and Britain, and has recently published part of her dissertation in *Tessera*, an interdisciplinary feminist journal.

MÉIRA COOK is a postdoctoral fellow at the University of British Columbia, where she is researching post-traumatic narratives.

SUSAN CRUTCHFIELD is an assistant professor of English at the University of Wisconsin at La Crosse, where she teaches cultural studies and film. She is co-editor of a collection of essays and creative work titled *Points of Contact: Disablity, Art, and Culture* (U of

Michigan P, 2000), and her article "Touching Scenes and Finishing Touches: Blindness in the Slasher Film" appears in *Mythologies of Violence in Postmodern Media* (ed. Christopher Sharrett, Wayne State UP, 1999). She is currently conducting research for a book project on the multiple media constructions of Helen Keller.

ANTHONY ENNS is a Ph.D. candidate in the Department of English at the University of Iowa. His essays on film and television have appeared or are forthcoming in such journals as *Postmodern Culture, Popular Culture Review, Studies in Popular Culture, Quarterly Review of Film and Video, Journal of Popular Film and Television*, and the anthology *Sexual Rhetoric: Media Perspectives on Sexuality, Gender, and Identity* (Greenwood Press, 1999).

OLIVER GAYCKEN studies cinema and media studies in the English Department at the University of Chicago. He is writing a dissertation on cinema and scientific visuality.

LAURIE E. HARNICK is currently working on a dissertation that considers the sociological and historical pressures that bear on the evolving narrative rooted in Victor Hugo's *Notre Dame de Paris: 1482*. She is also considering changes to the presentation of race and gender in film adaptations of Hugo's novel and is examining how themes evolve and emerge due to historical pressures and material concerns of their time. She teaches at the University of Western Ontario.

THOMAS B. HOEKSEMA is Professor of Education at Calvin College in Grand Rapids, Michigan. For twenty-five years he has been passionate in promoting the integration of people with and without labeled disabilities in schools, neighborhoods, churches, and places of work and play. For several years he has taught, published, and presented at professional conferences on the subject of film and disability.

PATRICK E. HORRIGAN is the author of *Widescreen Dreams: Growing Up Gay at the Movies* (Wisconsin UP, 1999) and the play *Messages for Gary*. He teaches English at the Brooklyn campus of Long Island University, and he lives in Manhattan. His essay "The Inner Life of *Ordinary People*" is part of a work in progress on mental illness and gay identity.

CHRISTIAN KEATHLEY is an assistant professor of English at Clemson Univeristy.

PAUL K. LONGMORE is Professor of History and Director of the Institute on Disability at San Francisco State University, specializing in Early American history and the history of people with disabilities. He earned his Ph.D. at the Claremont Graduate School and his B.A. and M.A. at Occidental College. Longmore's book *The Invention of George Washington* (U of California P, 1988; paperback UP of Virginia, 1998) is a study of Washington as a political actor and conscious shaper of his public image. Longmore has also written articles in scholarly journals and newspapers on themes related to Early American history and to the history of people with disabilities and their contemporary civil rights struggle. He is currently writing a study of three episodes in 20th-century disability history. With Lauri Umansky, he co-edited *The New Disability History: American Perspectives*, an anthology of essays, and is co-editing a book series, *The History of Disability*, both for New York University Press. He is researching three other books: "George Washington and the Invention of the American Nation"; "Presenting Tiny Tim: Telethons, American Culture, and the Making of Disability Identities"; and "Screening Stereotypes: Representing People with Disabilities in Motion Pictures and Television, A Cultural-Historical Analysis." He teaches courses at San Francisco State University on U.S. history, Early American history, and the history of people with disabilities. He has also taught at Stanford University, the University of Southern California, and the California Polytechnic University at Pomona. San Francisco State University's Institute on Disability is a pioneering multidisciplinary research, curriculum-development and community-service program. From 1983 to 1986, Longmore served as the administrator of the Program in Disability and Society at the University of Southern California, the first Disability Studies project in the United States. Longmore was featured in the historical documentary film "George Washington: The Man Who Wouldn't Be King" on the PBS series *The American Experience* in November 1992. He has been interviewed regarding disability-related issues on ABC's *Nightline*, ABC's *World News Tonight*, NBC's *Today*, and National Public Radio's *Weekend Edition*, and in *The Los Angeles Times*, *The New York Times*, *The Washington Post*, *McCall's*, and *TV Guide*. He has received grants from the National Endowment for the Humanities to conduct a Summer

Institute on Disability Studies, the Mount Vernon Ladies Association for research on George Washington, the National Institute of Disability and Rehabilitation Research to examine the impact of Disability Studies curricula, and the U.S. Department of Education to direct a mentoring project to facilitate the transition of students with disabilities from college to careers. He has also received an Andrew W. Mellon Post-Doctoral Fellowship in the Humanities, a Huntington Library Research Fellowship, and an H.B Earhart Foundation Research Fellowship. He has a physical disability.

NICOLE MARKOTIC is a poet and fiction writer from Calgary, Alberta. She teaches English Literature and Creative Writing at the University of Calgary, co-publishes the chapbook press, disOrientation books, is Poetry Editor for Red Deer Press, and is one of the editors on the collective of *Tessera* magazine. Her first book is the prose poetry collection, *Connect the Dots* (Wolsak & Wynn), her second book is a novel, *Yellow Pages* (RDC Press), and her most recent book is a collection of poetry, *Minotaurs & Other Alphabets* (Wolsak & Wynn). She is currently completing a novel set in the '70s in the U.S. and Canada.

MARTIN F. NORDEN is a Professor of Communication at the University of Massachusetts-Amherst. His work has appeared in such journals as *Wide Angle*, *Film & History*, *Journal of Film & Video*, and *Paradoxa* and in many anthologies. He is the author of *The Cinema of Isolation: A History of Physical Disability in the Movies* (Rutgers UP, 1994) and serves as book review editor for the *Journal of Popular Film & Television*.

CHRISTOPHER R. SMIT is a Ph.D. candidate and a former Carrol Arnold fellow in Communication Studies at the University of Iowa. His essay "The Creation and Corruption of Diversity in MTV's *The Real World*" was published in the October 1999 issue of *Studies in Popular Culture*. In 1999 Smit chaired the Cinema and Disability Group at the University of Iowa and organized the first conference on cinema and disability, which he documents in his essay "Notes on SCREENING DISABILITY: A Conference on Film and Disability (26-28 March 1999)," published in the Summer 1999 issue of *Disability Studies Quarterly*. His essay "Fascination: The Modern Allure of the Internet" was published in Oxford's *Web Studies*, edited by David Gauntlett.

LOU ANN THOMPSON is an associate professor of English at Texas Woman's University, where she teaches film, British Romanticism, and creative writing. Her publications include scholarly articles on a variety of topics in film and literature and also poetry and fiction.